WE ARE ALL EXPLORERS

WE ARE ALL

EXPLORERS

Learning
and Teaching
with Reggio
Principles
in Urban
Settings

Daniel R. Scheinfeld • Karen M. Haigh
Sandra J. P. Scheinfeld
Foreword by Lella Gandini

Teachers College,
Columbia University
New York and London

Published by Teachers College Press, 1234 Amsterdam Avenue, New York, NY 10027

Library of Congress Cataloging-in-Publication Data

Scheinfeld, Daniel R. (Daniel Richard), 1933–
  We are all explorers : learning and teaching with Reggio principles in urban settings /
Daniel R. Scheinfeld, Karen M. Haigh, and Sandra J. P. Scheinfeld ; foreword by Lella Gandini.
     p. cm.
  Includes bibliographical references and index.
  ISBN 978-0-8077-4908-1 (pbk. : alk. paper)
  ISBN 978-0-8077-4909-8 (hardcover : alk. paper)
  1. Early childhood education—Illinois—Chicago. 2. Experiential learning—Illinois—
Chicago. 3. Early childhood education—Parent participation—Illinois—Chicago.
4. Early childhood education—Italy—Reggio Emilia—Philosophy. I. Haigh, Karen M.
II. Scheinfeld, Sandra J. P. III. Title.
 LB1139.27.I3S34 2008
  372.2109773'11—dc22   2008024040

ISBN 978-0-8077-4908-1 (paper)
ISBN 978-0-8077-4909-8 (cloth)

Printed on acid-free paper

Manufactured in the United States of America

15   14   13   12   11   10   09   08   8   7   6   5   4   3   2   1

Contents

Foreword

On an evening in early May, 1993, Karen Haigh showed a group of us some preliminary drawings for a school to be built by the Chicago Commons Child Development Program in a desolate section of Chicago. Around the table were Daniel and Sandra Scheinfeld, various other colleagues, and Loris Malaguzzi. In fact, we were guests of Frances Donovan, who was part of this group of explorers who had recently gone together to Reggio Emilia, Italy, to discover the approach to early childhood education practiced in that municipality. She had invited us to celebrate in a friendly and intimate way something absolutely extraordinary: the presence of Loris Malaguzzi, the philosopher and founder of that noted approach to educating young children in Reggio Emilia, who had come to Chicago to receive the International Kohl Prize.

Malaguzzi was surprised by the city of Chicago. The daring architecture and the constant flow of people of all races and social classes on the move utterly amazed him. As his translator, I watched closely as he alternated between moments of great enthusiasm and admiration and moments in which he voiced doubts about the possibility of people living well at such high speeds and in such crowded spaces. But he was also moved by the welcome he had received in every school he visited and was truly enjoying the company now gathered in this warm home.

He was curious about the plans that Karen had brought. When I told him that Karen had hired an architect to whom she had shown photographs of Reggio schools and had given articles about Reggio to read, and that Karen was planning to guide the building of a school inspired by the ones he had created in Reggio, he was greatly pleased, although he wondered how this would be done.

That evening was an auspicious beginning to the journey that is described in this book. The proposed school did come into being in the form of the Nia Family Center, where many of the stories described in this book took place. To be sure, the importance of natural light and the use of large glass windows had to be translated, for reasons of security, into the use of glass blocks.

How fortunate for us that Karen Haigh and the Chicago Commons Child Development Centers had right at hand an experienced team of observers and researchers from the Erikson Institute, namely Dan and Sandra Scheinfeld, who could study this innovative enterprise in great depth and present their findings to interested readers everywhere. This well-constructed book, rich with stories and experiences of children, teachers, and parents, has matured over a long stretch of time, allowing the authors to observe change and to gain added perspective for evaluating the complex experience under investigation.

For the first time there is a narrative about teachers and children learning and working together that is accompanied by clear reference to the principles that are integral to the preschools of Reggio Emilia, with the principles having been translated so as to respect the culture and complexity in which Chicago Commons operates. For the first time we see the effects of thoughtful and dynamic professional support for teachers, who learn and unfold their potentials. We are offered the possibility of following how teachers' development as it is gradually and extensively constructed with the understanding of the value of relationships. This is what I have appreciated all along about the clear and creative mind, as well as the untiring determination, of Karen Haigh.

How do teachers learn to truly listen to children? How do teachers with diverse backgrounds open up to the possibility and discovery of the value of collaboration in order to understand their roles in relationships with the children? How does a group of teachers construct meaningful documentation day by day? How do teachers follow the principles of Reggio and respond at the same time to mandated requirements? What strategies can a school invent to make parents in an urban setting feel welcome and that they are true participants? These are just some of the questions dealt with here.

By the end of his stay, Malaguzzi had visited many different parts of the city and met a large number of people, not all of them necessarily connected with the field of early childhood education. Being a sharp observer and listener, he had become utterly fascinated and favorably impressed by the boundless energy and will to succeed that he encountered in Chicagoans during his stay. Shortly before leaving, he recalled his own skepticism and confided that he could now foresee the construction of good things for children in Chicago.

—Lella Gandini

Preface

This is a book about practice and theory in early childhood education. Its aim is to describe and analyze how the Chicago Commons Child Development Program explored the application of educational principles from Reggio Emilia within its own context from 1991 to 2003. The book focuses on the Chicago Commons' preschool classrooms, professional development experiences, relationships with parents, and administrative structures and processes. By Fall 1999, this initiative involved all 26 of the Chicago Commons preschool classrooms located in seven centers serving low-income Latino and African American communities. The book documents the work of many gifted staff and delves deeply into the meaning and value of the processes described. We limited this book to a manageable scope by concentrating on the preschool classrooms, even though Chicago Commons also explored Reggio Emilia principles in its infant–toddler and after-school classes. The Reggio Exploration at Chicago Commons continues to this day.

Our intended audiences are preschool teachers and administrators on the one hand, and university professors and students in the field of early child education on the other. In stating that this is a practical book, we mean that it conveys a rich set of ideas with which readers can interact and then create applications that fit their own situations. It is also a theoretical book in that it proposes underlying principles and processes that, in our view, illuminate the Reggio Approach as experienced at Chicago Commons.

The book is a description of how one organization responded to a set of educational principles from Reggio Emilia. Its intent is to help you construct an understanding of those principles so that you can apply them in your own context, in your own way. You may find many of the structures and practices that are described in the book directly useful in one form or another. Think of them as possibilities that can be translated to another context, reshaped, or transformed to meet your aims. What is most important is the relation between those structures and practices on the one hand, and the learning processes that they are intended to foster. In our view, the Reggio Approach is, above all, about processes of learning.

The book contains numerous descriptions of classroom teaching and learning sequences, learning environments, interactions with parents, staff development processes, and aspects of the program's overall organization. We often include dialogues in which learning by children and/or adults is taking place. The dialogues reveal interpersonal processes and the patterns of meaning expressed by the participants. They are useful both as a source of reflection for the individual reader and as a stimulus for group discussions.

Throughout the book we pose questions to the reader. We also provide our own interpretations. In this way, and in other ways, we invite you to engage with us in a dialogue about the meaning of what we present and what it might suggest for your own teaching and learning.

The book is based on several sources of information. First are data collected by Sandra and Daniel Scheinfeld from 1996 through 2003. These data consist of video recordings, audio recordings, and notes taken in classrooms; on field trips; in teacher collaborative meetings; in administrative meetings; in the monthly meetings involving parents, teachers, and administrators; and during in-service gatherings. Additional data were gathered through interviews conducted by Sandra and Dan with teachers, site directors, and staff support coordinators. Second are the myriad pieces of documentation created by program staff, including display panels, booklets on children's learning, and annual publications that document the work of the program through descriptions, photos, and dialogues. Third are numerous taped discussions with Karen Haigh, director of the Chicago Commons Child Development Program during the entire course of the study. Over the past 4 years, Dan, Sandra, and Karen have met frequently to collaborate in writing this book.

The Spencer Foundation provided a planning grant for the research in 1995. Data collection and early writing from 1996 to 1999 were supported by generous grants from the Pritzker Cousins Foundation.

Throughout the text, all names of children, staff, and parents have been changed. The exception is Karen Haigh, who is referred to as "Karen."

This has been an unusual kind of collaboration—one in which researchers (Dan and Sandra) and a community organization (Chicago Commons) combined efforts to create knowledge about teaching and learning with the intent of sharing it with others. The researchers and the program staff met regularly to strategize about directions in which to take the inquiry and coordinated their efforts in carrying it out. As a result, both the research and the writing phases of this book have benefited from a joining of inside and outside perspectives on the program. We invite you to bring your perspective to this ongoing dialogue.

Acknowledgments

We would, above all, like to acknowledge the enormous contributions of the entire staff of the Chicago Commons Child Development Program who made the Reggio Exploration a vital reality. We also want to thank them for their generous and enthusiastic support of the research for this book.

Dan and Sandra personally wish to give special thanks to staff members who contributed extra time to the research by participating in interviews, tapings of their classrooms, and special meetings. They include: Christine Alexander, Pauline Benton, Susan Budde, Tommie Butler, Jane Cecil, Sonia Class, Noberta Coria, Kimberly Cothran, Kofi Darku, Maria Espinoza, Nilda Feliciano, Rosita Feliciano, Carmen Garay, Graciela Gomez, Eva Hill, Priscilla Jones, Cara Julias, Jennifer Keldahl, David Kelly, Shannon Kimmel, Bonnie Kizielewski, John Koski, Rima Malhotra, Salud Martinez, Dorothy Miller, Claudia Rivera, Santa Rivera, Ozzie Robinson, GiGi Schroeder, Anne Sereni, Maria Viteri, Rosa Vizcarra, Liz Walsh, Rachel Weaver, Bertha Williams, Migdalia Young.

We are also grateful to the current administration at Chicago Commons, including Dan Valliere and Janice Woods, for their responsive support during the final draft of the book. Deepest thanks to the Teachers College Press staff, especially editors Marie Ellen Larcada, Wendy Weiss, Myra Cleary, and production editor Shannon Waite.

We wish to thank the many research assistants who made contributions to our work. We especially thank Amy Adamzyk and Karla Daye, who participated in the early phases of the research; Jeremy Bendik-Keymer, who helped lay the foundations for Chapters 5 and 6 and participated in the overall conceptualization of the book from 1999 to 2002; and Aaron Curtis and Elizabeth Graff, who made repeated and vital contributions through editing chapter drafts during the summers of 2006 and 2007. Finally, thanks to Suzanne Wagner and Nancy Wicker for their editorial advice.

In the spring and early summer of 2007, Lella Gandini and Lynn White spent countless hours reading and critiquing the draft of the book. Each had very special contributions to make: Lynn from a perspective of having implemented Reggio ideas in her classroom for many years, and Lella from the perspectives of her multi-decade engagement with the schools of Reggio Emilia and her long-term role as Reggio Children's Liaison to the United States. Their critiques made major contributions to the book. In addition, Lella critiqued several chapters of the book in 2004, prior to our contacting the publisher. In general, we are deeply grateful to Lella for her interest in the research over its entire duration. In addition, we wish to point out the enormous support given to the Chicago Commons Reggio Exploration by Lella and by Amelia Gambetti (also of Reggio Children) over many years.

We want to thank the Spencer Foundation and Pritzker Cousins Foundation for their vital support of the research. Special thanks to Gillian McNamee of Erikson Institute for her collaboration in the first year of the research and her continuing interest. Finally, we wish to give our warm thanks to the administration and staff of the Erikson Institute for their abiding and caring support of this work from its very inception.

WE ARE ALL EXPLORERS

Chapter 1

Introduction

Imagine you are a teacher standing on a corner with several preschoolers, and the following conversation takes place:

> *Latasha:* Cars have to stop when it changes to red light. I think someone lives in there because it always changes.
> *Kentrell:* There are coins that go in. They come from up there [the sky] and make it change.
> *Dewain:* There's a cord that go in there. And green light you go, red light you stop, and yellow light slow down.

This teacher was confronted with a wondrous moment: Three preschoolers showing an interest in the dynamics of traffic lights and how they affect the movement of cars. Furthermore, each child is expressing a distinct and imaginative theory about what makes traffic lights change colors.

> *What happened to this conversation?*
> *Did it end where it started?*
>
> or
>
> *Was it nurtured by the teacher into a*
> *rich and multifaceted exploration of the world,*
> *driven by the children's interests and curiosities?*

The *latter option* is what this book is about. This is an account of how an early child development program serving inner-city children and families in low-income areas of Chicago has been exploring, in its own context, an approach to preschool education known as the Reggio Approach, developed and flourishing in Reggio Emilia, Italy.

In the Reggio Approach, teachers provide rich learning environments for children. They listen to and observe children's expressions of interest, feelings, and thought as the children engage the environment. Building on these observations, the teachers challenge the children's thinking and join the children in constructing understandings about their world, often engaging environments beyond the classroom. Much of the learning occurs in small groups of three to five children in which they benefit from collaboration and dialogue with one another and with the teacher. They share and negotiate multiple perspectives as they co-construct understandings. The children use a wide variety of means, especially verbal and visual, to represent their understandings. They revisit their representations, often in collaboration with others, to reflect on and extend their inquiry.

Teachers systematically document children's conversations and representations. They meet regularly to use the documentation to interpret the children's emerging interests and ideas and to reflect on possibilities for extending the children's learning.

Children's deep desire to be listened to is fulfilled by the teachers, who create a space in their minds to reflect on the children's expression of feelings, thoughts, and interest, and engage in dialogue with the children about them. The children experience these reflections from the mind of the teacher and feel valued as the source of their own motives, thoughts, and perceptions.

Unlike other approaches to early childhood education, the Reggio Approach does not have a prescribed curriculum. Rather, the curriculum emerges from teachers' and children's collaborative responses to the expressed learning interests of the children.

In our view, this approach to teaching and learning is immensely respectful of children, their rights, and their desire to learn. In this process they gain a foundation for life. They internalize the pleasures and skills of constructing meaning together, taking into account many different perspectives. They become self-motivated learners, experiencing and developing their own agency through pursuing their learning interests and responding to challenges. They explore, experiment, and communicate in ways that strengthen their cognitive, linguistic, social, and emotional development, including the range of skills expected of preschoolers. In Reggio-inspired learning environments, children are resourceful, focused, engaged, collaborative, and expressive. The high quality of their work is visible and thoughtfully displayed on classroom walls and in hallways. Children, parents, teachers, and visitors can see the value, depth, and meaningfulness of the children's learning experiences and feel part of an evolving educational process.

SETTING OF THIS BOOK

The setting for this book is the Child Development Program of the Chicago Commons Association during the years 1991 to 2003. The director of the program was Karen Haigh. The program, then and now, serves predominantly Latino and African American low-income communities. The major sources of support are Head Start, state pre-Kindergarten, state-subsidized child care, and occasional private funders.

The Chicago Commons "Reggio Exploration" started in 1991, following Karen's first visit to the municipal preschools of Reggio Emilia. Classroom implementation began in 1993 in seven preschool classrooms, one from each center, and gradually grew to involve all 40 of the Chicago Commons early childhood classrooms by 1998 (see the Appendix). Beyond the period covered by this book, Chicago Commons staff have continued to explore the Reggio Approach and to make their learning available to others.

The aim of Chicago Commons is *not to replicate* the practices developed in Reggio Emilia, but rather to explore the principles underlying those practices (i.e., to reflect on their meaning, to be inspired by them, to adapt them to the Chicago social–cultural context, and to be open to developing new principles and procedures). It should be said that the schools of Reggio Emilia themselves also are continually evolving new insights and initiatives, transforming their own approaches on a day-to-day basis by collectively re-examining them. Continual transformation and renewal are inherent aspects of the Reggio Approach.

THE MUNICIPAL PRESCHOOLS OF REGGIO EMILIA

When Karen Haigh visited the Reggio Emilia schools, she found that her deepest educational convictions were reflected. She was struck by the learning environments, by the deep respect for children, by what the children were able to do, and by the thoughtfulness of the teachers in discussing their work.

The system of early childhood education of the Municipality of Reggio Emilia currently consists of 21 preschool centers (serving children ages 3 to 6) and 13 infant–toddler centers (serving children ages 3 months to 3 years). While the schools draw from every social context of the community, they give preference to children with special needs, to single-parent families, and to families who do not have a grandparent available for taking care of young children.

The life of the schools involves many participants, with teachers and families considered central to the education of children. The schools invite an ongoing exchange of ideas. Their open, democratic style encourages participation, exploration, and a sharing of goals and ideas through dialogue among staff, parents, and children.

The schools offer spacious, versatile, well-provisioned, beautiful, light-filled and thought-provoking learning environments tailored to facilitate the collaborative explorations of young children and to promote a sense of well-being for everyone who participates in them (Gandini, 1998).

A Reggio Emilia preschool center has three or more classrooms of children, usually organized by age level, and each led by two co-teachers who stay with the group of children during their 3 years at the school. Each preschool also has a studio teacher prepared in visual arts and/or other media such as music, dance, or design. The studio teacher, called the *Atelierista*, contributes to the learning experiences of children by planning and collaborating with the teachers. The use of multiple modes of communication plays a major role in the children's expression of their ideas.

EXPLORING REGGIO PRINCIPLES IN CHICAGO COMMONS PRESCHOOLS

As a point of entry for looking at Chicago Commons' exploration of Reggio ideas over a 12-year period, we will focus on 11 pedagogical principles that Karen first encountered during her 1991 trip to Reggio Emilia. These principles have remained salient to Commons' exploration of the Reggio Approach.

Image of the Child

"Strong, rich, and powerful" is a phrase frequently applied to children in the Reggio Emilia Municipal Preschools, in contrast to a view of the child as weak, dependent, and limited in capability. This image of the child is a way of being with children that orients adults to seeing strengths and capabilities that can be encouraged and built upon, rather than seeing the child as being comprised primarily of deficits. The teacher sees the child as capable, interested, rich in ideas, wanting to grow, and wanting to communicate with peers and adults.

The image of the child is an integral part of the teacher–child relationship, in which the teacher's aim is to empower children to explore the world and create meaning. The teacher's motive is to validate the children's curiosity, challenge their thinking, and facilitate their pleasure in connecting with the world and constructing understandings. Gradually, because this image of the child is in the teacher's mind, heart, and actions, the children take on this image of themselves and grow as active inquirers and constructors of personally meaningful information.

Listening/Observing–Reflecting–Responding

Teachers *listen* to and *observe* children's actions, interactions, conversations, statements, emotional expressions, and representations. They listen and observe in order to discover the children's interests and ideas, curiosities, strengths, feelings, and meanings. They *reflect* on what they have heard or observed, and *respond* by providing learning opportunities, challenges, and facilitative structures to children. A sequence involving listening/observing–reflecting–responding may occur within a few moments of time or over several days, weeks, or months. Engagements with children typically involve multiple cycles of this process (i.e., the teacher's response at the end of one cycle is followed by the children's response; this leads to further teacher listening/observing, which begins a new cycle).

Documentation

Documentation is an aspect of listening and observing. Teachers record moments in children's learning by writing notes, taking photos, making and transcribing audiotapes, videotaping, taking dictations, and collecting children's work. These records provide the focus for teachers' interpretations of children's interests, feelings, and ideas. Documentation is brought to teacher planning meetings and is often posted in the classroom or in accessible binders as an ongoing point of reflection for teachers, children, and parents. In time, some of the documentation is integrated into formal communications, such as display panels, slide presentations, and program publications in the form of booklets and posters.

Co-Construction of Understanding

People construct understandings together through collaboration and dialogue (e.g., teachers with children, children with children, teachers with teachers, etc.). The original Reggio principle is named "co-construction of knowledge." We prefer using the word *understanding* because it more strongly suggests a connection to personal experience, including one's feelings, and because it suggests a perception of how things connect with one another in the world around us.

Multiple Perspectives

Children and staff are encouraged to share and consider multiple points of view in relation to a question or object of inquiry. Doing so expands the range and/or depth of their understanding. A well-known Reggio example in this regard is to have one child observe an object from a ladder and another from a position on the ground. The two children compare their perceptions and discover that their descriptions of the object are significantly different.

Representation

Children represent and communicate their observations and ideas both during the process of engaging the world and from memory. An important aspect of children's representations is their *use of multiple symbol systems* (modes of communication) in their acts of representing; for example, communicating through some combination of verbal language, drawing, clay, wire, painting, gesture, and so on. Hence, the principal book on Reggio Emilia (Edwards, Gandini, & Forman, 1998) and the traveling exhibit (Reggio Children, 2005) are entitled *The Hundred Languages of Children*.

Revisiting

Children revisit and re-examine their experience and object(s) of study. They also revisit their representations and those of others. Revisiting invariably stimulates children to make further sense of their previous experience, to make new observations, and to evolve understandings and representations that go beyond the previous ones, utilizing additional perspectives and/or materials. Teachers revisit when examining and interpreting the documentation of children's learning or when re-examining some aspect of the classroom process or environment in order to listen and observe more closely.

The Learning Environment

The emphasis on the learning environment in the Reggio Approach starts with the classroom space, which is constructed carefully by the teachers to invite and guide children's explorations, to promote small-group collaborations, to encourage the making of representations, and to feature the children's ideas and identities prominently. The environment undergoes change constantly to facilitate children's exploration and learning. The learning environment also includes *other classrooms,* common areas in the *school building, the school grounds,* the *neighborhood*, and use of the *city* to provide rich opportunities for children's explorations.

Teacher Collaboration

Teachers reflect together *and* with other staff on their observations and documentations, then plan their responses to children and hypothesize possible outcomes. They also collaborate in implementing activities and in the overall management of the classroom.

Emergent Curriculum

Emergent curriculum is a joining of the nine previously stated Reggio principles. It is an extended learning process that is propelled by the children's interests, ideas, discoveries, and sense of wonder as they explore a particular area of inquiry, guided by teacher scaffolding. The focus and form of the learning process are emerging constantly as teachers take cues from observing and documenting what children are pursuing and representing, and from how the children are experiencing what they are doing. Although the emergent curriculum may be guided by a broad set of teacher objectives (such as strengthening children's powers of observation or introducing literacy skills), it does not involve a predetermined set of activities or predetermined outcomes because it is evolving constantly from the children's expressed learning energies and motives. It is made possible by teacher reflection and facilitation based on a sensitive entering into the world of the child, taking the child's perspective, and connecting these with the teacher's interests in children's learning. Chicago Commons uses the term *emergent curriculum* to refer to the process through which children's *in-depth studies* take place. In Reggio Emilia, the parallel term for emergent curriculum is *projettazione* (Rinaldi, 1998, 2006), and the term parallel to in-depth study is *progetto* (project).

Parent Participation

Parent participation emphasizes the pursuit of relationships with parents devoted to the development of the children and is characterized by *dialogue* and *collaboration.* Just as the image of the child is the propelling force in teachers' relationships with children, the image of the parent as competent, interested, and rich in ideas is at the center of the school's establishment of relationships with parents (see Chapter 9).

THE PIPES STUDY: AN EXAMPLE OF THE APPLICATION OF REGGIO PRINCIPLES IN CHICAGO

We invite you to enter into the Pipes Study, an example of an in-depth study with children that took place in April 1998. The Pipes Study will be referred to in various ways throughout the book. Here, it provides an example of how Reggio principles have been explored at Chicago Commons. As you read through the study, notice the ways that the Reggio principles are expressed.

The teachers were invited to choose one of the following topics to pursue with the children as an in-depth study: the City, Friends, the Family, and the Big School (the local elementary school at which many of the children would be attending kindergarten the following year).

A classroom team (teacher and assistant teacher) at Taylor House chose the City. Their decision was guided by their recent observations that the children, in block play, had been constructing buildings to represent some of the buildings currently being constructed in the neighborhood.

Walks in the Neighborhood

The study of the city started with a neighborhood walk in which the children were invited to notice as many things as they could. The children remarked about birds, rooftops, windows, bus signs, parking meters, and McDonald's. The teachers took notes on the children's thoughts and observations. After the walk, the teachers read their notes to the children in order to help them revisit, rethink, and expand upon what they had seen.

At the weekly meeting, the two teachers, another classroom team, the studio coordinator, the education coordinator, and the site director studied the children's responses.[1] They noticed that the children's observations during their walk could be divided into two categories: things that could be seen when looking up, and things that could be seen when looking down. So, wanting to encourage the children to focus more sharply during the next neighborhood walk, they made a plan to divide the children into a "looking up" group and a "looking down" group. The composition of each group would include older and younger children, more verbal and less verbal children, so that the children could maximally stimulate one another's thinking.

The Looking up and Looking down Walk. The looking up group was given binoculars to examine what was up, and the looking down group was given magnifying glasses to explore what was down. During the walk, the looking up group discovered things such as a man standing on a ladder, windows, the sky, a light pole, chimneys, and birds. The looking down group discovered flowers, grass, a fire hydrant, a water cap, and gas pipes. On their return to the school, the children were invited to draw what they had noticed on the walk.

---

1. The Education Coordinator role roughly corresponds to that of the "Pedagogista" in the Reggio Emilia municipal schools. The pedagogista works directly with the teachers in the schools to solve problems and make suggestions that help evolve the teaching learning process (Edwards et al., 1998). The Studio Coordinator role approximates the role of the "Atelierista," a studio teacher with a background in the visual arts who supports both children and teachers in processes of learning and visual communication (Gandini, Hill, Cadwell, & Schwall, 2005). In the Reggio Emilia preschools, there is an Atelierista located at each site. In the Chicago Commons program, one or two Studio Coordinators are shared across all seven sites and work mostly with teachers.

Reflecting on the Children's Drawings. In studying the drawings from the looking down group, the teachers noted patterns of parallel lines in several of the drawings. Through revisiting these drawings with the children and taking dictations, they determined that the drawings represented various kinds of pipes that had caught the attention of the children. For example, Jonathon said:

> You find gas pipes in the ground. They look like circles. They are underground. . . . There is grass on each side of the gas pipes. This is the dirt, there is another gas pipe, and this pipe is going inside the wall.

The teacher offered to write Jonathon's comments on his drawing (see Figure 1.1). The teacher then asked Jonathon to make another drawing showing "how the pipes work." She again took dictation from Jonathon.

> This is the house. There are pipes and drainpipes. It's like when real dirty oil comes out. You call the ambulance, the fire department, and the police. You just dial 9-1-1. The oil is coming from the pipes under the ground. Here is the gas pipe under the ground.

As he spoke, she again wrote his ideas on the drawing (see Figure 1.2).

Figure 1.1.
Jonathon notices gas pipes outside. He draws the caps of three gas pipes and shows how one gas pipe, in a grassy area, extends down into the ground, into the dirt, and inside the wall of a building.

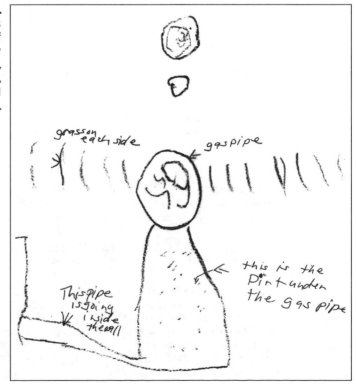

Figure 1.2.
Jonathon's second drawing
shows the movement of gas
and oil through two kinds of
pipes coming from under the
ground and into a house. He
also notes drainpipes that carry
dirty oil out, which he identifies
as dangerous.

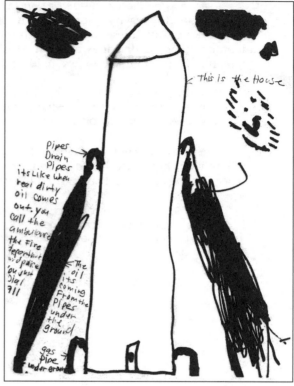

The Pipes Walk Through the Building

At the next weekly meeting, as a result of noting the pipes theme in Jonathon's and several other children's drawings and comments, the teachers decided to further focus the overall inquiry on pipes.

The pipes inquiry began with a walk around the inside of the school building to give a group of interested children a chance to notice different kinds of pipes.

David: It goes around and in here.
Nico: This is it. It looks like *a water* pipe. The pipe is coming into the hole and all the way in.
Salvador: It's going into the hole. I see something in there. It's turning, it's turning, and it's staying inside the wall. You see, it goes in the wall.

The group entered the bathroom. The teachers asked the children questions about what kinds of pipes they saw, where the pipes came from, and where they were going.

Nico (pointing to the pipe under the sink): These are for water. When we open this [the drain], the water goes down the pipes and into the wall. It goes into the pipe and into the ground.
Salvador: You see, just like I showed you [in the classroom]. You see this pipe. It goes under the ground and across under the school to the sewer. [Note the connections that Salvador is making between the previous explorations in the classroom and the current observations.]

The discussion shifted to the toilet.

> *Teacher*: When you flush, where does the water go?
> *Jalisa*: For the flush, for the water to go into the floor.
> *Salvador*: It goes in here, in this toilet part. You see this little hole. That's how it makes its flush.
> *Teacher*: And then where does it go?
> *Salvador*: Let's flush it so you can see where it goes.
> *Nico* (as they observe the flushing toilet): It looks like a tornado.
> *Salvador*: It goes in the wall and starts going down.

Finally, the exploration moved to the boiler room.

> *Jonathon*: These are bigger pipes. They're hot.
> *Salvador*: Hot air.
> *Jonathon*: And water comes down there, . . . and that leads to something hot. I don't know what kind of pipe it is, [but it's] draining to the sewer.
> *Teacher*: What's that pipe there?
> *Salvador*: The workers build it. See, look up there, teacher; it's connected to another pipe. It goes all the way up there. Look, it's going through the wall. It's going down into the ground.

The Pipes Area: Further Exploration of Pipes and Flow

At the next weekly meeting the group examined the transcript of the children's conversations from their pipe walk through the building. Based on the strong level of enthusiasm shown by the children, they decided to give the whole class an opportunity to explore pipes more directly. They collected a variety of pipes, such as long, short, copper, plastic, flexible, inflexible pipes, and set up a pipes exploration area in the classroom. The children played with the pipes, manipulated them on the floor, and put water through them (see Figure 1.3).

While documenting the children's activities in the pipes area, the teachers noticed that Jaime was holding a pipe over his head as though he was taking a shower

Figure 1.3.
Children collaborate and experiment when exploring how water flows through different kinds of pipes.

(Figure 1.4). They checked this hypothesis with Jaime and found that it was correct (Figure 1.5). The documentation that they took to the next weekly meeting included the Jaime photographs as well as photos of other children who were simulating shower taking. This led the team to suggest the next phase of the inquiry.

The Showers Study

Five children participated in the showers exploration. Each was asked to make three successive drawings in response to the question, "How do showers work?" After the first round of drawings, the teachers revisited each child's drawing with the child, who explained the drawing to the teacher. Children sometimes embellished their drawings to include thoughts that came to them while discussing their drawing with the teacher. Each child's explanations were written on the drawing by the teacher in order to give the children a reflection for their ideas and to provide the opportunity for them to revisit and reflect on their ideas on subsequent days. Jonathon's three drawings are presented in Figure 1.6.

The following dialogue between Jonathon and the teacher focuses on the third drawing. Notes in parentheses signal additions that Jonathon made to his drawing in response to the teacher's questions.

Figure 1.4.
Children experiment with connecting pipes in different ways in a newly designated pipes area of the classroom.

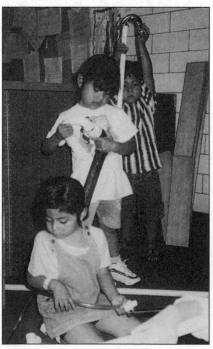

Figure 1.5.
Two children's exploration leads to creating showers, and Jaime acts out the flowing water.

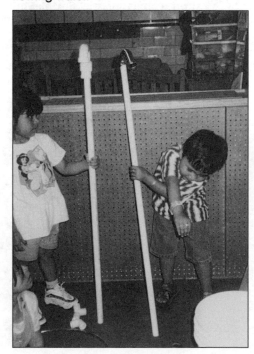

Figure 1.6. Jonathon's successive shower drawings (the words are written by the teacher).

Here is Jonathon's first drawing.

Here is Jonathon's second drawing, after revisiting the first.

Here is Jonathon's third drawing, after revisiting the second.

Jonathon: This is the shower. The water comes up and out. It comes from here [the faucet]. The water goes down into the tub.

Teacher: How does the water get out?

Jonathon: (Draws a drain in the tub.)

Teacher: And then where does it go?

Jonathon: (Draws a line out of the drain into the feet of the tub.)

Teacher: And then where does it go?

Jonathon: Out here. (Draws a line from the bottom of the tub to a cup). It goes into this cup. Then they put it in bottles and sell it to people.

The following questions are a way to reflect on the Pipes Study—or any other in-depth study—in relation to the Reggio principles:

- What image of the child is implicit in the teachers' actions and in their relationships with the children? For example, how do you think the teacher views Jonathon's competence in the dialogue just above?
- How did teachers' listening, observing, reflecting, and responding shape the learning process?
- What kinds of documentation did the teachers *collect* and how did they use it?
- What examples did you see of the co-construction of understanding among children and between teacher and child?
- What kinds of understandings were constructed? How were multiple perspectives brought to bear?
- What forms of representation did the children use to express and communicate their ideas? How were multiple forms of representation sometimes used to communicate the same idea?
- What appeared to be the benefits of children revisiting their representations?
- How did the teachers use various facets of the environment to stimulate and facilitate the children's learning?
- What role did teacher collaboration play in this sequence?
- What preschool learning standards were being met?

EXPRESSIONS OF REGGIO PRINCIPLES IN THE PIPES STUDY

Through the Pipes Study we can see the frequent interaction of the principles of *listening/observing–reflecting–responding, documentation, teacher collaboration,* and *image of the child.* For example, teachers collected the children's drawings from the neighborhood walk (listening, documenting) and reflected on them at their weekly team meeting (collaborating, reflecting). This resulted in their asking some of the children details about the mysterious parallel lines in their drawings (responding, listening). They wrote the children's explanations about pipes on their drawings and suggested to Jonathon that he make further drawings of "how pipes work" (responding, listening, documenting). The teachers then took these documentations to the next weekly meeting, where it was decided to focus the inquiry on pipes (collaborating, reflecting). They planned to offer a group of interested children the opportunity to take a pipes walk through the building (responding). The teachers recorded the conversations that took place during the pipes walk (documenting) and took a transcript from that tape to their next weekly meeting (collaborating, reflecting). At every turn, the teachers, through their words and actions, communicated to the children that they saw the children as keenly interested in the world, competent, rich in ideas, and motivated to communicate (image of the child).

In this study, the *co-construction of understanding* occurred in five different ways.

1. Teachers and children together co-constructed understandings of the children's interests (e.g., teachers returning to the children to discuss the meaning of the parallel lines in their drawings).
2. Teachers and children together co-constructed understandings about the object of study (e.g., teacher interacting with Jonathon about his third shower drawing). In these exchanges the teacher frequently communicated additional perspectives to consider through questions (e.g., "How does the water get out?").
3. Teachers facilitated the co-construction process among children and simultaneously participated with them in that process (e.g., the conversation during the pipes walk).
4. Children co-constructed understandings on their own (e.g., children's co-explorations in the pipes area; see Figures 1.3, 1.4, and 1.5).
5. At the weekly meeting, teachers co-constructed interpretations of children's representations and co-constructed ideas for scaffolding the next steps in the study.

Note that three of the above examples of co-construction focus on revisiting children's representations. The process through which co-construction of understandings takes place is *dialogue.*

Dialogue is when two or more individuals express their perspectives about something to each other, each party listens to, considers, and responds to the perspective(s) of the other in interaction with his or her own ideas, and the parties, through their interaction, work to connect and evolve their collective ideas to construct new understandings of the subject matter they are addressing.

Dialogue involves taking *multiple perspectives*. It must, by the very nature of the human condition, since no two people experience something from exactly the same position (Bakhtin, 1986, 1990; Holquist, 1990). The power of dialogue is that it promotes the expression of multiple perspectives and thereby leads to the co-construction of more differentiated and connected understandings in the minds of the participants than any of them likely would have rendered on their own. This happens precisely because they are sharing different perspectives and evolving new perspectives through considering the interaction of the perspectives that have been offered.

The children's conversations while exploring the pipes in various parts of the school building provide an example of how multiple perspectives contribute to a fuller grasp of an object of study. If you revisit their conversations (in the pipes walk), you will find one or more examples of the perspectives described in the list below. Each perspective in the list is accompanied by a single example.

- Pathway ("It goes around and in here.")
- Extent of penetration ("The pipe is coming into the hole and all the way in.")
- Contents that flow through the pipe ("It looks like a water pipe.")
- Removal of blockage to the flow ("When we open this [the drain], the water goes down the pipes and into the wall.")
- Connection to a larger carrier ("It goes under the ground and across under the school to the sewer.")
- Configuration ("It looks like a tornado.")
- Size ("These are bigger pipes.")
- Temperature ("They're hot.")

Note in the actual dialogue (pipes walk section) how the children's various perspectives build on one another and, when combined, contribute to a fuller understanding of the pipes in the building.

In the above case, the various perspectives shared by the children are complementary in the sense that they easily can be combined into a wider scope of understanding. Sometimes, however, a given perspective conflicts with the ones already expressed. Thus, the Reggio ideals include confronting children with two or more conflicting perspectives. The conflicting perspectives may be those of two children, as in the case of the ladder example (see "Multiple Perspectives" earlier in this chapter), or the conflict may be between the child's perspective and one introduced by the teacher (see Chapter 3, "Going Downtown" and "What Can Babies Do?"). In pointing out such conflicts, the teacher is playing what is called the "provocatore" role. The direct translation of this into English would be "provoker." Since a common English meaning of *provoke* is to anger, irritate, or annoy, the Commons staff chose to call this type of teacher provocation a "challenge." The broad meaning of *challenge*, as used in the program, is to stimulate someone to think more deeply about something. Challenges from the teacher provide a major stimulus to dialogue with and among children (see Chapter 3).

The Pipes Study is a clear example of an in-depth study guided by the emergent curriculum process. In the study, we see a continuous chain of listening/observing–reflecting–responding cycles. The emergent curriculum process is, in fact, an ongoing dialogue. Children and teachers continually are listening, observing, interpreting, and responding to one another's actions and meanings over an extended period of time.

In-depth studies are a very visible form through which Reggio principles are applied. At the same time, the Reggio principles apply to every moment of the school day. For example, they are expressed in dialogues between teachers and children engaged in spontaneous play (see Chapter 3, "How to Ride a Bike," "Going Downtown," and "The Beetle Borg"). They apply to exchanges during meal times and transition times, and at any other time of the school day. We will see examples of such applications in Chapters 2, 3, and 7, as well as further discussion of this subject in Chapter 6.

The learning environment facilitates all of the other processes that we have described above. For example, a well-constructed classroom environment stimulates children's interests and promotes small-group collaboration, which in turn frees up the teachers to work with one small group at a time and to collect documentations. A well-constructed environment communicates and promotes the image of the child through posting children's work, which in turn makes possible the kinds of revisiting processes described above. The importance of the learning environment and principles underlying its construction are described in Chapter 6.

THE SIGNIFICANCE OF DIALOGUE FOR HUMAN DEVELOPMENT

Dialogue characterizes communications between teachers and children, among children, among staff (see Chapters 10, 11, and 12), and between staff and parents (see Chapter 9). Accordingly, it pervades and illuminates every facet of the Reggio Approach and brings cultural unity to a program. This has major implications for the development of both children and adults. We would suggest that much of human development can be understood as a *growing capacity to engage in dialogue,* specifically:

- To be aware of and able to express one's own perspective as perspective, involving both feelings and thoughts
- To perceive that every other person's consciousness is distinct from one's own
- To be open to and listen carefully to the perspectives of others, both their ideas and their emotional experiences
- To be aware that any person's perspective, including one's own, is always limited
- To be able to juxtapose and negotiate one's perspective with those of others, with the result of challenging, broadening, and deepening one's own point of view on the one hand, and building more solid understandings on the other

A further aspect of human development that takes place through dialogue is the growth of each individual's capacities to see connections and construct more comprehensive models of reality in his or her mind. This capacity is vital to each person's adaptation and treatment of others, and to the collective decisions that societies make in their relationship to their citizens, to other societies, and to the natural environment.

CHALLENGING QUESTIONS

A number of key issues, historically and currently addressed in the program, will serve as organizing questions of this book. They include

- How can one enter a child's world and understand a child's deeper interests? Is it possible? How do we do it?
- How do we facilitate children's building on their interests once those interests have been identified?
- How can teachers promote and support children's development of their capacities for dialogue and the construction of understanding?
- How can the child's agenda and the teachers' agendas be effectively joined?
- What are our goals for participation of parents? Why are we pursuing those goals? How can we effectively go about engaging parents in relation to those goals?
- How can staff as a whole be guided and supported in their professional development?

- How does one structure, organize, and energize the program as a whole?
- Can all this be done within areas of urban poverty and government-funded programs?

ORGANIZATION OF THE BOOK

The next seven chapters (2–8) focus on the teaching–learning process. Chapters 2–6 are each devoted to one of the Reggio principles described earlier in this chapter.

Chapter 2 (Listening, Observing, Reflecting, and Responding) examines the process of teachers listening and responding to children's expressions of interests, feelings, and ideas. It documents how two teachers gradually learned to listen and respond to children in the context of a children's study of the local elementary school. The chapter then discusses what is meant by children's "interests" and invites the reader to reflect on a teacher–child dialogue that exhibits various degrees of listening and nonlistening by the teacher.

Chapter 3 (Co-Construction of Understandings with Children) addresses three questions: In what ways do teacher–child interactions facilitate children's thinking? What processes within teachers help them to facilitate children's thinking? How do teachers facilitate thoughtful dialogue with and among small groups of children? These questions are explored in the context of six dialogues between teachers and children.

Chapter 4 (Children's Representations) examines how children create representations such as drawings, three-dimensional constructions, and verbal expression to construct and communicate understandings that arise from their investigations of the world. The chapter also explains how children acquire knowledge and skills regarding the materials that they use when creating representations.

Chapter 5 (Emergent Curriculum) describes processes through which children's in-depth studies unfold over weeks or months. The chapter utilizes the concept of the emergent curriculum cycle to depict what teachers do to foster the evolution of an in-depth study. The emergent curriculum cycle, which is repeated several or more times during the course of an emergent curriculum process, consists of listening/observing, documenting, interpreting, projecting/deciding, planning, hypothesizing, scaffolding, listening/observing again, and so on.

Chapter 6 (The Learning Environment) discusses how the environments of classroom, school building, school grounds, neighborhood, and city can be constructed or utilized to stimulate the emergence of children's interests and to support children's interest-based learning engagements with one another, with their teachers, and with the environment.

The next two chapters (7 and 8) address two critical issues that often emerge in discussions about applying the Reggio Approach in American contexts.

Chapter 7 (Classroom Management) discusses how teachers can guide and coordinate activities in ways that promote the Reggio Approach throughout the day. Specifically, the chapter addresses the implementation and integration of five types of teacher actions: being available to listen, observe, and respond to children throughout the day; scaffolding children's learning; documenting children's learning; responding to upsets; and coordinating the overall flow of activities and routines. The chapter also discusses the processes of teacher collaboration within the classroom and how a classroom that is exploring the Reggio Approach can respond creatively to federal, state, and local government requirements.

Chapter 8 (School Readiness) asks how the Reggio Approach, as implemented by Chicago Commons, results in development that prepares children for learning in kindergarten and beyond. The chapter addresses the development of capacities for self-regulated, focused learning; skills in speaking, thinking, reading, writing, and math; and social–emotional development.

Chapters 9–11 look at the application of Reggio Emilia principles in three contexts that support the teaching–learning process: relationships with parents, professional development and support for teachers, and the overall organization of the program.

Chapter 9 (Parent Partnership) asks how a preschool program that is engaged in exploring the Reggio Approach with children can promote relationships with parents that reflect and support Reggio principles. The chapter examines six contexts in which the ideals of dialogue and collaboration with parents can be realized: home visits, the monthly meetings in which both staff and parents participate, drop-off and pick-up times, portfolio nights, involvement of parents in children's in-depth studies, and parent collaboration with teachers in the classroom and on field trips.

Chapter 10 (Professional Development and Support of Teachers) is a detailed examination of structures and processes that empower Chicago Commons teachers to embody Reggio principles in their teaching and learning. The chapter describes 11 contexts in which professional development of teachers occurs: weekly meetings, the ongoing experience of teaching and learning, collection and use of documentation, classroom collaboration, teacher research studies, monthly meetings, in-service experiences, learning tours, outside conferences, visits from Reggio Emilia educators, and visits to Reggio Emilia.

Chapter 11 (Organization of the Program) focuses on five questions: Who guides, supports, and inspires the activities of the coordinators and the site directors who, in turn, provide guidance and support to teachers? What is the role of the program's director? What is the administrative structure of the program? How are the teachers, coordinators, site directors, and others integrated into a learning community? How do children and parents participate in that learning community?

Chapter 12 (Lessons Learned) reflects on understandings gained from exploring the Reggio Approach in the Chicago Commons setting. The understandings are grouped under three categories: the spirit of the Reggio Approach, realities of exploring this approach in the Chicago context, and facilitating/supporting teacher thinking and action. The chapter concludes with suggestions for educational leaders who plan to introduce Reggio ideas to their teachers. Finally, the chapter asks, "Why explore ideas from Reggio Emilia?"

In the final chapters (9–12) we examine the idea of "parallel process," specifically, a proposition that the incorporation of Reggio principles into learning and collaboration among adults strengthens the implementation of the same principles in the adults' relationships with children.

The Appendix is a year-by-year account of the program's evolution over 12 years. It provides the reader with an opportunity to more thoroughly understand many of the events described in the book by placing them in their historical context. The account also allows the reader to make inferences about steps in the development of this Reggio Exploration over time.

Chapter 2

Listening, Observing, Reflecting, and Responding

When children feel they are not being listened to, they don't have anything to say.
—Sergio Spaggiari, Director, Reggio Emilia municipal preschools,
from a talk given at Reggio Emilia in 1994

When a teacher is listening to a child, she attends carefully to the meaning of what the child is saying and observes what the child is expressing or trying to pursue. She reflects the child's motives, interests, feelings, experiences, ideas, capabilities, and accomplishments back to the child in ways that fully recognize, endorse, and value them. She explores children's meanings with them in depth and is clearly aware of differences between her own perspectives and those of the children. She is an active partner with the child, often making suggestions or asking questions that build on and extend what she observes in the child's words, actions, and creations. Throughout this process, the teacher tries to have a clear awareness of why she is responding to a child in a particular way, even though the teacher's response may be intuitive.

Within this listening relationship established by the teacher, the children assume that they will be listened to and that the teacher's responses will reflect that listening. The children experience that their expressions of interests, motives, emotions, ideas, and capabilities are noted and embraced by the teacher and are causes of the teacher's responses to them. Thus, the children experience themselves as fully existing, valid, worthwhile, and cherished in the mind and heart of the teacher.

Listening, observing, reflecting, and responding are aspects of a single process; that is, the teacher responds through her understanding of what she has heard and observed, and the child responds to the teacher's response and thus gives her the opportunity to listen to the child and/or observe the child further. It is, above all, a dialogue. The child's meanings are not always expressed verbally; they may be implicit in actions, gestures, or facial expressions. But the process is a dialogue nonetheless.

When the above process extends over days or weeks in the form of an in-depth study, the teacher's responses to the children often are informed by conversations with other staff, either informally or in the weekly meetings (see Chapter 1, "Emergent Curriculum" and "Pipes Study"). When a teacher realizes she has missed an opportunity to respond to a child, she can always return to the child the next day or week to ask a follow-up question. This confirms to children that they are being listened to and taken seriously.

LEARNING TO LISTEN, OBSERVE, REFLECT, AND RESPOND

The process of teacher professional development begins with learning to listen to and observe children's expressions of their competencies and interests (see Chapter 10). There are two major aspects to this teacher development process. One is developing skills as a listener, observer, and interpreter; for example, learning to interpret the deeper lying interests being expressed in children's actions or drawings. The other involves the teacher coming to grips with the "agendas issue."

Teachers have learning agendas for children that come from their own school and family experience, from their training in education, and from requirements such as those of Head Start, state-subsidized child care, and state pre-K. Their agendas tend to be experienced as "shoulds." The crux of the agendas issue is that the teacher's primary focus on her own agenda can seriously interfere with her being able to listen and respond to the child's agenda (i.e., the child's interests and learning motivations). Teachers are encouraged to set aside their own agendas when those agendas interfere with listening to the children. However, this is not to say that teachers should not have agendas. An important distinction is expressed by Karen Haigh (director of Chicago Commons) in the following statement to her staff:

There is nothing wrong with the teacher having an agenda. It's just a matter of understanding that your agenda may not be the child's agenda. To assume that it is, is going to leave the child not being very interested in pursuing anything. *If teachers only follow their own agenda,* the child can become disinterested in learning. The learning becomes too disconnected from the child and his life. We want to support children's investment in learning, and there is a great danger in destroying motivation to learn when the interests being pursued are only the teacher's and not the child's. I want to say that this is much easier to talk about than it is to do.

THE WINDOWS STUDY AND THE AGENDAS ISSUE

The following description of the Windows Study is an example of how teachers in the Reggio Exploration gradually learned to listen to children's expression of their interests. The story illustrates a relatively early stage in the teachers' ongoing struggle to differentiate their own agendas from the agendas of the children.

Phase #1: The Big School

In early April 1998, two co-teachers at the ETC Center chose to pursue a Big School Study with their children, namely, a study of the local school where many of the children would be attending kindergarten the following year (see Appendix, Year 7). The two teachers made a list of all the things they wanted the children to learn about kindergarten. This procedure reflected their earlier, pre-Reggio training, and was strongly influenced by the traditional Head Start approach to preparing children for transition to kindergarten.

They engaged the children in large-group and small-group discussions on the topic of the Big School, asking questions that were guided by their initial list of things they wanted the children to learn.

The class visited the outside of the Big School and drew pictures. The next morning, they drew pictures about what they thought they would see on the inside of the school when they visited the following day. The teachers asked the children to think of questions that they wanted to ask when visiting the kindergarten room.

The class visited the inside of the Big School, including some kindergarten classrooms. One of the teachers reported, "When we went in the children were excited about how the school looked, especially the windows and the stairs, but we [teachers] were focused on the questions that they were going to ask about kindergarten."

On returning from their visit to the Big School, the teachers held conversations with the whole class about the visit. They posed two questions to the children: "What were some of the things you liked about the Big School and what were some of the things you didn't like?"

Following the discussion the children went to the studio in small groups to draw pictures of the school based on what they remembered from the visit. Audio recordings were made of their small-group conversations while they were drawing.

> *What patterns of children's interests or ideas do you see in the following dialogue?*

Lorenzo: I want to draw a big school.
Selina: Teacher, look what I did, a window.
Isaac: Look, teacher. This is a paper. Teacher, I want another paper.
Lorenzo: I'm done. Can I go back to the classroom?
Isaac: Windows, Windows, Windows. Teacher, I'm making a school.
Isaac: I saw clocks, chairs, and lockers.
Selina: Teacher, give me another paper.
Isaac: I draw a school, a window, and a door. I don't want to draw anymore.

Later on that day, when asked to engage in further conversation about the Big School, the children showed no interest in the topic: "I don't want to do this"; "I'm busy"; "Do we have to talk about this again?"

Feeling frustrated, the teachers took the drawings and transcripts from the dialogues to the weekly meeting. They had planned so many important things for the children to learn, and basically the children weren't interested. The weekly meeting team included the two teachers, a studio coordinator, an education coordinator, two teachers from another classroom, and the site director. The group decided to look at the children's drawings and at the accompanying dialogues to see if they could discern patterns of children's interests to build upon. This was a major turning point. In both the drawings and the children's comments, they noticed frequent inclusion of windows and stairs. They decided to focus their next explorations with the children on those themes.

Phase #2: The Windows Focus

The next school day, the teachers said to the children, "When we came back from the Big School, we noticed that you were drawing and talking about windows and stairs." The children's enthusiastic response confirmed their hunch.

The teachers went to the Big School after work the next day and took numerous slides of windows and stairs both at the Big School and in the neighborhood.

Several days later, they showed the children the slides of windows and compared them with the windows in the classroom. The children became excited at the idea of drawing their favorite windows in small groups. The learning sequence finally had shifted to a children's agenda.

The teachers then asked the children some questions about windows.

> *What ideas in the following dialogue
> might suggest next steps for the teachers?*

Teacher: Why are windows important?
Janette: If you don't have windows you can't breathe and you can die.
Lusio: Windows are for looking at the street. Looking at plants and grass and china.
Gena: They can go up and down.
Teacher: What are windows for?
Alex: To see.
Jaquelyn: That way you can see outside.
Alyssa: For looking at people.
Ruth: For look for see the cars.
Robert: So the children can see.
Angel: Because my Mom open the window.
Carmen: My father open the window and I got a flag.
Alyssa: You can open the window and get air. You can see airplanes, cars, flowers,
    and houses too, and people and the store.

The teachers took a transcript of the above dialogue to the weekly meeting. In exploring the dialogue, the group noted that many children were interested in what they could *see through* the windows. Consequently, they decided not only to focus on the children drawing their favorite windows, but also to suggest that they include in the drawings what they saw through the windows.

Phase #3: Drawing Windows

The children explored windows in several parts of the preschool building. The next day they drew pictures, from memory, of what they had seen through the windows the previous day. They talked with one another as they were drawing and showed their drawings to one another, sharing their experiences. The teachers audiotaped these conversations. At circle time the children shared what they were drawing and asked one another questions. This is Alyssa's drawing (see Figure 2.1).

Figure 2.1.
Children draw what they see through the windows. They enjoy working in a small group. Alyssa's (age 5) drawing shows her interest in both stairs and windows—interests that were first shown by several children after visiting the Big School.

↑   ↑
"This is the street"   "This is the stair to go upstairs from
                            the house across the street."

Several days later, the teachers selected some of the older children to do a "window hunt." With clipboards, drawing paper, and markers the children were stationed at windows in the preschool building. The teachers taped the children's ongoing conversations and took photos of the children's drawings. Gena's multiperspective drawing in Chapter 4 (see Figure 4.6) is an interesting example.

Thoughts on the Windows Study

The children's loss of interest in talking about the Big School alerted the teachers that they were on the wrong track. Until that point, their agenda of wanting the children to focus on the kindergarten classroom activities dominated their concerns. Although the teachers had achieved their goal of introducing children to kindergarten, their goal of working with the children to study the Big School was not easily pursued until they looked closely at the children's actual interests.

The children's interests became manifest when the teachers asked them to draw their experience. The teachers paid close attention to what the children drew and recorded what the children said while drawing. The teachers had begun to enter into a genuine dialogue with the children, by listening and observing.

In phase #2, the teachers responded by checking their interpretation of the children's interests with the children, taking slides of windows and stairs, showing the slides to the children, and inviting the children to draw their favorite windows. The process of listening and responding extended into the subsequent dialogue. Lusio says, "Windows are for looking at the street. Looking at plants and grass and china." A moment later, the teacher picks up on Lusio's perspective by asking, "What are windows for?" The rest of the dialogue revolves around that question and provides information for a further interpretation of the children's interest in windows, namely, an interest in what they can *see* through windows. In phase #3, the teachers responded to that interpretation by suggesting to the children that they draw both the window and what they see through it. The challenge was pleasurable and easily manageable for the children.

The observations and reflections of the weekly meeting team played an important role in helping the two teachers to reflect on and become more sensitive to the children's interests. Through that process all of the participants on the team grew in their ability to interpret children's interests and build on them. This attests to the importance of both documenting children's words and actions and collaboratively reflecting on the documentation with colleagues.

Months after this experience, the teachers made several public presentations describing the Windows Study and what it had taught them. This repeated revisiting and reflecting on the experience enhanced their learning and that of their colleagues (see Chapter 10, Documentation).

This episode, and those that occurred in other centers as the teachers engaged children in in-depth studies in the spring of 1998, marked a major turning point in the evolution of the Reggio Exploration at Chicago Commons.

CHILDREN'S INTERESTS

"Interests" are enduring motives to engage particular aspects of the world in particular ways. The following are some aspects of children's interests that a teacher might want to consider when interpreting and responding to them.

Surface Versus Deeper Lying Interests

When we speak of children's interests, sometimes we are relating only to the *surface* manifestation of interests. We may say, for example, that a particular child is interested in trucks, cars, babies, families, playing house, dinosaurs, and so on. But we have as yet to identify the *particular qualities* of those things that are drawing the child to them. Nor have we yet identified how the child *wants to relate* to them. We have yet to understand the *deeper lying* interests that give the playing out of the surface interests their form.

Patterns of deeper lying interests often can be identified through additional observation and reflection. For example, a revisiting of the children's conversations about pipes suggests that a deeper lying aspect of children's interest in pipes is that pipes go somewhere.

> *Jonathon:* This pipe goes inside the wall.
> *David:* It goes around and in here.
> *Nico:* The pipe is coming into the hole and all the way in.
> *Salvador:* It's going into the hole. I see something in there. It's turning, it's turning, and it's staying inside the wall. You see, it goes in the wall.

There also seems to be an interest in the pipes *going into* something (e.g., the wall), an interest in their *taking particular pathways*, and an interest in their path becoming *hidden from view* ("It's turning, it's turning, and it's staying inside the wall.").

Further, the children are interested in the contents that flow through the pipes.

> *Jonathon:* You find gas pipes in the ground.
> *Jonathon:* Drain pipes, like when the really dirty oil comes out.
> *Nico:* It looks like one water pipe.
> *Nico:* These are for water. When we open this [the drain], the water goes down the pipes and into the wall. It goes into the pipe and into the ground.

Later the children became deeply involved in moving water through the pipes provided for them in the classroom exploration and ultimately took an interest in exploring showers and the flow of water through the showerhead into the tub and beyond.

These observations suggest a hypothesis regarding the children's interest in pipes, namely, that a deeper interest is in flow and changes in the pathways of flow (i.e., motion along a path.) Their interest also would seem to be in the purposefulness of the flow, with the flow actually being intended by someone. This in turn may be rooted in what Johnson (1987) points out is a basic experience of children since infancy.

> Consider the common goal of getting to a particular location. From the time that we can first crawl, we regularly have as an intention getting to some particular place. . . . There may well be no intention satisfied more often than physical motion to a particular desired location. In such cases, we have a purpose . . . that is satisfied by moving our bodies from a starting point A, through an intermediate sequence of spatial locations, to the end point. (p. 115)

A deeper lying interest is likely to show up across a variety of surface interests of a child. An interest in motion along a path may be manifest in a child's interests in the movement of racing cars along a track, a gerbil through a maze, an ant across a terrain, or a rocket along a trajectory.

Finally, we might hypothesize that children's interest in pipes and the contents that flow through them, as well as the pathways of pipes inside of walls, reveals a pervasive, deeper lying interest in things that are hidden from view yet dynamic.

Child-Specific Versus Universally Shared Interests

Some interests (surface and/or deeper lying) are held by one or a few children, while other interests are shared by many of the children in a class. An example of the latter emerged in a Big School Study at another center. As the children's discussions of the Big School progressed, the teachers found that the strongest interest that the children expressed did not involve the details of the kindergarten curriculum (as the teachers had intended) but rather a concern about leaving their preschool friends when they moved on to kindergarten in the coming year. The older children, destined to leave in the fall, had concerns about parting from friends who were going to other schools and about leaving the younger children, who, in some cases, were their siblings. They also were interested in which friends would be going forward with them to the same school. The younger ones, for their part, had concerns about losing the older ones. In other words, the children were focused on universal issues of friendship and separation. This discovery led to the teachers inviting the children to participate in a study of Friends. The class enthusiastically responded (see Chapter 4 for children's drawings associated with this study).

Individual Ways of Relating to the Object of Interest

A further aspect of a child's interest is how the child is inclined to approach the exploration of the interest (e.g., through observation, talking about it, physical interaction, drawing, representation through clay, block construction, dramatic play, etc.). The desired manners of engagement are part of the interest and, ideally, will broaden and deepen over time.

Degree of Consciousness of an Interest

Finally, interests will differ greatly in the degree to which they are consciously present in the child's awareness. At one extreme are a child's general propensities to be drawn to certain topics, objects, and events. They are not yet crystallized into a conscious interest that the child can articulate or even fully recognize as his or her own. One often sees these implicit interests emerge and take form in relation to learning stimuli provided by the teacher. It is likely, for many of the children, that their interest in pipes grew from an implicit, preconscious propensity to a more conscious, formulated interest as the Pipes Study progressed. At the other extreme are interests that are fully present in a child's awareness.

CARMEN AND THE TEACHER

The following interaction between a child and a teacher gives us a chance to look closely at a child's interests. It also gives us a chance to look at both sides of the agendas issue, the teacher's agenda and the child's agenda. The episode swings between two extremes. On one hand, it is a *poignant case of contrasting agendas of teacher and child in which the teacher persistently pursues her own agenda in spite of the child's repeated messages that the teacher's agenda does not interest her*. On the other hand, the episode seems to be an *extraordinary case of sensitive listening* by the teacher and of mutuality between teacher and child. *Is this combination actually possible?* See what you think.

As you read this, it might be interesting to ask:

> *What is the teacher's agenda?*
>
> *What is the child's agenda?*

Carmen (4 years old) sits in a chair by herself with a box of shells in her lap. She looks up and smiles with pleasure as the teacher comes over and moves the chair closer to and parallel to her.

> *Teacher*: Would you like to make something with that? (While talking, the teacher looks at Carmen, but Carmen does not look up.)
> *Carmen*: Uhuh (continuing to look at the shells). Look at these . . . (Another child comes over and temporarily diverts the teacher's attention. Carmen waits expectantly.)
> *Teacher*: What would you like to make?

Carmen does not respond. Both the teacher and Carmen are now looking at the shells.

> *Teacher*: What would you like to do?
> *Carmen*: (Shows teacher one of the shells.) Do you see these sprinkles?
> *Teacher*: Sprinkles? I see a lot of lines.

Carmen puts the shell down and picks up another one, showing it to the teacher.

> *Teacher* (holding out the palm of her hand with the shell in it): Is it the same? (This seems to mean, "Is it the same as the previous shell?")
> *Carmen*: Uh-huh.
> *Teacher*: Why is it the same?
> *Carmen*: Because I like beautiful.
> *Teacher*: They're beautiful? (She takes the shell from Carmen.) Look. What do they have that is the same? What is it that's the same?

Carmen begins to place that shell and some other shells into the teacher's outstretched hand.

> *Teacher*: Why do they look the same?
> *Carmen* (placing shells on the teacher's palm): Because.
> *Teacher* (sounding less urgent, but still persistent): Can I see? Why do you think they look the same?

Carmen looks closely at the shell, drops it into the box, and then picks it up. She does not respond to the teacher in any other way.

> *Teacher*: Are these two blue? Why do you think they look the same?

> *What seems to be the teacher's agenda?*

> *Carmen* (picks up a shell and places it in the teacher's hand): Here's a big one.
> *Teacher*: Yes, that one is big. (She is endorsing Carmen's idea that the shell is big while helping Carmen to place the shell into the teacher's palm.) Look at this (pointing to one of the shells with her pen). What does that look like?

Carmen: I don't know.

Teacher: A flower. (She gives Carmen the answer that she, the teacher, has in mind.)

Carmen (looking and pointing at the shell): It's the Goo Goo Monster. (Note: Goo Goo Monster is a favorite chasing game that the children play outside. The Goo Goo Monster chases the others. Sometimes the children want the teacher to be the Goo Goo Monster.)

Teacher (leans in closer): It's the what?

Carmen: The Goo Goo Monster did this.

Teacher: The Goo Goo Monster did that?

Carmen: He ran away and bumped his head. (She lifts her arm in the air and looks into the distance, as if imagining a vivid scene. She smiles.)

Teacher: He ran away and bumped his head? He bumped his head here? (She points to a hole in the shell.)

Carmen: Yes.

Teacher: Hmmm. I see.

Carmen: I see another little hole. (She points to one of the shells.)

Teacher: Hmmm. This one has a lot of holes. (She turns the shell on her palm toward Carmen and points to it with her pen.) Does this one have holes? (She points to several shells in the palm of her hand.)

Carmen: No.

Teacher: This one, the big one, has holes. Can you find another one [with holes]?

Carmen: Look at the little baby. This is the little baby, and he is sleeping.

Teacher: He is sleeping? Yes, that's the small one.

Carmen (placing the baby shell in the teacher's palm): He wants his poppy and his mommy.

Teacher: Where are his poppy and his mommy?

> What would you infer about Carmen's interests
> based on what has occurred so far?

Carmen (pointing to two shells in the teacher's hand): Right here.

Teacher: Does this baby have brothers and sisters?

Carmen: Uhuh! See! Here's the mommy and the poppy. (She points to two new shells.)

Teacher: The mommy is over here and the poppy is over here.

Carmen: The kid's over here.

Teacher: Who's this? (She points to a shell.)

Carmen: The kid.

Teacher: What kid? Boy or girl?

Carmen: A boy.

Teacher: A boy.

Carmen (holding another shell): See. They painted it.

Teacher: They painted it? What color did they paint it? What color is that?

Carmen: I don't know.

Teacher: Is it purple? Is it the same color as this (pointing to the color purple on her own shirt)? Or is it the same color as your shirt?

Carmen: Shirt.

Teacher: Your shirt, yes. That color is white, the color of your shirt. Yes.

Carmen holds up another shell.

Teacher: What's this one? What are you going to tell me about this one?

Carmen (emphatically and defiantly): They painted it!

Teacher: How can you tell they painted it?

> *Carmen* (giving shell to the teacher): Because the Goo Goo Monster did it.
> *Teacher* (picking up the shell from her palm): The Goo Goo Monster?! Who is the Goo Goo Monster?
> *Carmen* (playfully): You are.
> *Teacher* (playfully): Me?!
> *Carmen*: Yes.
> *Teacher* (playfully): Nooooo!
> *Carmen* (placing another shell in the teacher's palm): Yes. I be the Goo Goo Monster.
> *Teacher* (holding up her palm, filled with shells): How many do you have? How many do you have, already, here? Hmmm?

Carmen picks up a shell from the box and blows into it. She does this twice, each time looking up at the teacher for a response to her blowing.

> *Teacher*: Why are you blowing in there?
> *Carmen*: Because. (She holds the shell and continues to look at it while the teacher leans toward her.) See? To get the baby out.
> *Teacher*: Do you think it is to blow in there? What happens when you blow in there?
> *Carmen* (holds the shell up to her mouth and blows on it): Because the baby can't get out. (She is trying to help the baby.)
> *Teacher*: Are you trying to get those little black things out? (She leans close to Carmen, pointing at something on the shell.)
> *Carmen* (enjoying herself, continues to blow into the shell and a sound comes out): Teacher, look! (She taps on the teacher's arm.)
> *Teacher* (finishes talking with another student and bends toward Carmen, encountering the sound resulting from Carmen's blowing): Wow!
> *Carmen* (giving the shell to the teacher): Now you blow it.
> *Teacher* (takes the shell and blows into it): Where? I have to blow in the little hole? (The teacher tries blowing again.) It makes a funny noise!
> *Carmen*: Let me do it. (She takes the shell back and blows into it. Her face is cheerful.) Makes a funny noise.
> *Teacher*: A funny noise.
> *Carmen*: Now you blow in my ear.
> *Teacher*: You want me to blow into your ear? (She picks up a shell, holds it near Carmen's ear, and blows into it.)
> *Carmen* (covering her ears): I hear it.
> *Teacher*: Let me see. Now do it to me.

Carmen takes a shell, holds it near the teacher's ear, and blows into it.

> *Teacher*: Oh! I see. (Teacher is interrupted by another child but keeps her hand outstretched to Carmen while she is turned away from her.)

Carmen looks intensely at the shells in the teacher's hand.

> *Teacher* (turning back to Carmen): Look at this one. This one has holes. Like this one—one hole?
> *Carmen*: I don't like no holes. (She takes the shell from the teacher's hand and puts it into the box, symbolically ending the exploration.)
> *Teacher*: You don't like it when you have holes in there?
> *Carmen*: Nope. (Drops another shell into the box.)
> *Teacher*: Okay.

> *How do you interpret Carmen's "I don't like no holes"?*

Thoughts and Questions on the Teacher and Carmen

Here are a few perspectives on this episode.

At seven different points, the teacher attempts to introduce her agenda (compare/contrast of attributes, counting, colors, etc.) and each time Carmen ignores the teacher's idea or question and introduces something from her own agenda.

The teacher recovers the breach each time by listening and responding to *Carmen's* reassertions of *Carmen's* agenda. Each affirmation by the teacher is then confirmed by Carmen. Further, the teacher frequently builds on Carmen's idea/interest by expanding on the spirit of it in some way (thus confirming it in an especially strong way).

The teacher's persistence in introducing her agenda is striking in that it continues after many signs of disinterest from Carmen and after frequent successes in responding to Carmen on Carmen's own terms. In fact, the teacher's agenda seems to persist to the very end of the episode, when she asks Carmen to compare shells by the number of holes they have.

> *What is your theory about why the teacher*
> *is so persistent about advancing her agenda?*

Seen in the context of this child's development and this teacher's development, there is a dual process taking place. Carmen expresses some of the personal meanings she attaches to the shells, while the teacher is trying to get a grasp on the process of listening and responding.

Two Aspects of Dialogue

> *How could this episode have succeeded as well as it seems*
> *to have succeeded when the teacher persistently kept returning*
> *to an agenda in which Carmen was not the least bit interested?*

During the middle and later portions of the exchange, the teacher corrected herself each time she saw that Carmen was not interested in her agenda by momentarily responding to Carmen's agenda. Toward the end of the episode, the teacher was listening and responding fairly consistently, with only occasional attempts to return to her former agenda.

There was a spirit of mutuality underlying large parts of the episode. By "mutuality" we mean a feeling of emotional sharing between persons such that each person is reflecting and accepting the other person's feeling and, as a result, the persons are feeling a sense of pleasurable bonding between them. The emotional sharing may be about each other (e.g., love, mutual admiration) and/or about a shared feeling in relation to an object, event, or idea.

This leads us to reflect on two aspects of teacher–child and child–child exchanges: cognitive and social–emotional. *Cognitive* refers to the ideas communicated by each party and the relationships between those ideas. *Social–emotional* refers to the feelings, both individual and shared, that are experienced in response to the content of a message, the choice of words, the relation of a message to previous communication, voice tone/inflection, body language, smiles, and so on. For example, the teacher's body position (sitting angled toward Carmen, frequently leaning over toward Carmen, forming a unit with her), the smile in the teacher's voice and on her face (expressing pleasure in being with Carmen). The playfulness in Carmen's responses and Carmen's expressions of pleasure reflect and engender in both of them a sense of pleasurable mutuality.

The cognitive and social–emotional aspects of dialogue do not function independently of each other. They infuse each other.

Carmen's Interests

> *What would you conclude are Carmen's interests*
> *as they are expressed in the episode?*

We would hypothesize that, in one way or another, her interests revolve around relationship. Carmen's interest in the shells involves her relationship with them. She wants to experience the shells mainly through her senses and aesthetically.

Perhaps Carmen wants to experience the shells in terms of her impact on them: She talks about the Goo Goo Monster's physical impact on the shells. Then the Goo Goo Monster turns out to be herself. She blows on the shells to create sounds and listens for the shells' response.

Carmen also is interested in the shells as an expression of her relationship with her parents; for example, she identifies the shells as the little baby in relation with poppy and mommy. This may reflect a broader interest in relationships between babies and parents.

Carmen is very interested in receiving *the teacher's confirmation of Carmen's experience* of and with the shells. This runs through the entire episode. She is interested in experiencing mutuality with the teacher. She wants to share sensations, appreciations, and feelings of pleasure. The experience of pleasurable mutuality seems to reach its height with each blowing into the shells near the other's ears (initiated by Carmen), sharing their resultant feelings that confirm each other's experiences, and sharing the overall experience of mutual pleasure in the exchange.

In sum, Carmen would seem to be predominantly interested in her relationships with people and things, rather than in the abstract, conceptual relationships among things. At root, her interest is in the discovery of *self* through exploring relationships between herself and others (Bakhtin, 1986, 1990; Holquist, 1990).

> *How might you go about extending Carmen's interests in a way that*
> *challenges her to reflect on her experiences and ideas?*

CONCLUSION

When teachers are listening and responding, children become animated and involved, their cognitive and creative processes are energized, and their belief in themselves is deepened. Something similar happens when children listen to one another.

There is a particular image of the child associated with teachers listening, observing, and responding: namely, teachers seeing that young children are natural inquirers. They have motivations to explore the world through direct interaction with it and through constructing some kind of understanding of what they are encountering. Further, they have a strong motive to communicate the results of their explorations and to receive reflections from adults and other children for their discoveries. Their communications can take many forms: talking, drawing, gesturing, role-playing, and so on. All of these contribute to their ongoing dialogues with teachers and peers. The more avenues of communication that are offered, the better.

The most significant kind of interaction with the world for children of preschool age is in exploring their relationships with it. They explore their relationships with family, teachers, and friends. They explore sensory relationships with animate and inanimate objects. They explore the way objects, animals, and all facets of nature respond to their physical actions. They are explorers and researchers.

An important lesson that the Windows Study and the Carmen episode teach us is that teachers have to work diligently to put aside their agendas for children in order to see children in the full richness of their possibilities as motivated learners. The teachers' agendas are tenacious. In the Windows Study, the teachers almost lost the children's interest entirely before the teachers started to reflect on the contents of the children's drawings and documented conversations. Once the teachers started to listen, observe, reflect, and respond, the children's responses became focused and energized. In the exchange between the teacher and Carmen, we see the tenacity of the teacher's compare/contrast agenda for Carmen alongside her ability to respond to Carmen at the sensory, relational, metaphorical level in which Carmen was truly interested. The latter contributed to a warm, rich exchange between them. The teacher at times persisted with her agenda, however, despite numerous signals from Carmen that the teacher's agenda did not interest her.

These initial realizations about the inherent agendas of teachers and the potential of those agendas to get in the way of teachers' listening to children are an important step in teachers learning to achieve their Reggio ideals.

At the same time, we want to restate the point made at the beginning of this chapter that it is natural and appropriate for teachers to have learning agendas for children. The important thing, however, is that the teacher not assume that the child's agenda is the same as hers and that the teacher not let her own agenda interfere with listening to the child. The Carmen–teacher dialogue specifically raises the question of how teacher agendas such as literacy and math learning can be implemented without obstructing teachers' abilities to listen to, observe, and respond to children's learning motivations (see Chapter 8).

In the next chapter we take a close look at what teachers can do once they have identified children's interests. Namely, how can teachers build on the children's interests to facilitate the development of children's thought processes and their ability to engage in thoughtful dialogue and exploration with teachers and with one another?

Chapter 3

Co-Construction of Understandings with Children

In this chapter we focus on processes that develop children's thinking abilities and capacities for dialogue in interaction with the teacher and/or other children. We will explore three major questions.

1. In what ways do teacher–child interactions facilitate children's thinking?
2. What processes within teachers help them to facilitate children's thinking?
3. How do teachers facilitate thoughtful dialogue *with* and *among* children in small groups?

IN WHAT WAYS DO TEACHER–CHILD INTERACTIONS FACILITATE CHILDREN'S THINKING?

The three episodes that follow are examples of a teacher facilitating children's thought development in the context of children's spontaneous play activities (in contrast to the more structured small-group work typical of in-depth studies). In each case, the intention of the teacher is to embrace the children's interests, understand their thinking, and help them to extend their thinking. The teacher poses challenging questions that assist the children in *making connections* and combining those connections into more comprehensive frameworks of understanding.

Making connections is about noting or inferring *relations* among things; for example, sequential relations, causal relations, functional relations, or relations of similarity, difference, or containment.

> As you read the first episode, look for ways that the teacher helps Vance to make connections and to combine those connections into a more comprehensive conceptual whole.

How to Ride a Bike

Vance (playing at the water table, calls over his shoulder): Teacher, I can tell you something different.

Teacher (as she begins to walk over to Vance): What can you tell me different? (She sits down next to Vance.)

Vance (pauses a little in getting started as teacher waits patiently): When I show somebody how to ride a bike, you put your feet on the pedals. (Vance moves his feet up and down as he continues to play at the water table while glancing at and talking with the teacher.)

Teacher: So what are you going to do when they put their feet on the pedals? Do they put their feet like that . . . ? (The teacher places her hands flat on the rim of the water table to indicate someone putting their feet on the pedals.) And then they know how to ride? What do you have to do?

Vance: And then they ride. (Vance continues with his hands in the water play but moves his feet to suggest pedaling.)

Teacher: Okay. So if I put my feet on the pedals like this . . . (Teacher puts her hands out flat again, stationary, to indicate feet resting on pedals.)

Vance (turning his head to see her hand gestures): And pedal like slow. (Moves his hands straight up and down to represent pedaling.)

Teacher: Oh, so I've got to pedal.

Vance: Uh huh.

Teacher: So how do I know what to do?

Vance: Easy.

Teacher: How?

Vance: Like pedal down the street. (Vance makes pedaling hand movements against the inside of the water tub as he talks.)

Teacher (again trying to get Vance to more fully express his thoughts): It looks like your hands are going like this, look. (She picks up on Vance's nonverbal communication and moves her hands up and down, mirroring his former hand movements, only more slowly and more deliberately.) Up and down. Is that what you're gonna do?

Vance nods in agreement.

Teacher: What if I want to go real fast?

Vance: You have to go real slow. (Vance demonstrates, moving his hands slowly, while copying the upward–downward circular movement that the teacher used.)

Teacher: If I want to go real fast, I have to go real slow?

Vance nods yes.

> What do you think Vance means when he says that you have to go real slow in order to go real fast?

Teacher: What if I want to go real slow, what do I have to do?

Vance: Go just a little bitty slower.

Teacher: Go just a little bit slower if I want to go slow?

Vance nods yes.

Thoughts on the How to Ride a Bike Episode. In this exchange, the teacher helps Vance to make two types of *connections*.

- Sequential steps in riding a bike
- Causal relations (actions that make the bike move, go fast, and go slow, respectively)

In facilitating Vance's making of connections, the teacher uses two types of prompts.

- *Statements,* in words and gestures, that mirror back to Vance the idea that he has just communicated and stimulate further thought
- *Challenging questions*, usually in a conditional form:
  "So what are you going to do *when* they put their feet on the pedals?"
  "So *if* I put my feet on the pedals like this . . . (then) . . . ?"
  "What *if* I want to go real fast?"

Note that through her questions the teacher is facilitating the development of Vance's language and thought in tandem. For example, in using clausal connectors such as "if" and "when," she is teaching him language for expressing conditional relations.

The teacher is listening and responding to Vance's interest. She takes his interest and his ideas seriously and wants to know more about how he is thinking.

The teacher challenges Vance to think more deeply about what he is proposing. Her questions ask him to build on his statements, to extend them, to elaborate on relations between ideas, and to think in terms of cause and effect as well as sequence. Through her questions she also introduces additional perspectives for him to consider, for example, speed (fast and slow).

She asks clarifying questions to help herself understand Vance's point of view. Early in the exchange, she changes perspective, imagining that she herself is following Vance's instructions; that is, she questions him as to what she needs to do to ride the bike. This makes the focus of the dialogue more concrete, direct, and personal.

Throughout the exchange, she mirrors Vance's thoughts back to him through verbal language and body language, the same combination of communication modes that he used in relating to her. Her mirroring provides *thought platforms* from which she and Vance can further extend his thinking.

Each is learning from the other. Vance is learning how to explain his ideas to another person (especially how to include more detail) and he is learning how to have a conversation in which both participants are listening to each other and contributing. The teacher is learning how Vance thinks, for example, about pedaling slowly in order to go fast. She also is learning about how to facilitate a child's thinking.

The end result of this discussion is that Vance and the teacher have co-constructed a procedure for teaching someone to ride a bike that is far more extensive, complex, and integrated than the idea with which he seems to have begun. This construction tends to form a conceptual whole made up of relations among elements and relations among relations (see Chapter 4).

Going Downtown

Desiree and Edwina have entered their "car" that consists of two cubbies situated behind a door (opened against the cubbies) that has upper and lower glass windows in it. Thus, they can sit in the cubbies (front seat of the car) and look through the window of the door at the rest of the classroom. Desiree is holding a doll wrapped up in a blanket (her "baby") in an apparent plan to take the baby with them on a trip.

Teacher (approaching the two girls and standing at the periphery of their activity area): That's your car?

Desiree and Edwina nod yes, as they sit behind the glass door in their two cubbies.

Teacher (to Edwina): Where are you and Desiree going?
Edwina: The Rainbow [a clothing store in downtown Chicago].

> *Teacher*: Where's that at, Desiree?
> *Desiree*: Downtown.
> *Teacher*: Downtown. That's where the Rainbow is? Wow! What street is it on?
> *Desiree*: Madison.
> *Teacher*: Oh, Madison Street, downtown. . . . Okay. (To Edwina) You're driving downtown, to Madison Street?
> *Desiree*: No. I'm driving. She's in the car.
> *Teacher* (to Edwina): It's your car but she [Desiree] is driving?
> *Edwina*: No. I'm driving.
> *Desiree* (still holding her baby): I'm driving!
> *Teacher* (to Edwina): She says she's driving. (To Desiree) So if you're driving, what's the baby going to do?
> *Desiree*: Her rocker. She needs her rocker, but I don't have it.
> *Teacher*: She needs her rocker, but you didn't bring it. How is she going to sit down in her rocker then?
> *Edwina*: This [is] her rocker (lifting up a plastic dishpan).
> *Teacher*: That's her rocker.

Desiree starts to put the doll in the "rocker."

> *Teacher*: Okay, let me see her go in the rocker. (She waits until Desiree begins to fit the baby, still wrapped in a blanket, into the rocker.) A baby carrier! (The teacher acknowledges that the baby is placed fully into the carrier and then walks off with Quincy, who has been urging her to come to see his new creation.)

Desiree and Edwina finish their preparations and begin their drive downtown.

Thoughts on the Going Downtown Episode. The teacher explores the girls' interest with them, prompting them to fill in some of the details about their destination. She mirrors back her understanding of what they have said: "Oh, Madison Street, downtown. . . . Okay, you're driving downtown." This creates a stimulus to the girls to respond further.

In stating the details of their trip and in resolving the baby safety problem, the girls, with the teacher, have created an enriched and more complex conceptual model of how to conduct their imaginary trip downtown. Among other things, they now leave on their trip with a firm destination in mind and with their ideas about logistical procedures more developed.

> What kinds of thought is the teacher facilitating in this episode?

The teacher's questions challenge the children to construct several types of relations.

- By asking where things are located, the teacher establishes with them that the Rainbow is *contained* within Madison Street and both are *contained* within downtown.
- Then the teacher creates a dilemma: "So if you're driving, what's the baby going to do?" Her question is about "functional fit," a relation in which two or more parts of a whole are compatible with one another and contribute to the functioning of a whole. Her challenge to the girls is that driving the car and holding the baby at the same time are *not* compatible. Their solution of the "rocker" creates the functional fit.

The conceptual whole that emerges is a plan for a successful trip downtown. In communicating her challenge, the teacher uses a conditional language form, "if . . . then": "So if you're driving, (then) what's the baby going to do?" The teacher's question prompts Edwina to come up with her invention of using a dishpan as a rocker.

The Beetle Borg

Quincy asks the teacher to look at his "Beetle Borg" construction. (A Beetle Borg is a creature in the Power Rangers video series.) Quincy has made it out of hollow blocks. It is wider than and almost as tall as himself. Quincy holds a cymbal in each hand and bangs them together periodically.

> *Teacher* (picking up on Quincy's action): What does that do? (She points to the clashing cymbals.)
> *Quincy* (clashing the cymbals once more): This makes the power. It makes the noise that goes to each color. (He refers to a chain of red and yellow plastic links lying on top of the construction.)
> *Teacher*: Oh, it makes the noise that transfers to each color.
> *Teacher:* I'm really curious, where does it [the power] run out to?
> *Quincy* (while adjusting the chain of yellow and red plastic links into a crack in the top of the construction): When you hear somebody, the power runs out. (He continues running the plastic links over the top of the structure.) One, two, three, four, five, six, seven, eight, nine, ten. That would mess it up.
> *Teacher*: That would mess it up?
> *Quincy*: Yes. Cuz the power is all out right now.
> *Teacher*: Now the power is all out?

Quincy nods.

> *Teacher*: Oh, that's what happened before, when you had to put the power in. That's what messed it up. And where does the power run out?
> *Quincy*: Down, down, down, and out the two holes.
> *Teacher*: Down, down the two holes. Where are the two holes?
> *Quincy*: It goes down, down there and out here. (He places his fingers next to two holes at the bottom of the structure.)
> *Teacher*: Wow! That's a lot of power. That's a lot of movement, too.
> *Quincy*: Watch, watch. (Quincy goes behind the Beetle Borg and demonstrates the power by making shooting noises.)
> *Teacher*: When the power goes out. Does it go out fast or slow?
> *Quincy*: Fast. (He makes more shooting noises.) The power comes out.
> *Teacher*: I've got one more question. When the power goes out, does this stay still or does it move? (She points to the red and yellow plastic chain at the top of the construction.)
> *Quincy*: It's got yellow, red, red, yellow, yellow, yellow, yellow. (While saying this, Quincy points to each piece in the chain as he names its color.)
> *Quincy* (going to the side of the Beetle Borg): I've got to fix my key.
> *Teacher*: Oh, you've got to fix your key?
> *Quincy*: Yes, I'm going to the key store. (He leaves to pursue his mission.)

Thoughts on the Beetle Borg Episode. The teacher's facilitation of Quincy's thinking has several dimensions. She asks him a series of questions that reflect her interest in his creation. At each stage of the conversation she mirrors Quincy's ideas back to him by rephrasing what he has told her, asking him (implicitly or explicitly) to expand upon the meaning, or asking him a question that acknowledges and builds on what he has just said. Through this interaction, Quincy is mentally constructing and verbally articulating the Beetle Borg's components and relations among them, including the Beetle Borg's process of power generation, power transmission, triggering of power release, and exiting of power. Together they are constructing a complex whole made up of elements and dynamic relations among them.

Prompted by the teacher's questions, Quincy makes *functional connections* (e.g., "This makes the power. It makes the noise that goes to each color") and *causal connections* (e.g., "When you hear somebody, the power runs out"). He also describes the pathway of the energy flow (Teacher: "And where does the power run out? Quincy: "Down, down, down, and out the two holes").

Some Perspectives on the Three Episodes

Note the importance that *movement* plays in the above three episodes: riding a bike, riding downtown, the flow of power in the Beetle Borg. As noted in Chapter 2, movement and flow seem to be an important in-depth interest for many preschool children.

These three episodes illustrate that the teacher's facilitation of children's powers of thought and expression can happen both in reality-based contexts (teaching someone how to ride a bike) and in imaginary contexts (the Beetle Borg). Further, in all three episodes, the teachers' questions prompt the children to use their imaginations to make connections that they can't actually see in front of them. They need to imagine the dynamics of riding a bike, taking a trip to specific locations downtown, and the flow of energy through a configuration of blocks.

The children also are learning to engage in a dialogue: to respond to the questions and ideas of others, to verbalize their ideas, and to elaborate and re-represent them through multiple symbol systems (verbal, gesture, drama, sound, etc.). Through this process, the teacher is helping the children to construct and articulate an interconnected set of relations.

A close examination of these episodes finds the teacher simultaneously inside and outside of the situation that the child has created. She is involved with the child, in the child's own streams of thought, and at the same time takes the role of the curious external observer, keenly interested in learning about the child's world through the child's own explanations. A viewing of the videotapes of these episodes shows how this inside/outside position is expressed physically by her standing just inside the periphery of the children's play settings.

Note that in the Vance and Quincy episodes, the children were seeking the teacher out to share and confirm their ideas, theories, and imaginative constructions. In other words, she is acting not just as a classroom manager but as co-constructor of understandings with the children. In general, she gives the message to children that she is approachable and open to engaging with them around their interests.

Valuing of the Child's Mind

Thus far, we have approached these episodes from the standpoint of the teacher's role in helping children develop abilities of thought and expression. We now turn to a further aspect of these exchanges, namely, the teacher valuing the children's minds through the great interest and enjoyment she shows in engaging their motives and thoughts. Children experience that the teacher's motive is to embrace their motives, feelings, and thoughts. This is a powerful reflection to the children's experience of their own minds. Through the repeated process of teachers valuing children's minds, combined with the children experiencing the use of their minds in responding to challenges, the children develop the ability and propensity to value their own minds. They experience themselves as having important motives and powers of thought. They take their learning motivations seriously, experiencing pleasure in using their minds to reason and reflect.

In the above three episodes, the teacher communicates her valuing of the children's minds in six ways.

1. Carefully following the children's interests and initiatives
2. Encouraging the children to express their own ideas and showing a genuine curiosity about them
3. Mirroring her understanding of the children's idea(s) back to them through words and gestures
4. Challenging children to extend and connect their ideas (within the focus that the child has set for the interaction) by posing thought-provoking questions and bringing in new perspectives
5. Reflecting on the children's thoughts in her own thought process and reflecting that process back to them
6. Sharing the enjoyment that the children are feeling in using their minds

Taken together, these six aspects of valuing children's minds communicate to the children that the teacher is carefully listening to, reflecting on, internalizing, and cherishing their expressions of motivation, thought, and enthusiasm. The result, on a cumulative basis, is growth in children's inner capacity to explore and enjoy their own interests, feelings, and thoughts. The development goes beyond intellectual skills to include children experiencing themselves as self-regulating agents who think, feel, and act in the world with well-grounded purposes and a sense of their own competence (see references to sense of agency in Chapter 5, "The Developmental Goal for Children" and Chapter 8, "Identities as Actively Engaged Learners").

WHAT PROCESSES WITHIN THE TEACHER HELP HER FACILITATE CHILDREN'S THINKING?

Why doesn't this teacher "get stuck" when she attempts to engage children in a thinking process? What helps her to manage a sustained, thoughtful conversation with children? In our estimation, there are four kinds of thinking/feeling going on within the teacher that help her to facilitate children's thinking.

- *Believing that children have interesting ideas and wanting to understand their thinking:* For example, when asked what she was trying to do in the How to Ride a Bike episode, the teacher responded, "I was trying to understand what his thought was, what was his idea."
- *Viewing children as having the power to make connections:* This is reflected in her challenging all of the children to extend and connect their ideas in ways that move them toward a more elaborated set of interrelated ideas.
- *Believing that children have a motive to communicate their ideas to others:* For example, in response to a question about what she thought was important to Quincy in the Beetle Borg episode, the teacher responded, "Expressing his ideas; sharing it with adults and being able to tell what it does or what he wanted to it to do."
- *Creating a space in her own mind that allows for the child's idea to grow:* The teacher creates a space within her mind that is defined by the child's chosen

focus of interest. She then imaginatively puts the child's initial idea somewhere in that space. The space is larger than the space occupied by the child's idea. This allows the teacher the possibility of imagining directions in which the child's idea might extend/expand outward. The space is now a mutually shared space with the child. She tries, in her conversation with the child, to imaginatively construct, within this space, an extended picture of the child's ideas and the relationships among them. In doing so, she asks herself questions about the child's emerging ideas that she in turn poses to the child. Thus, for example:

— In the How to Ride a Bike episode, she is imagining herself to be the recipient of Vance's instructions and is trying to create a workable picture of how she actually is going to ride a bike.

— In the Going Downtown episode, she starts with the girls' idea of packing up the car to go somewhere and tries to fill out a more complete picture by asking where the girls are going, where that place is located, and how they are going to ensure the safety of the baby.

— In the Bettle Borg episode, she is trying to fill out a picture of how the power generates, is transformed, travels through the Beetle Borg, and exits.

As she creates with the child a model in her mind of the child's emergent thinking, she poses questions to the child that communicate additional perspectives to consider. Through the ongoing interaction between her questions and the child's responses, they co-construct a more differentiated and complex understanding. Note that in all episodes, the system of understanding that emerges is organized as a *sequence* of events in which each event causes or enables the next.

HOW DO TEACHERS FACILITATE THOUGHTFUL DIALOGUE WITH AND AMONG CHILDREN IN SMALL GROUPS?

Each of the following episodes is about a small-group conversation revolving around a particular *type* of question or problem: Janell and the Brick is a *problem-solving* dialogue. The Missing Knife is an attempt to *resolve an interpersonal conflict*. What Can Babies Do? is a conversation that addresses a question of *fact*. As we explore each of these episodes, we invite you to ask with us:

> *What does the teacher do*
> *to facilitate thoughtful dialogue among the children?*
>
> *What kinds of understanding are*
> *being constructed through the dialogue?*

Janell and the Brick (Problem Solving)

Children were collecting materials to use in the classroom. Janell brought in a brick that generated excitement in the class. It was displayed, examined, and shown with great pride. However, the brick presented a safety problem. It had crashed several times into other children's materials, was tossed into the air, and had dropped to the floor. In the discussion that follows, the teacher is facilitating a dialogue among several 4-year-olds in search of a solution to the problem presented by Janell's brick.

Teacher: Could you store the brick in a cubby? What do you think?

Janell: No, it would break it up. It would bust it up with that brick. We could keep it here [on the table]. It could stay right here. I could hold it a while.

Martel (putting his hands on the brick as well): It could stay right here for a while.

Janell: I could cover it up like this [with paper] and then we could put it on the table. Martel could keep his hand on it to hold it [the paper] down.

Marisha (following the conversation, looks skeptical and shakes her head at the suggestion that the paper would prevent anyone from finding the brick): It would hurt somebody. It might hit somebody because they would pick it up.

Martel agrees with Marisha that the brick wouldn't stay on the table.

Janell: You could put it on the ground, keep it there, and then you could kick it like this. (Janell demonstrates.)

Janell (returning to his previous idea): This is how you could wrap it. Then you've got to hold it here like this.

Martel: You've got to stay by the table and then keep it there.

Janell: You can stand here and hold on to the brick like this.

Teacher: Do you think the brick would stay there?

Marisha: No, it would hurt somebody. It might hit somebody on the head because they would pick it up.

Janell: But we should kick the rock [brick]. We would keep it on the floor and we would kick it around like this. (He demonstrates.) It's on the floor, then it wouldn't hit somebody in the head.

Marisha (looking skeptical): It shouldn't stay here 'cause you'd have to say you are sorry, say you are sorry for hitting someone with the brick.

Teacher: Do you think we could find any place in the building where we could keep the brick and it would be safe? (Everyone agrees that they should look for a place in the studio. They walk into the studio, searching for the perfect place to "hide" the brick.)

Janell: We should keep it right here, in the chains.

Marisha: People would see it. It's not hiding.

Janell: It's got paper on it; it's covered good. I like it here.

Marisha: It should go under the table, next to the two other rocks. Then people wouldn't see it.

Janell: I have a plan, another plan. We could keep it in the paper and cover it with this box right here.

Marisha: You could put it under the table!

Janell: Look, we could cover it like this, take the box and put the box on it like this. Then cover it with a towel like this.

Marisha: We could come back and see if anyone finds the brick. See if the brick is still there.

Janell: We should leave the room and come right back to see if the brick is there.

> *What do you think were the most important things that the teacher did to facilitate dialogue in this conversation?*

Thoughts on Janell and the Brick. The discussion among the teacher and the three children is a genuine dialogue: That is, the group kept focused on the problem, shared multiple ideas, listened and responded to one another, and were influenced by one another's thinking. They also stated reasons for their ideas, challenged one another's ideas, and earnestly worked together toward achieving a resolution.

The teacher made three interventions in this episode.

1. His first was to suggest a *possible solution* to the problem and to invite responses: "Could you store the brick in a cubby? What do you think?" This question triggered considerable discussion. Note how the teacher framed the question with "Could you . . . ?" This feels open, inviting a variety of possible responses. It also paves the way to critical thinking since one of its meanings is "Would this solve the problem?"

   "What do you think?" communicates the teacher's image of the children as thinking beings, places a *value* on their thinking, invites them to become aware of their own thinking, and reinforces the emphasis on openness to ideas. Also, it implicitly invites them to be partners in thinking with one another and with the teacher.

2. The teacher then posed a *challenge* to the group to reflect critically on Janell's proposed solution: "Do you think the brick would stay there?" This question was open enough to invite both positive and negative responses and thus provided Marisha with an opportunity to critique Janell's idea. Janell responded and Marisha did not accept Janell's argument, backing up her position with a prediction.

3. Finally, the teacher offered an *invitation* for the group to consider a much wider range of possibilities for places to store the brick: "Do you think we could find any place in the building where we could keep the brick and it would be safe?"

What were the cognitive and the social–emotional aspects of this exchange? (See Chapter 2, Two Aspects of Dialogue, regarding the cognitive and social–emotional aspects of the Carmen–teacher exchange). During most of this exchange, both Janell and Marisha appear to be strongly committed to their respective, very divergent positions (as judged by their constant repetition of their perspectives).

The intensity of Marisha's position is expressed through her continual reference to the dire consequences that would result from Janell's proposed solutions. The atmosphere feels charged as Janell makes only slight concessions to Marisha's arguments and, in response, Marisha becomes increasingly emphatic. Then the teacher suggests that they consider the entire school building as a context for possible solutions. This seems to create a greater sense of space, both physical and psychological, and that may have contributed to the final process in which each makes major concessions to the other, arriving at a tentative solution.

The Missing Knife Episode (Conflict Resolution)

This episode revolves around an interpersonal conflict at the lunch table, where the teacher is seated with seven children.

> *What role does the teacher play this time?*

Abrielle (reaching across the table and taking a plastic knife that was near Sara's plate, while announcing): Hey, that was mine!
Sara: No, it was mine!
Abrielle: No!

Sara frowns hard at Abrielle.

Abrielle (to the teacher): Look, teacher, she got my knife. I put it right here [near her own plate] and Sara is getting it. I put it right there.
Teacher: Then you need to talk to Sara.

Abrielle (to Sara): I didn't like that. I didn't like it. (She bangs the knife down.) I'll get one! (As she gets up and leaves the table, she yells over her shoulder.) Teacher, Sara's bad.
Teacher: Why is she bad?
Abrielle: She takes my knife.
Teacher: Maybe she didn't know that it was yours, Abrielle.

Sara deepens her frown.

Josephina: Abrielle, Abrielle, you're hurting her feelings.

Abrielle puts her hands over her ears to block out what Josephina is saying.

Teacher: Abrielle, Josephina is talking to you.
Josephina (leaning closer to Abrielle): You are hurting her feelings.
Abrielle: But she took my knife.
Josephina: She probably didn't notice that . . . she probably didn't notice that was yours.
Abrielle: Nooooo.
Josephina (after exploring her area of the table): Teacher, I have two! (Holds up two knives.)
Teacher: Is that two knives?
Josephina: Yeah.
Teacher (nodding yes in return and smiling knowingly): Maybe one was Abrielle's?
Abrielle: No, aaaaa (to Sara). You took it from there.
Josephina (leaning forward to Abrielle and holding one of the two knives): This was yours. Look at it. (Josephina puts down the knife next to Abrielle.)
Abrielle: I don't take knives like this. No. That wasn't mine. (She picks up the knife, wipes the blade with her napkin, and looks at Josephina.) Look. (Then to the teacher) Teacher, look, it's clean now.
Abrielle (trying to cut her banana with the knife and looking at the teacher): Teacher, I need help cutting my banana.
Sara (to Abrielle): You want me to help?
Teacher (to Abrielle): Ask someone to help you.
Sara (taking the knife from Abrielle and successfully cuts the peel from the banana): There we go. There we go, Abrielle (in a cheerful voice).
Abrielle: Thanks so much.
Sara (shaking her head and hands as if she is celebrating the pleasure of the moment and the end of tensions with Abrielle): Thank you.

> *What does the teacher do to facilitate
> thoughtful dialogue among the children?*
>
> *How is the teacher's role in this episode
> different than in Janell and the Brick? How is it similar?*

Thoughts on the Missing Knife Episode. The episode had a positive outcome, due in part to Josephina's empathic interventions and to her discovery of the missing knife.

When Abrielle complained to the teacher about Sara, the teacher framed the interchange as a conversation between the two girls: "Then you need to talk to Sara." In other words, she kept the situation focused on the exchange between the children, rather than between herself and individual children.

The teacher tried to support the ongoing dialogue by asking Abrielle to examine her assumptions about Sara ("Why is she bad?") and then by trying to give Abrielle a different perspective on Sara's possible intentions ("Maybe she didn't know that it was yours, Abrielle.").

The teacher tried to get Abrielle to respond to the perspective that Josephina was bringing to the situation when Abrielle shut Josephina out: "Abrielle, Josephina is talking to you."

Then Josephina explores her area of the table and finds an extra knife: "Teacher, I have two!" The teacher responds by highlighting the relevance of Josephina's finding for the current interaction: "Is that two knives?" "Maybe one was Abrielle's."

Finally, when Abrielle asks the teacher to help her cut her banana (with the notorious missing knife), the teacher uses the opportunity to connect Abrielle to another child: "Ask someone to help you." This provided the opportunity for Sara to proactively heal the tension between herself and Abrielle in an act of forgiveness.

In sum, every move of the teacher was devoted to encouraging the children to address one another, listen to one another, reflect on their own assumptions, and consider one another's motives and feelings. While the conversation did address a question of *fact*, what else was going on? Here are the teacher's comments after viewing the video clip of this episode.

> I want them to learn how to resolve conflicts on their own, verbally, because it's something that they are going to need for their whole life. . . . I was trying to redirect the questions so that they can answer it on their own, instead of me giving them the answer and how to do it.

What Can Babies Do? (A Question of Fact)

The third episode occurred as part of an Ages Study at New City Center in 2002. The study began after one child asserted that a person has to be 8 years old to ride a bike with two wheels. This reminded the teachers that children often talk about and differentiate between what babies can do and what big people can do. So they gave an invitation to all those who were interested to participate in a study of "what people can do at different ages." Five children responded to the invitation. In the opening dialogue, the teacher posed the question, "What can babies do?" Lucero was the most articulate on the subject.

> A baby can't do anything, and in the night the baby wakes up and starts crying. Anyways, he can't do anything. All he can do is sleep and eat. He's too small.

The next day the teacher took the small group to visit the infant–toddler room at a nearby Chicago Commons child center. When the children returned, they talked about their experiences and drew pictures about their observations. The following day the teacher convened the group for further discussion.

> *Teacher*: Remember what you said, that all babies can do is sleep and eat? What do you think now after we have had the opportunity to visit them?
> *Lucero*: These babies were bigger than just sleep and eat.
> *Teacher*: Then what size are the babies that just sleep and eat?
> *Lucero*: Very small, like this (demonstrating with his hands).
> *Teacher*: The babies that we saw, can they play?
> *Jonas*: They can play with the balls and they can jump.
> *Armando*: Yes, they can also sing.
> *Jonas*: No, Armando, babies can't sing.

Teacher: Why not, Jonas?

Lucero: They can't sing because they have small mouths.

Daisy: No, Lucero, they can't sing because they can't even talk.

Lucero: I know that, Daisy. But babies can still walk.

Teacher: All the babies we saw yesterday can walk?

Daisy: No. Some of the babies were still too small.

Teacher: Can somebody else tell me something that you saw in the babies' room?

Lucero: I saw that one of the teachers was feeding a baby because he was still too [little] to eat by himself.

Daisy: I saw one of the teachers singing while the kids were dancing.

Armando: Yes, the kids were dancing.

Daisy: Some of the babies were looking out the window.

Teacher: What do you think the babies were looking at out the window?

Daisy: Because there were birds outside on a tree and a little mouse. (The children had seen a mouse outside on their way into the center.)

Lucero: Yes, but when the mouse see us he run.

Jonas: It's because it got scared.

Teacher: Why?

Lucero: Maybe because it only likes to see babies, not big kids.

Thoughts on the Babies Discussion. *What did the teacher do to facilitate thoughtful dialogue among the children?* The teacher opens the discussion with a challenge, "Remember what you said, that all babies can do is sleep and eat? *What do you think now* after we have had the opportunity to visit them?" When Lucero responds with, "These babies are bigger than just sleep and eat," the teacher takes the opportunity to lead the children into differentiating the category of "babies" into sizes of babies: "Then what size are the babies that just sleep and eat?" Midway through the discussion the teacher offers two more challenges to the children's thinking. When Jonas says, ". . . babies can't sing," she asks, "Why not, Jonas?" This results in some spirited discussion. A bit later she challenges Lucero's statement that babies can walk with, "All the babies we saw yesterday can walk?" Toward the end, she asks the children a question that communicates a valuing of their capacities for thoughtful reflection: "What do you think the babies were looking at out the window?"

The episode as a whole contains numerous indicators of dialogue. The participants focus on a question. They share multiple perspectives, they listen and respond to one another, they state reasons, they ask for reasons, they challenge and build on one another's ideas. In one way or another, all of the teacher's questions served to keep the children focused on the pivotal question of what babies can do.

What kinds of understandings were constructed during the conversation? Aided by the teacher's questions, the children made their way toward the possibility of differentiating babyhood into two broad categories.

"Very small" babies:

- "Just sleep and eat"
- "Still too little to eat by himself"

"Bigger" babies:

- ". . . play with balls . . . jump"
- ". . . walk"
- ". . . were dancing"
- ". . . were looking out the window" (at birds and a mouse)

By the end of this dialogue, it is likely that the children's categories for thinking about babies were considerably more differentiated than they had been prior to their visit to the infant–toddler room.

It also is likely that the children grew in their understandings about learning. For instance, they experienced that after observing carefully and reflecting on their observations, they changed their minds about some things. They also experienced that when they shared their observations with one another, they learned from one another and came away from the encounter with richer memories and new understandings.

Comments on the Three Small-Group Episodes

In these three episodes, virtually all of the teacher interventions were stimulating to the children's thinking. The large majority of the interventions were *open-ended questions* that served to elicit additional perspectives or asked children to extend a thought that they had expressed. Further, in most or all cases, the teacher did not have a preset idea of what the full range of possible answers might be. Hence, the question was a stimulating one to the teacher as well as to the children. On some occasions, rather than posing a question, the teacher drew the children's attention to a piece of information that could facilitate the children's thinking about the salient question at hand. Finally, each teacher's choice of language for framing the question served to encourage and scaffold the children's thinking.

CONCLUSION

While the six episodes presented in this chapter are very different, we see certain commonalities in the teachers' facilitation strategies.

- Listening to children and, through questions and statements, reflecting back what they said
- Challenging children through posing thought-provoking, open-ended questions that are rich and clear, and that push at the edges of the children's development
- Fostering the basic principles of dialogue with and among children; that is, engaging in and promoting discussions in which children are generating multiple positions and perspectives, listening and responding to ideas, giving reasons to support ideas, and co-constructing understandings with the teacher and/or other children
- Helping children to make a wide range of connections utilizing a variety of thinking skills and helping them to integrate those connections into coherent understandings
- Communicating a clear and consistent respect for children's powers of observation, powers of reasoning, and abilities to create new understandings by joining observation and previous knowledge through reasoning

In the next chapter we will take our exploration a step further by examining how the children's use of various forms of representation strengthens their ability to make observations and connections, and provides a focus for their dialogues with teachers and one another.

Chapter 4

Children's Representations

In this chapter we examine how children use representations such as drawings, three-dimensional constructions, and verbal expressions to construct and communicate *understandings*.

By "understandings," we mean constructs in a person's mind, which include:

1. Something that a person identifies as an *entity*, such as a rabbit, a family, or the moon
2. The *elements* that constitute that entity, along with the *attributes* of those elements (e.g., one of the elements that constitute a rabbit is the rabbit's ear; the attributes of the rabbit's ear include shape, color, and texture.)
3. *Relations* among those elements (e.g., spatial, causal, or comparative relations) and the relations *among* those relations, combining to form the entity as a whole
4. The relationship between the entity and its *environment*
5. The relationship of the entity to its *past*; that is, the events that influenced its form, process, and relationship with its environment

For an example of how different understandings of something are communicated through different representations, let's revisit Jonathon's drawing of a shower (see Chapter 1) and compare it with Tony's drawing of a shower that was made during the same study (see Figure 4.1).

In our view, there are two types of closely joined relations that make up Jonathon's understanding of the shower expressed through his drawing: The first is the physical sequence of hardware that makes up the shower system; the second is the flow of water through the hardware, going up the vertical pipe to the showerhead, out into the tub, down the drain, and into a cup. The understanding communicated through the drawing is about the nature of the various mechanical parts making up the shower, relations of the parts to one another, and the flow of water through the related parts.

Tony's understanding, portrayed in his drawing, is organized primarily around the relation between the shower taker and the shower. The person has a smile on his face, suggesting pleasure in the process of taking a shower. There are few mechanical details and those are largely eclipsed by the human experiential emphasis.

In short, we are suggesting that Jonathon's and Tony's drawings communicate quite different understandings about a shower. Although these drawings probably do not exhaust each boy's understandings of showers, they do reflect very different interests and perspectives. This in turn has implications for how a teacher might help each child extend his inquiry beyond this point by asking questions that suggest additional perspectives or by encouraging the boys to combine their perspectives in a joint enterprise.

Jonathon's and Tony's portrayals are highly complementary. Tony's perspective picks up where Jonathon's perspective leaves off. The two boys' perspectives, taken together, provide for a richer, fuller understanding of a shower than either perspective taken alone.

Figure 4.1.
Two different
perspectives on showers.
On the left is Jonathon's
drawing depicting the
way the shower and
tub work. On the right is
Tony's drawing, which
emphasizes the pleasure
of being in a tub with
the shower on.

> *What might you do to challenge the boys
> to extend their investigation further?*

REPRESENTATIONS IN THE PROCESS OF LEARNING

In the pages that follow, we will look at seven cases in which children create representations that help them to guide and organize their learning. The following questions are used to structure our descriptions:

- How do the children's creation and use of representations contribute to their processes of learning?
- What is the teacher's role in helping the children to connect their acts of representing to their processes of learning?
- What kind of understanding does the representation communicate and how is that understanding organized and communicated by the representation?

Jazmin and the Ant

Jazmin was one of five children who were interested in ants. On the first day of this study, the teacher asked the group: "What do ants look like?" The children had difficulty verbally describing ants, so she asked them each to make a drawing of an ant from memory. This would tell her whether they could communicate more effectively through drawing and would reveal something about their knowledge of ants (see Figure 4.2, Jazmin's first ant drawing).

Two days later the group revisited their ant drawings.

Figure 4.2. Jazmin's ant drawings, showing her increasing understanding of the structure of an ant's body.

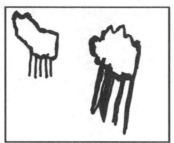

Jazmin's first ant drawing, which Paolo said "looks like a sheep!"

Jazmin's second depiction of an ant, drawn while looking closely at a live ant.

Javiar (referring to Jeremy's drawing): That looks like an airplane!
Paolo (referring to Jazmin's drawing): That one looks like a sheep!
Teacher: Would you like to go outside and find some real ants and draw what they look like?
All: Yes.

Each child was given a clipboard with paper and pen. On the first trip outside, they did not find any ants, so they drew imaginary "ant houses." On the second trip, Jazmin, Marisela, and the teacher located a live ant on the sidewalk alongside the school.

Teacher (to Jazmin): Can you draw him before he gets away?
Jazmin (observing the ant closely): Circle! . . . He has a circle!
Teacher: He has a circle?
Marisela: It's a circle. It's a circle.
Jazmin: Yeah! Look! Have circle, have circle.
Teacher: Okay, draw the circle on your paper.
Jazmin (drawing an oval body and a circle within it): This is a circle, this is a circle. (She then draws three legs on each side of the body.)
Teacher (challenging her further): How many circles does the ant have? (The teacher helps Jazmin to find the ant again.)
Jazmin (examining the ant closely): Three. He has three circles. (Jazmin draws an additional two circles within the body, to make a total of three; see Figure 4.2.)

The drawing reflects Jazmin's understanding of some elements of the ant and the spatial relations among them (i.e., relations among the body, the head, the legs, and the body segments). She took on a difficult task of representing a tiny, three-dimensional, fast-moving object on a two-dimensional plane.

In the process of constructing understanding through observing, Jazmin moved back and forth between observation and drawing. The task of drawing the ant provided a stimulus and reference point for the process of observation. In doing so, it promoted Jazmin's having a *dialogue with the object* in which she asked new questions each time she returned to her observation of the ant. The clipboard, pen, and paper assigned to each child set the stage for that process.

The teacher's scaffolding played a very important part in the process as she repeated Jazmin's verbal observation and prompted her to draw her discovery. She then challenged Jazmin to further observe the ant in order to make her representation more complete: "How many circles does the ant have?" The teacher was teaching Jazmin how to use representation in her observations and, hence, how to be a better observer.

Amber's Flowers

The classroom had been exploring paints for several weeks. The children mixed their own colors and shades of color, picked their favorite color, and explored a range of materials as their knowledge about painting grew. The teachers decided to take the children to the gardens of a local park to study the flowers so that they could further develop their understandings of color.

Before leaving the preschool, the children painted pictures of what they thought the flowers in the park would look like, using brushes and watercolors. Amber drew a row of long green stems, parallel and equidistant, with one round blob of a contrasting color on the top of each stem.

It was a damp cold morning in the park. The teachers provided blankets for the children to sit on while they observed and painted the flowers. Each child was given watercolor pencils, paper cut to various sizes, water, and a clipboard.

In her drawing, Amber fully embraced the range of vibrant colors in the large garden she saw beyond her, portraying the intensity of the colors. Unlike her classroom drawing of flowers, she no longer depicted the individual shape of each flower, but chose to represent the effect of all the flowers. She used contrast and repetition of colors and broad shapes to create a visual whole and the perspective of seeing a garden from afar. The contrasting of particular colors increases the viewer's sense of their vibrancy. It is a study in color.

Amber commented on this experience:

We had to go on the trip and we had to draw some flowers. And the grass was green. They had yellow flowers, pink flowers, orange flowers, and purple flowers. And then the red flowers. All these kinds of flowers. I see a lot, a lot, a lot of flowers. Not just one flower.

Age Progressions

When beginning a study of the Big School, the children of one classroom talked at length about the age of entry into kindergarten and the timing of birthdays in relation to the fall. This led to a discussion about what children can do at different ages. The discussion was tape-recorded, transcribed, and brought into the weekly meeting. The team decided to invite children to talk about what they could do at different ages and make drawings to accompany their descriptions. The teacher asked each child, "Could you tell me what you could do when you were a baby?" then wrote down the child's response. The child then drew a self-portrait as a baby. On the next round the teacher asked, "Could you tell me what you could do when you were 1 year old?" The sequence of questions and drawings were extended to age 12. After the statements and drawings were completed for a series of ages, the teacher revisited the child's statements with the child to convert the initial statements into captions for the pictures (see Figure 4.3).

The learning process here consists of the child bringing together numerous memory fragments and projections into an age progression framework provided by the teacher. In the child's mind, the progression is about becoming bigger and being able to do more things.

Five types of relations are communicated in the above representation:

1. The relation between age and associated capabilities
2. The progression from small to increasingly larger size
3. The progression from very limited capability to increasingly greater capability

Figure 4.3.
Joshua, 4 years old, draws himself and his perception of what he was like in the past, what he is like in the present, and what he will be like in the future. He changes his ability to draw according to the age he is drawing.

This is me when I am 12 and I go to the really big school. We do homework at the really big school. We draw numbers sometimes. We draw letters. When you are twelve, you go by the really big school.

That's me. I'm 4 years old. I'm bigger than 2 years old. I can draw and read books and play cars and go to school and run real fast and ride by Batman bike. I got it for my birthday.

Me. I am 2 years old. I can walk now 'cause I am bigger. Toys, I play with toys.

Me, I am 1 years old. I play with baby toys. I can't walk 'cause I am too little.

I'm a baby. When you are a baby you drink a bottle.

4. The progression of increasingly more complex drawings associated with increasing age (note that the baby figures are drawn in the style of a younger child)
5. The time progression itself, represented through the vertical sequence

In some cases, children made clay figures to parallel their age progression drawings.

The Chicken Community

Dion arrived at school with three chicken eggs. He wanted to hatch them and had the idea of putting them in the butterfly house where butterflies currently were hatching. The class agreed. After placing them there, they waited and waited but nothing happened. Dion concluded that maybe the eggs wanted their own house. That led to the idea of making a house for chickens.

Ten children showed an interest in the study. The teachers invited them to each draw the sort of chicken house they might like to make. The following discussion led into the drawing process:

Teacher: What kind of house would the chickens want?
Dion: A circle.
Monica: A stick house.
Teacher: What would our circle house look like? What would it have inside?
Dion: A bathtub, they have a couch, and watching T.V. The kids are playing around and the kids build cars; penny racers and it jumped over the penny racers.
Teacher: Why do you want to make a circle house?
Dion: Because I never made a circle house. (Dion draws a circle for the house and

comments as he draws.) Their television is a triangle. The kid is blowing gum. That's the cereal.

Ana: I want to draw a chicken house, like an egg, a big egg.

As they drew, children collaborated in forming their ideas.

Monica: I'm going to make a big egg because I am going to make something for the room. I'm going to make a beautiful house for the chickens. All the stuff.

Teacher: What kind of stuff?

Ana: I'm gonna write [draw] the T.V. and I'm gonna write the couch. I'm gonna make the kitchen and the room. (See Ana's drawing, Figure 4.4.)

Following this, the whole class was introduced to the study and all of the children were invited to draw pictures of their ideas for a chicken house. The teachers decided that children would use clay to construct the house because it easily lends itself to three-dimensional circular constructions and because most of the children previously had worked with clay. Dion drew a large circle on a piece of paper. The children rolled pieces of clay, placed them on an outline of the circle, scored them with a fork as they stacked coils on top of each other, shaped the construction, and used water to smooth out the seams. Each night they wrapped the construction in wet towels to keep it moist and workable. Younger children learned from the older, more experienced children.

Whole-class discussions were held at group time. As this process progressed, all the children eventually became involved in building the chicken house. After several weeks' work, it was left to dry, then fired, glazed, and fired again.

Next the teachers conducted discussions with the children about what the chickens would *need in* their house. Each child thought of a different idea. They first drew their ideas and then made them out of clay. There were many discussions as they worked side by side. They succeeded in making the items to scale so they would fit into the house. They made a toilet, bookcase with books, couch, refrigerator, sink, and stairs to enter the house. Aaron, who was making the toilet, decided he wanted to take a close look at an actual toilet before creating one for chickens. Monica made the refrigerator and then pumpkins and tamales to place inside it.

Two weeks later the teachers introduced another question, "What do chickens *need outside* their house?" The children were invited to first draw their ideas. Then they

Figure 4.4.
Ana's plan for a chicken house. A house "like an egg, a big egg" with a "kitchen and a room." She drew flowers in the yard, and a chicken outside the house. A common strategy used by teachers is to ask children to create plans in order to develop their ideas.

took a walk to observe what was in the neighborhood around the school. This led to several discussions.

> *Teacher*: Let's think for a moment about when we went for a walk around the community. What were some of the things that we saw?
> *Terence*: Sidewalk. I see a street.
> *Teacher*: What do you need in a community?
> *Terence*: Cars.
> *Teacher:* Why?
> *Terence*: So they can drive on the street.
> *Teacher*: Why?
> *Terence*: So they [other people] can walk on the sidewalk. So they do not crash.
> *Teacher*: Why is that important?
> *Terence*: So they can't run over the people.
> *Teacher*: What is a chicken community like?
> *Terence*: Like a floor and a street.
> *Teacher*: Tell me more about a floor and a street.
> *Terence*: So they can go on the sidewalk and don't crash on the sidewalk.
> *Teacher*: You think chickens will have cars?
> *Terence*: Yes, so they can drive and don't crash.

In response, the teachers suggested making cars for the chickens. None of the children had constructed cars before. The teachers suggested that they use toy cars as models, but the children said they wanted to make a "real car." So, one of the teachers took the children outside to look at cars parked along the street. The children noticed that some had two doors and some had four. Some had circle-shaped seats, others were square, and still others were rectangles (all concepts that the children had been taught earlier in the year). After discussing their observations, the children created a clay car together, using the same methods that they had used to construct the house. The rectangular car was made with seats for "mom," "dad," and "baby;" seat belts; a steering wheel; windshield wipers; and wheels. The children were able to make the inside components of the car at a scale that fit their car's interior space. This encouraged them to interact with their creations. Eventually, a separate car roof with an open sunroof section was made out of clay.

Finally, the teachers suggested that the children consider the *stores* that chickens would need in their community. They mentioned eyeglass, food, hat, and donut stores. After going on a walk to look at stores in the community, they reviewed their findings together.

> *Teacher*: Where did we go on our walk?
> *Monica*: We went to see stores.
> *Teacher*: What kind of stores did we see?
> *Monica*: I saw a pizza store.
> *Terence*: I saw a haircut store.
> *Damaso*: I saw [where] my tita (grandmother) works.
> *Teacher*: What do they sell at the store?
> *Damaso*: They sell candy. They sell carpet.

The children then drew pictures of what they had seen. The teachers decided that instead of having the children make the surrounding community out of clay, they would suggest creating a mural, painted on a long plywood board, to be placed in back of the chicken house. The mural would extend the study while offering an opportunity for children to have experience with other materials.

To help the children create the mural, the teachers showed them a map and an aerial photograph of the area around the school where they had taken their walks into the community. Using these as references, the teachers pointed out the location of each of the stores the children had noticed on their walks. They then had the children label, on the plywood board, where they wanted to place each street and store that they had identified. The children drew the street nearest the school. Then they drew, on paper, the playground, McDonald's, the pizza place, and the carpet store. They re-created their drawings on paper and then on the designated places on the plywood, first with pencil and then with black marker. Finally, they painted the drawings.

The completed mural was placed behind the clay house with some of its furnishings (not all of which could fit inside at one time). The car roof and the car were placed beside it. Children enjoyed playing with it (see Figure 4.5).

In the construction of this representation, numerous skills were utilized:

- Drawing from imagination
- Thinking/discussing in the context of observation
- Drawing from observation
- Using numerous clay techniques
- Designing and constructing to scale
- Drawing for planning purposes
- Reading maps
- Planning out the use of a large surface by sketching in the location of various components in advance
- Moving from sketching the surface to painting the surface

Further, each of the above skills was integrated with the use of verbal language.

The understandings that were generated through the overall process were underpinned by personal meanings; for example, the children's projection of human needs onto the chickens, the inclusion of the children's own immediate community, and connections to stores where members of their families worked.

The teachers scaffolded the process at each phase, incorporating children's previous learning into the process, such as knowledge about shapes and previously learned skills in clay construction and glazing.

The progressive construction of this representation extended over a 3-month period and provided a tangible focus for integrating numerous inquiries and ideas. The

Figure 4.5.
The chicken house, furnishings, car, and neighborhood; a collaboration propelled by questions about what chickens need.

background mural provided a community context and visual unity to the whole representation. The study also had a conceptual unity around the idea of "need." Decisions about what to include, at every stage, were guided by consideration of what the chickens needed in their lives: a house, furnishings, car, stores, streets, stoplights, and sidewalks.

Gena's Three-Perspective Drawing

Gena's drawing was made during the final phase of the Windows Study, described in Chapter 2. Gena and three friends decided to draw what they could see through a second-floor office window (see Figure 4.6).

Gena, referring to the upper half of her drawing, said: "This is a window in Carmen's room. The grass, the flowers, the tree. This is the house and the tree next to the house and the other tree." She then commented on the lower half: "This is Alyssa and me and Serina and Janie. We are drawing the window in Carmen's room." Finally, she mentioned the three arrows she had drawn: "Those are arrows to point to everything."

Gena's drawing includes three very distinct visual/spatial perspectives:

1. Her view of three windows and what she can see through them. Like Jazmin's representation of the ant (see above), this part of the drawing organizes and records her observations looking through the three-paned window.
2. An imaginary bird's-eye view from the ceiling, looking down at her group drawing what they saw out the window. It involves not only imagining herself high up in the air but also imagining what the group would look like from that perspective. This would seem to reflect a major stage in Gena's development of an understanding of multiple, simultaneous spatial perspectives.

Figure 4.6.
Gena spontaneously chose to depict several different perspectives in her drawing. The perspectives include looking at and through a three-paned window, a view from the ceiling, and considering the perspective of the viewer by using arrows to point to everything.

3. The perspective of the audience in relation to the drawing as a whole. Gena included arrows in the drawing to bring attention to various facets of the drawing that she wanted viewers of her work to notice. In her dictation she says that the arrows "point to everything." By drawing the arrows, and verbally explaining their intent in her dictation, Gena enters into a dialogue with the viewers of her work. She anticipates that people will view her drawing and she is asking them to notice everything in it.

The next two examples of representations touch directly on the children's relationships with friends and family. In these examples, the paramount emphasis is on the use of representations to express social–emotional understandings and enhance the experience of mutuality in social relationships.

Gifts

Many children in the class showed great interest in what was going on in the room across the hall, and vice versa. As a result, the teachers of the two rooms introduced the idea of gift exchanges between pairs of children across the two classrooms.

In each pair, the children interviewed each other about likes and dislikes. Then, in response to what they learned about each other in the interviews, they made gifts for each other from various media: clay, colored paper, paints, and colored markers.

One boy drew a tractor to give to his friend so that he could cut the grass. Then he made it out of clay (see Figure 4.7). In another gift study, a boy made a clay telephone for a friend who said that he missed his mom when he was at school. The purpose of the phone was to allow the friend to communicate with his mother.

The children's goal of making gifts for their partners led to learning the concept of an interview and the procedures involved in carrying out an interview. The interviews generated understandings about the interests and concerns of the other child.

The understandings associated with each gift were threefold: the content of the other child's likes, wants, and concerns; an understanding that the other child's likes, dislikes, wants, and concerns exist independently of one's own; and an understanding that the gift exchange promotes a sense of closeness with the other child. For the child who made the telephone for his friend, two additional types of understanding were involved: the causal relation between the mother's absence and the friend's discomfort, and the idea that the use of a telephone potentially could relieve the discomfort.

Figure 4.7. Empathetic gift giving and friendship. Keith first draws a tractor for Ronaldo, then he makes a clay tractor.

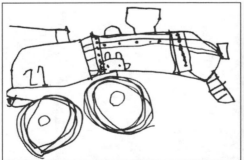 

"The tractor, it's a gift for Ronaldo. Ronaldo is gonna to use this to cut the grass. After Ronaldo cut the grass he's gonna water. Then he's gonna put in flowers and plants." (Keith, 5 years old)

Friends

The Friends Study grew out of children's concerns about leaving their preschool friends to go to the Big School the following fall (see Chapter 2, "Child-Specific Versus Universally Shared Interests"). As part of the study, the teachers suggested that the children make drawings of themselves with their friends. The children's comments about the drawings were written down by the teacher and attached to the drawings. These were posted in an area where the children could revisit them frequently (see Figure 4.8).

The creation and frequent revisiting of the drawings served a number of functions.

1. Through creating the drawings the children were able to affirm their relationships with one another, express their feelings about their relationships, and possibly diminish some of the concerns they had about entering kindergarten. Note that two of the children, in their dictations, mention that they will be with their friends when they go to the Big School.
2. Friends had the opportunity to re-experience their friendship by making the drawings and by revisiting the drawings after they were posted.
3. Through the posting of the drawings, the friendships were acknowledged by the teachers and the rest of the class, thereby affirming and celebrating the relationships.

Figure 4.8. The meaning of friendship.

Me, Keith, Dan, Jesco, they my friends playing with cars. (Haraldo)

We're friends. We painting and you are laughing because your mommy's here. Jolene is your mommy. Now, can I get out of here? (Yvette)

We wear long dresses, long dresses and we holdin' hands. We gotta wear black shoes 'cause we wearin' dresses. We walkin' all by ourself. We play with ninja turtle puzzles and computers. And we big. (Yvette)

This is me playing with Jazmin and Aldo inside the Big School. It's my family. I have a whole bunch of family. They're my friends. One big kid named Bruce. He played at the Big School with Jazmin and Aldo. (Joshua)

Joshua, it me and you. We're holding hands. We goin' to the Big School. Me and Joshua gonna play with the blocks and my dad's gonna pick me and Joshua up. And [I] asked my dad to go to his house and he let me. (Isaac)

In addition to affirming actual friendships, some of the understandings communicated by the drawings and dictations are that friendship is about doing pleasurable activities with one another, supporting one another, feeling close like family members, being included in one another's families, and feeling grown-up together.

THE TEACHER'S ROLE IN FACILITATING CHILDREN'S REPRESENTATIONS

In the various examples above, we see representations done before observing, while observing, after observing, and from recall.

Some of the most important things that teachers do to promote the children's creation and use of representations are

1. Inviting children to draw something before they observe it. This sensitizes children to observing the object of study when they eventually encounter it, by reflecting in advance on details and by experiencing conflicts between their initial representation and what they then observe (Roopnarine & Johnson, 1993). Later they can compare their first and later representations and reflect on the developments in their understanding.
2. Conducting discussions with the children in which they brainstorm what they are about to observe.
3. Scaffolding children's observations by asking questions and providing tools.
4. Organizing the children into small groups so that they can share knowledge and stimulate one another's observations and representations. Later, organizing them into groups to discuss their representations.
5. Asking children to comment on their representations.
6. Asking children questions that stimulate them to include additional perspectives.
7. Suggesting to children that they revisit their representations for purposes of reflecting on them, extending them, transcending them with newly formulated representations, or using them as stepping stones to the next phase of an inquiry.
8. Posting children's representations to facilitate revisiting.
9. Using the children's representations as vehicles for moving an inquiry from a small group to the whole class and back to a small group.

The Meaning of "Perspective"

We often have used the term *perspective* in this and previous chapters to mean the type of *relations* that one brings to bear in thinking about and representing an object of study. We saw earlier in this chapter, for example, that Tony and Jonathon emphasized different relations in their respective depictions of showers.

A second meaning of *perspective* is the relationship of the observer to the object of study. This might be a *spatial* relationship of person to object (as in Gena's perspective from the ceiling). Or it could be the perceiver's *purpose* for engaging the object, *sentiments toward* the object, or *assumptions about* the object. The observer's relationship *to* the object usually affects the elements and relations that the observer emphasizes in the representation of the object.

Multiple Modes of Representation

The phrase "multiple modes of representation" (also referred to as "multiple symbol systems" in Chapter 1) refers to children using a variety of communication modes to represent an object of study (e.g., drawing, painting, clay, wire, gesture, dramatic enactment, etc.). The emphasis on multiple modes of representation has at least five rationales.

1. Utilizing multiple modes of representation provides children with opportunities to employ multiple aspects of themselves in perceiving and representing the object. This expands their range of perception and their overall powers of observation and communication.
2. The use of multiple modes of representation promotes the taking of multiple perspectives on the object of study. For example, paints and oil pastels stimulate attention to color. Use of pencil draws attention to line. Use of voice stimulates attention to emotion.
3. In using multiple modes of representation in relation to the same phenomenon, children's ability to use each of the modes is strengthened. For example, the development of children's verbal communication is enhanced by their combining it with drawing and gesture. Conversely, their capacities in drawing, block work, and clay are strengthened by joining them with verbal communication.
4. The encouragement to use multiple modes of representation opens special opportunities to children who have not been able to express themselves well in the modes that they are accustomed to using.
5. Children's use of multiple modes of representation to communicate about a particular object or idea gives teachers a better opportunity to understand children's meanings.

EXPLORING MATERIALS: CHILDREN LEARNING REPRESENTATIONAL SKILLS

In 1997, the teachers and coordinators concluded that the children's ability to represent their ideas would be greatly enhanced by giving them prior experience in the use of materials that typically are employed in making representations, such as drawing materials, paper, wire, clay, paints, and so on. They introduced a two-phase process for strengthening children's abilities to use materials: exploring the material and using the material to communicate meaning.

Phase #1: Exploring the Material

In the exploration phase, teachers challenge the children to develop a greater awareness of the properties and possibilities in the material. For example: "What's the longest line you can draw with a pencil? The hardest line? The fastest line you can make? The thickest line? The most wiggly line?"

These explorations are in themselves a type of construction of understanding, namely, understanding what materials can do and how one can make them do it. The teachers encourage the children to share their discoveries with one another.

The following example of exploring clay is useful for understanding the care with which a materials exploration can be conducted.

- Step 1: With encouragement, and prompted by teacher suggestions, the children use their hands to manipulate the clay, feel its texture, smooth it out with water, pound it, smear it, poke it, make balls from it, roll it, make snakes, or coil it.
- Step 2: The children then use tools such as forks, plastic knives, rolling pins, and sticks to explore the clay's possibilities for being shaped and marked.
- Step 3: The children begin to shape and use the clay in practical ways. They write messages on clay slabs and make cups as a way of experiencing digging, pressing, and reshaping clay with their hands.

As they explore the materials, children are encouraged to verbalize their experiences and observations.

Ioli: We pour water, and then we make little sticks and balls.

Vanessa: Some of the balls are smaller and some are bigger.

Yesinia: You push down on the clay. I pinch it. I could make a line with the pencil for you. Could make your mommy and daddy. I wet the clay for you, for to stick the legs together.

Skye: Scrape it, write it, and getting to mark it. Bake it and scrape it and get it for the teacher and me.

Each medium that is explored by the children opens up a new set of experiences along with their skill development. For example, with regard to drawing with markers, Deandra said:

I wrote airplanes, skinny lines, and squiggly lines. I used all these colors; yellow, orange, blue, brown, green, and red. The marker smells like chocolate and I like chocolate cake.

As the children's explorations of a particular material progress, the teachers encourage them to move further into their inquiries by asking questions like, "What other materials do you think you can use along with this one?" They also challenge the children to explore further uses of the same material; for example, to link short pieces of wire to make long pieces or experiment with different ways to connect two pieces of wire. Responding to these challenges develops in the children an openness to creatively adapting materials to their needs. Soon children become adept at choosing materials and combinations of materials to use in particular representations and inquiries (see Figure 4.9).

Phase #2: Using the Material to Communicate Meaning

After children acquire skills using a material, teachers often suggest that they use those skills to make identity representations. Sometimes children make two representations of themselves, using different materials in each, for example, pencil and clay. Or, a child may be taught to use two different materials in the same representation; for example, superimposing wire on a self-portrait initially drawn in black marker.

Identity representations are not limited to self-portraits. Identity also includes representations of family, home, and things a child likes to do. After using their newly acquired skills with materials in their identity representations, it is an easy transition to use those same tools to represent their ideas in the context of in-depth studies.

Figure 4.9. Tashima cuts wire in the studio to create a fish based on close observation of a dead fish. She uses a drawing of the fish as a guide. The completed sculpture is hung over the fish tank shown in Figure 6.6.

RELATIONSHIPS AMONG REPRESENTATION, LEARNING, AND UNDERSTANDING

In this chapter, we have documented the role that children's representations play in constructing and communicating understandings about their world. In doing so, we have been looking at relationships among *representation, learning,* and *understanding.*

We began the chapter by defining *understanding* as the constructs in a person's mind that form a *whole,* which is made up of the elements of an entity, the relations among those elements, and the relations among those relations.

Our first examples were the contrasting understandings of showers communicated in the drawings of Jonathon and Tony. We proposed that the predominant relations that made up Jonathon's understanding of a shower (as reflected in his representation) were relations among the physical components of the shower system and the relation of the water flow to the configuration of physical components. By contrast, we suggested that the predominant relation in Tony's understanding of a shower was the relation between the shower taker and the downward flow of water, with special reference to the shower taker's pleasure in experiencing water flowing down upon him.

The account of Jazmin and the Ant allowed us to get a glimpse at how *representation, learning,* and *understanding* can be connected. In this episode, we saw two primary aspects of representation: representation as *process* and representation as *product.*

The representation process consisted of Jazmin using drawing as a vehicle for recording her observations of the ant (aided by and combined with verbal representations, such as voicing the concept of "circles"). The representation process was an integral part of her learning process, which involved moving back and forth between observation and representation. We described that learning process as a dialogue with the object (see also Chapter 12, "Dialogues with the World").

Other representational processes connected with children's observations were Amber's Flowers, Gena's multiperspective drawing, and some aspects of the Chicken Community Study, such as the construction of a car for the chickens.

Sometimes, a representation process responds to memories in the mind of the learner, rather than to observations. Examples in this chapter were the Ages Study and aspects of the Chicken Community Study. In these cases, learning takes place when the learner constructs wholes in his or her mind by connecting memories and then communicating those memories through one or more modes of representation. The process of creating the representation contributes to the construction of understanding in the learner's mind and vice versa.

In Jazmin's case, the representation as *product* was her final drawing. If Jasmin were to revisit that drawing and modify it on the basis of further observation of an ant or on the basis of her reviewing her memories of the original ant, the drawing would then once more be part of representation as process.

In Chapters 1 and 3, we proposed that having multiple *perspectives* of an object of investigation contributes to a richer, more complex understanding of the object. In the present chapter, we suggested that using multiple modes of *representation* ("multiple languages") to represent an object of study also contributes to the construction of a richer, more complex understanding. We also proposed that using multiple modes of representation contributes to taking and representing multiple perspectives.

The bottom line in all of this is that children's experiences in creating representations of their objects of study, strengthened by incorporating multiple perspectives and multiple modes of representation, empowers them as learners. That empowerment becomes part of their overall sense of agency as learners. In the next chapter, we will discuss what we mean by sense of agency and look at the critical role that children's representations play in the emergent curriculum.

Chapter 5

The Emergent Curriculum

An "emergent curriculum" is an extended learning process in which the direction and content of children's learning activities are driven by the children's interests and ideas (see Chapter 1). It is the process through which *in-depth studies* occur, as in the Pipes Study (Chapter 1), the Windows Study (Chapter 2), and the Chicken Community Study (Chapter 4).

An emergent curriculum process begins with teachers observing and *documenting* children's actions, interactions, and representations through note taking, photography, tape-recording, collecting children's work, and so on (see Chapters 1 and 10). In reflecting on the documentation, the teachers interpret one or more interests being expressed by one or more children. The interest might be expressed during the children's engagement in an activity introduced by the teacher or through their drawings and dialogues following the activity. Alternatively, it may be expressed in the context of spontaneous play activities or through an object that a child enthusiastically brings to school.

Once an interest has been interpreted by the teachers and confirmed with the children, the teachers invite children to participate in an activity that relates to that interest. In the context of the activity, children interact with the teachers and with one another to co-construct understandings about the topic or object of interest. The teachers observe and document children's engagement in the activities and interpret the interests and ideas that are being newly expressed through those engagements. On the basis of those interpretations, they design and implement further activities. And so the process unfolds through ongoing cycles of activities involving teachers and children listening, observing, reflecting, and responding to one another.

Thus, the emergent curriculum is an extended dialogue between teachers and children and among children, lasting over days, weeks, or months (see Chapter 1). The term *emergent*, in addition to meaning that the curriculum emerges from the children's interests and ideas, has a further meaning: namely, the emergence of *understandings* reflected in the minds and representations of the children and teachers.

In guiding an emergent curriculum, teachers have many *choice points* along the way. For example, when they interpret documentation of children's conversations, they are likely to hypothesize a number of children's interests, not all of which can be followed at any one time. So, they make a decision based on what they think will interest enough children to form a group and what the teachers are curious about in regard to the children, teaching, and learning.

The emergent curriculum process requires teachers to be thoughtful and reflective. In general, it is important for them to be aware of why they *are* or *are not* choosing to take a particular action and what they are learning from their experience. The emergent curriculum is a major context in which they function and develop as researchers and learners. If they know why they are choosing one thing over another, they can learn more from the outcome (see Chapter 10, "Goals for Teacher Professional Development," and Chapter 11, "A Learning Community, A Learning Culture").

THE DEVELOPMENTAL GOAL FOR CHILDREN

In our view, the emergent curriculum process embodies a major child development goal underlying the Reggio Approach, namely, the child's development of *a sense of agency.* A sense of agency is defined as: Experiencing oneself as an active, self-directed agent who can, individually and in collaboration with others, formulate personally meaningful learning goals, figure out strategies to achieve them, engage the world to pursue them, construct understandings, and communicate the newly developed understandings to others. A sense of agency combines a sense of efficacy and personhood. It means: I stand in relation to others with my own motives and ideas and I have the competence to pursue them.

Specific developmental goals connected to this sense of agency include the ability to have an idea and act on it; the ability to engage in focused, sustained learning; observation skills; reasoning skills; the ability to make connections and integrate them into comprehensive understandings; representational skills; and the ability to collaborate and communicate with others (see Chapter 8).

THE EMERGENT CURRICULUM CYCLE

Figure 5.1 depicts a *cycle* in the emergent curriculum process. The cycle, described in terms of teacher actions, is a more differentiated version of the listening/observing–reflecting–responding principle described in Chapter 1. In the model of the emergent curriculum cycle, listening/observing is accompanied by *documenting*. The concept of reflection is differentiated into *interpreting, projecting/deciding, planning,* and *hypothesizing.* The concept of responding is expressed as *scaffolding.*

As with all models, the emergent curriculum cycle can be shaped to fit specific circumstances. For example, on some occasions, a teacher might go directly from observing to interpreting without engaging in formal acts of documentation.

Revisiting the Pipes Study

The Pipes Study (see Chapter 1) is a useful starting point for examining what teachers do to foster an emergent curriculum process. In revisiting and summarizing the Pipes Study, we will insert markers that denote the particular actions in the emergent curriculum cycle that are taking place. In reading the following analysis, please keep this question in mind:

> *What actions did the teachers do
> to facilitate the unfolding of the study and why?*

When given a choice of several broad topics within which to engage children in an in-depth study, the teachers chose the City because they noticed that the children, in their block play, had been constructing representations of new buildings in the neighborhood (*listening/observing, interpreting*). They decided to take the children for a walk in the neighborhood (*deciding/planning*).

On the walk, the teachers asked the children, "What do you see in the city?" (*scaffolding*) and took notes on the children's responses (*documenting*). When the class returned to the school, they read the notes back to the children (*scaffolding*) to help them rethink what they had experienced on the walk.

Figure 5.1. The emergent curriculum cycle.

Listening/Observing:
Listening to and observing children's activities and communications.

Documenting:
Recording what one hears and observes through note taking, tape-recording
and transcribing, photographing, videotaping, collecting children's representations,
posting children's representations, and so on.

Interpreting:
Reflecting on the documentations for the purpose of inferring children's interests and ideas.

Projecting/Deciding:
Brainstorming possible next steps for responding to the children's
interests and ideas and choosing one or two of the projected possibilities.

Planning:
Extending the choice into plans for implementation, including logistics.

Hypothesizing:
Imagining likely responses of the children to the planned activities.

Scaffolding:
Implementing the planned activity by preparing the environment, facilitating
children's engagement with the environment, engaging in dialogue
with children, fostering dialogue among children, facilitating children's
creating of representations, and responding to contingencies as they arise.

Listening/Observing:
Entry into another cycle that builds on the previous cycle starting with
listening to and observing the children's responses to the scaffolded activity.

The teachers then took the notes to their weekly meeting, attended by themselves, another teacher team, a studio coordinator, an education coordinator, the site family worker, and the site director. The group's analysis of the notes (*interpreting*) led them to conclude that the children could benefit by making observations in greater depth (*deciding*). So they planned the next walk in a way that would help the children to focus more sharply. Each child would be assigned to either a "looking up" group or a "looking down" group (*planning*).

After the walk, the teachers asked the children to draw what they had noticed on the walk (*scaffolding*) and wrote the children's explanations on their drawings (*scaffolding/documenting*). They collected the drawings (*documenting*) and took them to the weekly meeting, where the group noticed that the drawings fell into two broad categories: "nature" and "things that work in the city" (*interpreting*). The teachers, aided by the rest of the team, brainstormed a number of possible responses (*projecting*) and planned the following: to focus initially on "things that work in the city" and to revisit some of the drawings from that category with individual children to further explore their ideas with them (*deciding/planning*).

In revisiting the children's drawings with them, the teachers took dictations of the children's further explanations (*scaffolding/documenting*). The drawings included gas pipes, fire hydrants, and a water cap.

At the next weekly meeting, the group analyzed the results of the revisiting the teachers had done with the children (*interpreting*). They observed that most of the drawings and/or dictations involved pipes in one form or another. Since this appeared to be a pervasive interest (*interpreting*), they decided to focus on pipes as a major object of study (*deciding*). They made a plan to take interested children on a "pipes walk" through the school building (*planning*).

During the pipes walk, the teacher asked the children questions, including, "What pipes do you see?" "When you flush, where does the water go?" "And then where does it go?" (*scaffolding*). They tape-recorded the entire conversation (*documenting*).

At the next weekly meeting, the group listened to the audiotape from the pipes walk (*interpreting*). They were impressed with the strength of interest and depth of thought that the children's observations and voice tones reflected (*interpreting*). So they decided to set up a pipes exploration area in the classroom. This consisted of a wide variety of pipes along with a water table and workspace for exploration of the pipes (*planning*). As children explored the pipes, the teachers took photographs (*documenting*).

While taking photos, the teachers noticed Jaime holding a long pipe attached to a short curved pipe over his head. They guessed that he might be representing a shower (*interpreting*) and asked him about it. Jaime confirmed their interpretation. That led to the team's decision to offer the children an opportunity to make drawings of "how showers work" (*deciding/planning*). The result was the Showers Study (see Chapters 1 and 4).

> Now that you have read about the actions that teachers took to facilitate the Pipes Study, which of the steps in the emergent curriculum cycle do you think might be difficult for you? Which would be easy? Why?

We now turn to two further examples of emergent curricula, the Hands Study and the Dinosaur Study.

The Hands Study

The children were exploring drawing materials (see Chapter 4). As they worked with charcoal, they discovered that they could make handprints by pressing their charcoal-covered palms on paper. The teachers noticed that this delighted the children. They photographed the children making handprints and took some notes (see Figure 5.2).

As the class experimented with other drawing materials, the teachers noted that the children frequently used the materials to trace the outline of their hands on paper.

Spontaneous hand printing and hand tracing became popular activities among the children. This suggested the possibility of a study of hands (Chicago Commons, 2002). The teachers decided to pursue this with the children to see where it would go. They invited the children to trace their hands with white pastels on black paper. At circle time they introduced the idea of differences between different people's hands. The dialogue led to identifying attributes such as color, lines, and marks on hands. They also engaged the children in discussions such as "What are your favorite things to do with your hands?" "How do we use our hands?" "What if we had no hands? How would we eat; how would we write?" They invited the children to work in pairs, tracing large outlines of their hands with the use of an overhead projector: A child in each pair put his or her hand down on the projector glass, resulting in an image of the child's hand appearing on a large vertical sheet of paper placed in front of the projector. The

Figure 5.2.
Discovering that charcoal-covered
hands can be used for printing.

other child, using a marker, traced around the image of the hand projected onto the paper. The children enjoyed collaborating and experimenting with the size of the images projected on the wall.

> *What other activities might you introduce to deepen or broaden the children's exploration of hands?*

The teachers next invited children to trace the outlines of their hands on 8" × 11" white paper, observe the details on their hands, and draw some of the details on the traced outlines. To help children spot the details on their hands, the teachers pointed out that the details were made up of lines and circles. The children traced around their hands well, but they did not draw many details on these outlines. When they did, it tended to be stereotypic lines and circles that did not seem to actually represent observed details (see Figure 5.3, left side).

The teachers wondered whether they had overestimated the children's ability to recognize and draw the details of their hands or whether they had wrongly assumed that children would be interested in such details. They decided to suggest to the children that they compare hands with one another to see if their hands were different. The children engaged in this activity enthusiastically, but reported that they didn't see any differences.

> *Why do you think the children weren't noticing differences when comparing their hands?*
>
> *What else might have been tried at this point?*

The teachers had an intuition about what might be a more successful activity. They took photographs of the children's hands and laid them out on a table for the children to examine, asking them if they could recognize their own hands. The children were excited and asked if they could examine the photos with magnifying glasses. They were all able to recognize their own hands. The teachers then organized the children into small groups to share their discoveries. The children's most frequent observations were of birthmarks, scratches, lines, and circles. By using the photographs, they seemed better able to recognize and verbalize details.

In the next planning meeting the teachers realized that it is important to take time to repeat activities, slow down, consolidate, and then go deeper into the investigation. Again, they invited children to trace around their hands and draw in the details. They suggested that they use both the photos of their hands and their actual hands as combined reference points. The drawings that resulted reflected a remarkable leap forward in detail and accuracy (see Figure 5.3, right side).

> *Why do you think this worked so well?*

Just when the teachers were wondering what to do next, one of the children asked: "Can I draw my friend's hand?" The teachers noticed that many children expressed an interest in doing this. They invited the children to work in pairs to draw each other's hands. During this process, many of the children whose hands were being drawn coached their partners about what to include in the drawing. There was a strong investment by the coaches in having their hands drawn accurately. In fact, the coach often became a vociferous critic of the final product. Under these conditions, the children were quite able to represent details in each other's hands without the use of the photographs.

The teachers, after reflecting on the children's work and noting their continuing interest in hands, decided to challenge the children further. They invited them to do free-style drawings of their hands, suggesting that they use their hands as well as the photographs as reference points. As an introduction to this process, the teachers reviewed the idea that hands are made up of shapes, triangles, circles, and lines. Many of the children picked up on those ideas when doing their freehand drawings. However, the free-style drawing was a difficult task for them. They were able to produce drawings, but not with the same accuracy in shape and detail that was present in their previous set of drawings (see Figure 5.4).

Figure 5.3. Moving from stereotypic drawings of details to more refined actual details based on looking closely at hands and photographs of hands and discussing details with friends.

Before using photographs as reference points for drawing onto a traced hand.

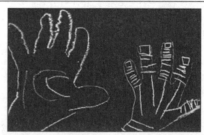

Using photographs and actual hands simultaneously as reference points for drawing details onto traced hands.

Figure 5.4.
Drawing hands directly, without the benefit of tracing the outlines first, challenges children in new ways.

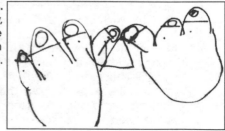

The teachers reflected on possible next steps. They decided to extend the Hands Study into the surrounding community. They started by asking the children how people in their community use their hands. The children's responses included places in the community where family members worked and places where their families shopped. From these conversations, the teachers chose three destinations to visit: a department store, a bakery, and a restaurant. After the visit to the stores, they discussed with the children what they had observed about how people work in these shops with their hands. The children drew pictures and used clay to represent their observations.

Comments on the Hands Study. This sequence was shaped by the teachers' interpretations of children's interests and by their ongoing assessments of children's observational and drawing skills. At three points in the study, children's initiatives propelled the study forward.

The Hands Study involved all or most of the class. The activities fostered a great deal of small-group communication and collaboration among the children, both of which contributed to the children's continued interest in studying their hands.

The addition of the photographs greatly enhanced the developmental benefits for the children and was an important learning experience for the teachers. In our view, the game of matching hands to photographs was an ingenious way to help the children notice the details in their hands. First, it strengthened their motivation to notice details. Second, in order to match their hands with the photographs, the children had to become aware of the details in their hands. Third, by thoughtfully taking the photographs, the teacher communicated to the children that she shared their interest in their hands. Finally, the photographs were two-dimensional, in contrast to the actual hands. This enabled the children to move from observing a two-dimensional plane to creating a two-dimensional representation.

The Dinosaur Study

This study grew out of the interests of four boys in Godzilla and "Sharp Tooth" (*Tyrannosaurus Rex*) during a Monster Study. This led to a whole-class discussion about dinosaurs in which the teachers asked, "What are dinosaurs?" and "What do dinosaurs do?" The teachers then invited interested children to represent dinosaurs on half sheets of paper using fine black markers. The combination of the small sheets and fine markers encouraged the children to make detailed drawings. Many of the drawings had human features. For example, Paulina drew a round face, including hair, teeth, and fangs (see Figure 5.7 later in this chapter).

The teachers revisited all the drawings with the whole class and asked: "Do dinosaurs have heads? Do they have hair? Do they have ears?" The children's interest began to pick up.

Teachers and children started to examine the dinosaur books in the classroom. Three-year-old Justin selected a dinosaur book and brought it to the teacher. Four-year-old Jake joined them. Together, they began an animated discussion about the various types of dinosaurs illustrated in the book, most of which were known to Jake by name. The conversation continued as both boys drew many pictures depicting different dinosaurs.

The next day the teacher invited Justin and Jake to share their work with the class. They explained and named the types of dinosaurs they had drawn and acted out the way a dinosaur moves. They also showed the class pictures from the book they had used. At this point, all the children became extremely interested, crowding around as Jake pointed out claws and teeth.

The next day the teachers offered the whole class an invitation to draw dinosaurs, this time using the dinosaur picture books and figures as references.

Mario was one of the children who responded.

He picks up a T-Rex figure from the shelf where a number of different dinosaur figures are arranged and begins to play with it, making it come alive. The teacher
calls him over to draw his dinosaur at the table (see Figure 5.5).

He begins drawing T-Rex so that the head is well situated and proportioned on
the page, leaving enough room for the whole body. Another child takes the book
back to her side of the table. Mario continues drawing, looking across at the now
almost upside-down dinosaur picture, and translates what he sees upside down to
the perspective he had begun drawing from. The teacher suggests that he go and
get the T-Rex figure. He quickly retrieves the figure and places it beside him to use
as a reference. He realizes the dinosaur figure is looking in the opposite direction
from the profile he is drawing on the paper. Instead of repositioning the figure, he
simply turns his paper over and the black outline of T-Rex's head shows through the
white paper. Now it faces the same direction as the figure.

Mario uses his black marker to trace the head showing through from the reverse side of the paper. He looks closely at the figure and sees that there are three,
not two, holes (nostril and eye) on the figure. He includes the third hole (an ear) on
his drawing. Then he adds marks on the head that represent the texture of the skin
that he noted on the rubber figure. He finishes his drawing, completing the entire
figure so that it fits well onto the paper.

Mario shows the completed drawing to the teacher, who asks him where the
tail is. He quickly returns to his seat, looks again at the figure, and adds the tail that
is visible from behind the figure.

From this point on, dinosaur drawing became a common practice during activity
time, as did leafing through dinosaur books and doing dramatic play with dinosaur
figures. The teachers introduced a set of small dinosaur figures to the small block area.
Children started bringing additional dinosaur figures and dinosaur books to school.
The rich variety of dinosaurs increasingly dawned over the class.

When the teachers announced that they would take the children to the Field Museum to see dinosaurs, the children's interest levels intensified. The day before the trip
they were surprised to find a set of four dinosaur skeleton books that the coordinator had left for them to discover. This stimulated spontaneous animated discussions.
Children were now combining information from several sources, and sharing details
of different dinosaurs with one another.

Figure 5.5.
Children use a variety
of reference points,
including books and
figures, as they draw
dinosaurs.

Anticipation was great the day of the trip. Four parents arrived and the teachers briefed them on the importance of letting children make their own discoveries at the museum and respecting the way children made their drawings. The teachers saw this as another opportunity for children to experience their own learning motivations and sense of agency as learners.

At the museum, children took time to look closely at the dinosaur exhibits. When they arrived at the room with large dinosaur skeletons, the teachers handed each child a clipboard, paper, and black felt-tipped pen. With their full attention on their work, each child began making detailed drawings of the skeletons. A ramp allowed them to switch perspectives and look down on giant dinosaurs, or up at flying dinosaur skeletons. Two boys acted out dinosaur fights and gestures in front of a large dinosaur that hovered over the bones of another dinosaur as if they had been in battle. A 3-year-old spent 20 minutes observing and carefully drawing a nearby dinosaur while his mother held the clipboard steady for him (see Figure 5.6).

Each child did several drawings. Paulina, who had drawn the human-like picture of a dinosaur prior to the museum visit, now focused intently on drawing a large dinosaur figure on display. Prior to the museum trip, Paulina's interest in sharp teeth and fangs was expressed in her drawing and when she and her friends played with dinosaur figures. At the museum, her interest in teeth continued and guided her careful observations and detailed drawing of a dinosaur skeleton (see Figure 5.7).

Figure 5.6.
A 3-year-old shows a sustained interest in observing and drawing a dinosaur skeleton in the museum.

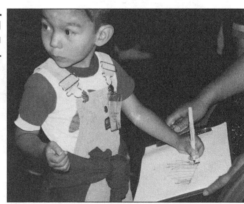

Figure 5.7.
Paulina's idea of a dinosaur (left), drawn without any visual reference before the museum trip, and her drawing (right) as she observed a dinosaur skeleton at the museum.

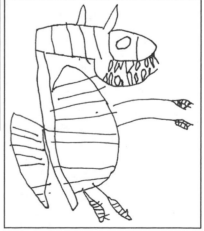

The next day, at circle time, the class revisited their museum dinosaur drawings. The teachers were impressed since each child's drawings showed an increase in understanding—conveying different complex forms, details, and different perspectives—from their pre-museum drawings. The children also had become more critical of one another's drawings. They pointed out key features that were missing. They also became focused on building museum-like block structures in which big dinosaurs were separated from small dinosaurs, meat-eating dinosaurs from plant-eating dinosaurs, and those with spikes from those without spikes.

After the 2-week school break, teachers surprised the children by projecting slides of the museum dinosaurs, including scenes of dinosaur families and habitats, onto the wall beside the block area. The children enjoyed playing dinosaurs, moving through the projected light, and continued building dinosaur habitats with blocks.

As the study progressed, children developed particular interests. For instance, Mario, in his first drawings, featured big jaws with rows of teeth. After the museum visit, he became more interested in studying and depicting large plant-eating dinosaurs with small heads and long necks.

Five boys decided to make clay dinosaur figures. They encountered the problem of how to maintain the upward angle of long-necked dinosaurs. Teachers helped by suggesting they use wire supports inside the clay figures (see Figure 5.8).

In response to the children's interest in the large size of the dinosaurs at the museum, teachers invited them to take turns projecting their museum drawings onto large sheets of paper on the wall. Each child traced around the enlarged drawing to create big dinosaur images, some measuring 4 or 5 feet tall or wide (see Figure 5.9).

Figure 5.8.
Five children
spontaneously
created dinosaur
figures out of
clay, a material
they always have
access to and the
properties of which
they continually
explore.

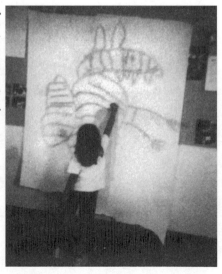

Figure 5.9.
Impressed with the
size of the dinosaurs at
the museum, Paulina
enlarges and traces
her dinosaur skeleton
drawing using the light
projector.

Several days later, when the children had traced their drawings, the teachers cut out the large figures after class, mounted them on foam board, and placed them around the classroom. The next morning, as the children entered the room, they were astounded to see the enlarged dinosaur drawings standing in the classroom. The room was full of dinosaurs. The children went wild with joy as they engaged with the enormous dinosaurs, interacting with them and helping one another move them around. The teachers noted that the specific children who had traced the dinosaur images were not claiming them solely as theirs. Rather, the figures were shared among all the children. The individual processes had become a group process. As in previous play, both boys and girls were aware of which were the most aggressive dinosaurs. They acted out encounters between the figures, shouting the dinosaurs' names, making dinosaur noises, and lifting some into the loft. Through their play, they showed and further internalized their knowledge of names, attributes, and relations among dinosaurs. They knew which dinosaurs could attack others successfully and what defenses to use against particular attackers.

The world of dinosaurs came alive in that moment, and in making it come alive, the children took another step in their construction of understanding.

> *What surprised you about the children in the course of the Dinosaur Study?*

Comments on the Dinosaur Study. Throughout the Dinosaur Study, children took initiatives to pursue their interests. The teachers supported and challenged the children as the study progressed and learned about dinosaurs along with them. Many of the children developed new capacities to communicate their ideas. For example, Jake began to draw whole figures for the first time. Previously, he had not drawn whole figures of anything, only random lines. Justin began to talk and even presented his work verbally to the class.

The study led to greater communication and collaboration among the children. Beyond the events described above, the curriculum continued to emerge as children exchanged letters about dinosaurs with one another, with friends in other classrooms, and with family members.

OBSERVATIONS ON THE THREE IN-DEPTH STUDIES

In each of the three studies discussed in this chapter (Pipes, Hands, and Dinosaurs), children's representations played a pivotal role in the process of exploration and learning. The representations served as a point of focus for each child's reflections about the object of study and as a stimulus to further investigation. They also provided a major vehicle for communication among children and vital information for the teachers.

Small groups of two to four children served as the primary context for children's learning. The groups served as the nexus for sharing ideas, extending interests, and creating representations.

Teachers fostered the construction of understandings among the children by entering into dialogue with them before, during, and after their explorations and by introducing additional ways of stimulating and facilitating their co-construction of understandings. In each case, the teachers transformed the classroom environment to spark the children's imaginations and challenge them to consider their objects of study from new perspectives. They also took the children into environments beyond the classroom, such as the boiler room, the museum, and the community, to extend and deepen the children's learning experiences and provoke the construction of new understandings about the attributes, relationships, and contexts of the phenomenon they were studying.

In the Showers Study and Hands Study, we saw important examples of how children's studies can be focused on very familiar facets of the children's experience. Much of the curriculum can be generated through the study of ordinary, everyday things, applying multiple perspectives to them, considering contexts and connections, and creating opportunities for tangible and imaginative discoveries. The exploration of the familiar sets an important example for exploring the wonders of one's immediate surroundings throughout life.

The studies also incorporated the children's previous learning and experiences; for example, children's previous work with clay, light projectors, and shapes strengthened their work in the Chicken Community, Dinosaur, and Hands studies, respectively.

In all the studies, the children experienced a great deal of joy. They clearly were doing things that interested and intrigued them. They also experienced enjoyment in interacting with one another, in their growing powers of investigation and communication, and in constructing new understandings that they could share with one another, with their families, and with the teachers.

The teachers, for their part, noticed that the emergent curriculum process always went deeper and farther than expected when they began each study. Further, they learned more about the value of taking time to document and to reflect on their documentation to inform their next steps.

Our motives to explore and construct knowledge about the world are already in our being at birth. The purpose of an emergent curriculum in particular, and the Reggio Approach in general, is to encourage those motives and teach children the skills and perspectives that promote their realization. This gives children the opportunity to develop *agency* as learners, collaborators, and constructors of understanding about the world, their relationships with it, and themselves.

With our observations about emergent curriculum processes in mind, let's move to Chapter 6, where we will examine how the construction of the learning environment supports many of the processes we have described.

Chapter 6

The Learning Environment: Classroom, School, Neighborhood, and City

This chapter explores five contexts that constitute the children's learning environment:

- Classroom
- School building
- School grounds
- Neighborhood
- City

In distinguishing these different zones of engagement, we keep in mind that they are not separated in the learning process; that is, children's understandings that are constructed in one context are extended to inquiries in others. Ultimately, everything returns to the classroom, ideally to be revisited and connected.

THE CLASSROOM ENVIRONMENT

Teachers construct the classroom environment to function as an ongoing *partner* in the teaching–learning process. For this reason, the classroom environment sometimes is referred to as "the other teacher." A carefully designed classroom environment greatly facilitates the implementation of Reggio principles. We will show how and why that is the case throughout this section.

In its role as "the other teacher," the classroom environment is constructed to meet five major goals:

1. Promote learning processes in which children are engaging with one another and with objects of interest, exploring in a focused manner, constructing and representing understandings
2. Communicate the identities of the children and the image of the child
3. Invite children to take multiple perspectives and make multiple connections
4. Promote a sense of well-being in everyone
5. Encourage parents to engage with the life of the classroom

Once a classroom environment has been constructed with these goals in mind, teachers make ongoing changes in it for a variety of reasons; for example, because children's interests or ideas are moving in new directions, because the teachers see new possibilities for stimulating children's interests, or because they see a better way for the environment to serve one or more of the five goals stated above. The teachers are supported in constructing and transforming the environment by workshops and by assistance from coordinators, the site director, and other teachers. They also engage the children as collaborators in brainstorming potential changes.

Goal #1: Promote Children's Collaborative, Focused Engagement with One Another and with Objects of Interest

On any particular day, children are either pursuing in-depth study activities (see Chapter 5) or are engaged in a wide variety of other activities that we can broadly describe as "focused play." Examples are the Going Downtown and Beetle Borg episodes of Chapter 3, cooking and serving a pretend meal in the housekeeping area, creating patterns of shapes on the light table, writing letters to friends, and creating a large balance beam and exploring it with various types of weights.

A distinctive characteristic of focused play activities is that the children, individually and in small groups, are engaging the environment on their own. Teachers may interact spontaneously with the play at times, but it is predominantly the children's domain. When teachers do interact with the children's play, they frequently engage them in dialogue about what they are doing (see Chapter 3, How to Ride a Bike, Going Downtown, and the Beetle Borg).

The activities associated with *in-depth studies*, on the other hand, often are described as "work," because there is a formal emphasis placed on the children constructing understandings and creating representations of their ideas and discoveries. These activities involve more teacher scaffolding, are part of an emergent curriculum process that has continuity over time, and are carefully monitored, documented, and facilitated by the teachers even though the children may be working on their own much of the time.

Nevertheless, focused play activities may show many of the characteristics of in-depth study activities for two reasons: First, since all of the children experience in-depth studies during the year, they are likely to bring a focused, systematic attitude to their other activities as well. Second, the classroom environment is constructed by the teachers to encourage and support children's focused explorations.

It is important to keep in mind that the children's focused play activities are frequently the seedbed for potential in-depth studies. Teachers perpetually are observing and documenting new indicators of children's interests, wherever they may occur.

Small-Group Learning Areas. Children's explorations typically take place in a network of small-group learning areas, each of which is organized around activities and materials that are inherently interesting to preschoolers. Common examples are large blocks, small blocks, books, housekeeping, dress-ups, light table, water and sand table, writing table, loft spaces, shadow screen, painting area, and construction area equipped with wire, clay, and recyclables.

Each of these small-group areas is designed to encourage children's collaborative interaction in exploring, co-constructing understandings, and representing their ideas. Accordingly, each area provides the following:

1. Interesting objects (including materials to read)
2. Collaborative work surfaces
3. Materials for creating representations, attractively sorted and easily accessible
4. Display and storage of children's work
5. Thoughtful use of light (when possible)
6. Inviting atmosphere

The following description of a writing area (see Figure 6.1) is an example of a small-group learning place that embodies the above six characteristics. The table comfortably accommodates three children sitting along its length and one child at the end. The racks on and above the writing table can be reached easily and hold a variety of writing materials carefully sorted into removable wire baskets. These include a variety of pens, pencils, pastels, and markers, along with different sizes and colors of paper, envelopes, rulers, stencils, erasers, a stapler, and a telephone—all chosen by the children with the teacher's help. The triple-light pole beside the desk offers focused, warm yellow light. Natural light spreads from a large window across the room, and soft light from the hallway comes into the area through windows, doors, and the transom beside the writing table. A fluorescent ceiling light offers white light over the entire space. (In general, when fluorescent lights are used, it's good to use additional light to break up the monotony.)

The writing table invites participation. There is easy access from the rest of the room and openness to movement within the space. Special features include an aquarium with goldfish and plants, which might inspire thoughts of water and lakes. There is a talking tube that connects to the classroom across the hallway, as do several windows. A wastebasket next to the table suggests that one can discard and start work over or try something else. Above the area umbrellas and crystals are suspended from the ceiling, creating a special sense of place and wonder. Five feet back from the writing area is a bench containing the children's loose-leaf binders where they store the writings and drawings that they do at the table. Alongside it is a low table where a group of children can revisit their binders together.

Figure 6.1.
The children dictated a list of twenty writing-related items, which were then placed in this writing area.

Positioning of Areas. Teachers frequently position particular small-group learning areas near one another to encourage children to join the resources of adjacent areas. For example, in one classroom, teachers located the dress-up area, the housekeeping area, the book area, and the writing table near the large-block area. This arrangement encouraged children to bring items from those adjacent areas into the block area in order to furnish the "room" that they were constructing out of large blocks. The closeness of the writing area encouraged them to communicate about the things they were creating in the block area.

Other considerations that enter into the placement of areas within the classroom are access to natural light (as in the placement of the painting area), access of lofts to windows (in order to observe objects and events in the external environment), placement of light boxes in darker areas of the room, the grouping of "wet" areas (e.g., water table, painting, clay) versus "dry" areas (e.g, blocks, dress-ups), and the locating of wet areas near a water source.

Ongoing Enrichment. Learning areas frequently are augmented by placing objects of current interest into them. For example, in the course of the Dinosaur Study (described in Chapter 5), the teachers placed dinosaur figures in the block area. The presence of blocks and dinosaurs together resulted in the children articulating a set of connections informed by what they had learned about dinosaurs.

New learning areas sometimes are created to respond to and extend freshly emerging interests; for example, the creation of the "pipes area" during the Pipes Study (see Chapter 1).

Freeing up Teachers. When classrooms are designed in the above manner, small groups of children can function relatively autonomously. This allows a teacher to relate extensively to one small group at a time and to document children's activities while the other teacher engages the rest of the room. Low boundary markers, such as shelves, benches, and rugs, are used throughout the room, enabling both children and teachers to see virtually anywhere in the room at any time.

Dual-Function Areas. The large-block area often serves as the whole-class meeting area since block construction and whole-class meetings both require a large, uninterrupted space and the two activities don't take place at the same time. A low-napped rug covering the floor of the area is appropriate for both functions. Some classrooms have risers on one side of the block/meeting area, which allows the class to sit at different levels when a teacher reads a book so that everyone can see the pictures and the teacher's face. A number of other areas in the room may serve multiple functions, such as eating, drawing, and working with three-dimensional materials (clay, wire, recyclables, etc).

Goal #2: Communicate the Identities of the Children and the Image of the Child

The Environment Communicates the Identities of Children. The classroom environment has the feeling of an alive, ongoing endeavor. The visibility of the children and their work; the presence of items that reflect the children's interests, thoughts, and discoveries; photographs of children engaged in activities; and display panels about children and their families create an identity and history of the classroom. They tell you about the people who live there, the things they are pursuing, the relationships among them, and their connections beyond this immediate space.

- The walls and low shelves, both painted in *neutral colors*, allow the children and their work to stand out.

- Children decorate their cubbies with personally meaningful objects and images, photos of families and friends, and personal symbols.
- Children's self-portraits, drawings, and dictations are displayed in the classroom in interesting ways.
- Individualized mailboxes on which children have written their names and taped a drawing, self-portrait, or personal symbol signify that children are in active communication with one another and the teacher.
- Children's writing, drawings, and photographs stored in journals, binders, or portfolios are kept in visible, accessible places in the classroom.
- Full-length mirrors are placed vertically to reflect a child's whole body and horizontally to show a child's face, hands, and torso while working.
- A personal photograph or drawing is placed alongside each child's nap time location.

The Environment Communicates the Image of the Child. In addition to the design of the learning areas that invites children's active, collaborative engagement in learning (Goal #1), many other facets of the environment communicate the image of the child:

- *Ladders and lofts* send the message that children are capable climbers (see Figure 6.2).
- *Adult-sized* benches and antique dressers indicate that children are capable of using adult furniture.
- *Real utensils* are included in the housekeeping area; for example, a table set with cloth table mats and real silverware and glassware, a beautiful vase with flowers, and so on. These send the message that children can take care of beautiful things and learn how to handle breakable objects just as adults do.
- *Materials are made fully accessible* to children by being easy to reach, easy to lift, and stored in transparent containers that are attractively organized to allow children to see the whole range of choices at once. The open access to materials sends the message, "It is up to you when you want to use it; if you're painting, you can take the water colors to a table or to an easel" (see Figure 6.3).

Figure 6.2.
A loft with clear plastic sides offers children different visual perspectives, spatial experiences, and climbing opportuniites. Note the binoculars, the images of children under the rolled-up shadow screen, the music tape player, and the elongated floor mirror (bottom right), which offers a different perspecitve on small-block constructions.

Figure 6.3. Accessible, inviting materials with work surfaces nearby. In the photo on the left, well-displayed clear containers with colorful contents invite children to investigate, sort, and use familiar and recycled materials creatively. In the photo on the right, a child carefully experiments, measures, conceptualizes, and plans as she integrates the very different materials she has chosen into a whole design to create a collage.

- A *variety of work surfaces,* including different floor surfaces, encourages children to make choices. For example, tables are of different heights so that children can stand, sit, kneel, or sit on the floor when using them. Some are at coffee table height with cushions around them.
- *Numerous opportunities for flow of movement* are made possible by the arrangement of furniture and by teacher decisions to avoid cluttering the environment with unnecessary furniture.
- *Space is used flexibly.* For example, in the Going Downtown episode (see Chapter 3), the two girls use cubbies as the seats of their "car." They pretend that the glass-windowed classroom door, opening against their cubby seats, is the windshield of their car. They use items from the adjacent housekeeping area to accompany them on their journey downtown. In Figure 6.4, two boys make themselves comfortable as they work.
- *Children are invited to revisit and discuss their work* through the location of display areas near regular traffic pathways.

The environment is well organized, so that children can find inspiration and make thoughtful choices as to how, when, and where they engage the materials and spaces available to them. The environment tells children that it is there for them to use and that they are capable of valuing and using its interesting and beautiful objects.

Goal #3: Invite Children to Take Multiple Perspectives and Make Multiple Connections

Multiple perspectives and connections are encouraged in many ways. Unusual mirrors placed in unexpected places, such as on the ceiling, invite children to see themselves in a different way. Lofts sometimes include both stairs and ladders, and a pulley system to transport goods or messages from one loft to another. Binoculars, magnifying glasses, mirrors, shadow screens, and overhead projectors all provide different perspectives. Children can experience multiple spatial perspectives from lofts, high and low seating, risers, and windows between rooms at different levels. A wide variety of accessible books and

Figure 6.4.
Two boys choose to use the floor to stretch out as they work on their self-portraits together.

materials in different areas of the classroom allows children to make multiple connections. Contrasting textures such as a brick wall, soft rug, linoleum floor, embroidered pillows, and wood bench offer children different sensory experiences.

Multiple perspectives also are encouraged by inviting children to make meaningful connections to the world beyond the classroom:

- Connections to *other classrooms* through windows, speaking tubes, and inter-classroom mail deliveries
- Connections to *nature* through plants, animals, shells, beautiful stones, natural colors, and many varieties of wood
- Connections to *home* through items such as big chairs, couches, wall clock, and potted plants, promoting feelings of continuity and comfort
- Connections to the *community* through open access to windows at different heights and through children's representations of life in the neighborhood
- Connections to *one's own and other cultures* through pictures and meaningful objects

Goal #4: Promote a Sense of Well-Being

A variety of niches in the classroom relate to different states of being. A child can find a quiet, private space, a stimulating place of sounds, a comfortable spot with soft objects, and places to climb safely. Different types of lighting create a space that is either more private and focused, on the one hand, or more brightly lit and encouraging of action, on the other. If a child takes a book, she has some real choices about where to read it. Special places are created on and under lofts. From a loft, a child can see what's going on in the room.

The attention to detail throughout the room reflects a caring aesthetic and communicates to the children that they are valued. For example, one or two beautifully presented things in a loft, such as a few plants and two science books relating to plants, invite children to inquire. The selection and placement of photos reflects thoughtful intention. A balance scale is equipped with a variety of small found treasures to weigh. The carefully constructed environment invites children to choose from a variety of beautifully displayed materials and objects arranged for their use.

An inviting feeling is created through spaciousness, natural light, neutral wall colors, diversity of heights and types of furniture, a variety of floor coverings, handcrafted objects, natural objects arranged in interesting ways, and a range of objects to look at, arrange, sort, count, and explore. The classroom also contains surprising items such as unusual shelving, unique stools or chairs, or an oversized easel to accommodate two children and encourage them to exchange ideas.

Goal #5: Encourage Parents to Engage with the Life of the Classroom

The *entry area* of the classroom and the *hallway* outside the room together constitute a zone in which parents have most frequent contact with the classroom. Therefore, it is important that these areas be welcoming, engaging, and informative.

The entry area is inviting and tends to be near the cubbies where children store their coats and belongings. There is ample space for parents to stand and have a conversation with the teacher, to see new developments in the room, and to relate to their children while they take off their coats and get settled. Displays of children's work are clearly visible from the entrance, encouraging parents, teachers, and children to enter into a dialogue about children's current interests and ideas. There is a bench for parents to sit on. Children's binders and journals are stored nearby, so that parents can look through children's work and become closer to the life of the classroom.

The hallway just outside the classroom typically has wall displays that connect parents to the classroom; for example, display panels that document children's learning sequences (see Chapter 10, "Documentation") or parents' statements of "hopes and dreams" for their children, accompanied by family photos (see Chapter 9).

Teachers' Reflections on the Evolution of Their Classrooms: Then Versus Now

The following is an account of how the teachers of two classrooms at the New City Center transformed their classroom environments after becoming part of the Reggio Exploration. They were influenced both by ideas from Reggio Emilia (Gandini, 1998) and by a seminar by Anita Olds, a gifted and comprehensive designer of environments for young children (see Olds, 2001).

The "Sunshine Room" and the "Rainbow Room." The first classroom had glaring yellow walls that were overwhelming. It was known as the sunshine room. The areas within the room were divided by bright picket fences painted blue, yellow, pink, or green. Holly Hobby wallpaper decorated the hallway. Brightly colored plastic children's furniture and plastic dishes were the norm. One's attention was drawn to the vivid walls, furniture, and colorful teacher-created borders around the bulletin boards. Visitors hardly noticed the quality of natural light from large windows or the children's work since the brightly colored furnishings competed for the viewer's gaze. In fact, the room distracted one from focusing on the children at all.

The second room was known as the rainbow room. Each wall was a different color, with pink and blue dominating. Yellow, blue, green, and red bookshelves defined the areas within the classroom and distracted one's attention from the many objects on the shelves. A feeling of clutter pervaded the room. Objects were not carefully selected and placed in the room, making it hard to determine the real choices one could make when interacting with objects and within spaces. The top third of each window was covered by opaque industrial plastic.

Transformations. The teachers wanted to create environments that recognized children's interests, ideas, and capabilities and that were pleasurable, engaging, thought provoking, and safe.

Their first changes were painting the walls a neutral off-white, taking out the brightly colored fencing, repainting shelves a neutral color, bringing in some natural wood shelving, and taking out the teacher-designed borders. These changes allowed the children and their work to become the color in the room. Attention was paid to displaying and building on the children's ideas and expressions. The emphasis also shifted to creating choices in the environment that invited children to extend their interests and build on knowledge they already had.

The teachers wanted to include some furnishings that were like home and some that were different and would stimulate the children's curiosity and aesthetic sensibilities. They took out the plastic furniture and some of the child-sized furniture, replacing it with home-like furniture, observing that children enjoy using things that grown-ups use and are very capable of climbing onto a bench or into a rocking chair. Each room now offered a greater variety of furniture, including many antique pieces that were beautifully crafted. The teachers eliminated all clutter and overcrowding of furniture.

The children and teachers together decided which items to have in the housekeeping area. Children did a study of the things in their homes and kitchens. Families began contributing items such as glass bowls, tortilla makers, pots, and vases, and teachers found some items at resale shops. When introducing special items to the classroom, teachers drew children's attention to their beauty and suggested how to take care of them. They found that when children are part of the process of choosing the items, children feel the items are theirs and treat them with care.

Overall Thoughts on the Classroom Learning Environment

After thinking about all they learned in the ongoing process of changing their classroom environments, Chicago Commons staff had the following advice for teachers:

- Don't just follow formulas. Think about what you are doing and why you are arranging something the way you are. Take time to reflect and make changes as needed. It is okay to make mistakes. It is a learning process. You can keep working on something and find the best arrangement.
- Observe how children are using various areas in the room as one of your major clues for change, and think about changes from the child's point of view. Remember what it was like for you as a child.
- Take photos of your space before you make changes. This helps to first objectify it and then re-create it.
- It is an ongoing process. Environmental changes need to be anchored to the children currently in the classroom. Over the years, you see differences in how children respond. Changes need to be made accordingly.

LEARNING ENVIRONMENTS BEYOND THE CLASSROOM

The learning environments beyond the classroom include the school building, the school grounds, the neighborhood, and the city beyond.

The School Building

Three locations in the school building play important roles in the experience of children, parents, and visitors: the studio, halls and stairways, and the entry area.

The *studio* is a room that is richly furnished with useful materials, tools, and stimulating objects where teachers or coordinators work with small groups of children. One studio serves all the classrooms in a center. Typical uses of the studio include a small group of children working with a teacher on a collective representation of their learning, or a teacher meeting with a small group of children to discuss their thoughts about that morning's field trip or a new inquiry. Because it provides wonderful materials and an abundance of good work surfaces, the studio serves as a very useful space beyond the classroom. It is an inspiration for all who use it (see Figure 6.5).

The *hallways* are alive with carefully prepared display panels portraying children's learning explorations (see "Documentation" in Chapters 1 and 10). Examples include a study of birds, showing children's drawings of birds that they observed in the neighborhood near the school; a study of children's identities, including self-portraits in wire and drawings of what each child's family likes to do together; a dandelion study in which children discovered that some dandelion leaves are rounded and some are pointed; a hair study in which children compared their own hair with that of their parents, siblings, and staff; and photos of children exploring the sensory qualities and physical capacities of clay, accompanied by their dictations. Parents and visiting educators find these panels highly informative. They convey the spirit and depth of learning that takes place in the school.

Hallways are places of wonder, furnished with items that invite people to stop and explore. Examples include

- Surprise boxes (with closed flip tops) hanging from the walls. These contain interesting small objects that are replaced periodically so that children can delight in discovering them.

Figure 6.5. A very small studio in which four or five children can focus and where quality art supplies, audiovisual equipment, and thought-provoking materials are available.

- Fountains with flowing water
- A fishpond with accompanying notepads and pencils that encourage children to write messages to the fish (see Figure 6.6)
- A bathtub filled with soft baby dolls (see Figure 6.6)

In the *stairwells*, which are more subject to fire code restrictions, one finds displays of children's clay work or tile drawings.

The *entry area* of the building provides an opportunity to display important messages that welcome people and provide insight into the values, philosophy, and cultural identity of the center. Messages about children, teachers, and parents are beautifully conveyed through words and photographs. Children's work is thoughtfully displayed. In one center, the staff wrote memories of their early childhood that were displayed alongside their baby pictures.

The entry area contains something unique that engages people's curiosity. It may be an interesting arrangement of natural objects, such as sticks or pine cones. There may be objects relating to a current study, for example, a sawhorse with a saddle and a wide-brimmed cowboy hat. There are usually some cultural references, for example, handmade Mexican furniture. The area is constructed with great care and kept clean and attractive. Entry areas are spacious enough to offer several objects to interact with and places to sit. Figure 6.7 shows an entrance area thoughtfully furnished with unusual mirrors, plants, a loom inviting children to weave strips of fabric, a gazebo with movable parts to explore, and a large bench.

Learning activities also take place in other parts of the building. The kitchen, basement, and offices of various staff are locations where children can carry out special inquiries.

Figure 6.6. Hallways can be places provoking wonder, curiosity, and active engagement.

Figure 6.7.
An entranceway
offering places to
sit and things to
explore.

The School Grounds

The yard of each center contains a relatively unique set of learning opportunities in addition to swings, slides, ladders, and low balance beams. Examples are natural dirt areas where children can dig to discover what lies beneath, trees and shrubs they can explore, a path with interesting architectural forms arranged alongside it, an extensive hard surface where children can make large chalk drawings and ride tricycles, areas for running, a playhouse that encourages rich fantasy play, an old boat serving as a sandbox, and an outdoor studio (see Figure 6.8).

The area surrounding the school building often provides an ideal setting for the extension of an in-depth study; for example, as part of a Camping Study the children explored experiences of tenting and camping beside the school, including making a fire and cooking outdoors. The area surrounding the school also provides opportunities for the study of insects, birds, and other animals.

Opportunities like these for children to have full-body, imaginative engagements with the outside and natural environment are a key part of exploring their relationship with the world.

The Neighborhood

In previous chapters, we have seen several examples of ways in which the neighborhood offers rich opportunities for children's inquiries; for example, the Pipes Study, the Windows Study, What Can Babies Do?, Jazmin and the Ant, and Amber's Flowers. A major resource in the neighborhood are stores, as we saw in the Chicken Community Study and the Hands Study.

The most successful neighborhood explorations are carefully scaffolded by the teachers in ways that help the children to focus and at the same time give them wide latitude to exercise their interests and motives. An example is the creation of the "looking up" and "looking down" groups for the second neighborhood walk in the Pipes Study (see Chapter 1).

Thus, in neighborhood and city settings, the structuring is not achieved by constructing the environment itself, but by structuring the children's *interactions* with the environment.

Figure 6.8. Outdoor areas were redeveloped to make interesting pathways, connections with nature, outdoor studios, and grassy areas to run and play on.

The City

Engagements in the city include visits to institutions such as the natural history museum and the zoo. In the Dinosaur Study, teachers equipped children with clipboards and pencils, encouraging them to make sketches of dinosaur skeletons and other dinosaur exhibits (see Chapter 5, "The Dinosaur Study"). In the Chicken Community Study, children visited chickens and their home at the zoo. Some children met with the zookeeper, whom they interviewed using their own written questions (see Chapter 4, "The Chicken Community"). Other examples of using the city to extend children's learning included: pursuing their interests in stoplights, traffic, trucks, other vehicles, ramps, and highways while riding a bus on the expressway; extending their study of pirates by attending a pirate play at the children's museum and presenting the actor-pirates with messages in bottles; and exploring color by visiting a city park, where the children encountered flowering plants and reproduced the colors, patterns, and forms they observed in the gardens (Chapter 4, "Amber's Flowers"). Similarly, visits to the Art Institute, the public library, and the aquarium were responses to children's particular interests. They provided new information, experiences, and opportunities to stimulate and extend the children's observations and understandings within emerging in-depth studies.

ASKING QUESTIONS ABOUT LEARNING ENVIRONMENTS

Here are some questions that may be helpful to you regarding the various learning environments:

- In what ways does your classroom environment invite children to collaborate in their learning activities?
- Does a visitor have a sense of who lives in this classroom and something of its history?
- Where is the "color" in your classroom? Does it come from the children and their work?
- How do you use wall space in your classroom? Is there a rich array of children's work, voices, and ideas? Is there a balance between display of past work, recent work, and ongoing work?
- How do you maintain a balance between open and furnished space in your classroom? What might you do to simplify and open up more space, or utilize space in more meaningful ways?
- In what ways do you sort and display materials so they are visible, accessible, and interesting to children?
- Is there a flow to the classroom that respects children's motivations?
- What messages do classroom furnishings send? Do you have unique and interesting furniture? Does it remind children of home? Does it enrich children's experience and deepen their awareness of different meanings, uses, and possibilities?
- What connections to home life are visible in this classroom?
- How are parents represented, or present, in the classroom?
- Does your classroom invite children to take different perspectives?
- In what ways is the classroom environment connected to other classrooms, to the "outside" world, and to the local community?
- In how many ways have you incorporated nature into your classroom?
- Are there places in the classroom that respect children's different states of being? Can a child find a quiet, comforting, private place, a stimulating place of sounds, places for dramatic action, physically challenging places?
- How and why might you use different qualities of light in your classroom?
- How does the classroom environment greet visitors and parents, teachers, and children when they enter? What implicit and explicit messages does the environment send? What changes might you try, and why?
- In what ways do the building and the grounds engage the interests of children and parents, encourage meaningful interaction and dialogue, stimulate wonder, provide opportunities for exploration, and offer safety, warmth, and comfort?
- When you take your children on neighborhood or city field trips, how do you scaffold the learning process? In what ways do you enhance their sense of purpose and focus? How do you document children's observations and experiences? In what ways do children revisit these experiences? When and how do you record your reflections on the trip?

Chapter 7

Classroom Management

In this chapter we address the question of how teachers can guide and coordinate classroom activities in ways that support and promote elements of the Reggio Approach throughout the day. In the previous chapter we considered ways in which teachers construct the classroom learning environment to meet five major goals:

1. Promote and facilitate children's engagement with one another and with objects of interest
2. Communicate children's identities and the image of the child
3. Encourage children to take multiple perspectives
4. Promote children's sense of well-being
5. Encourage parents to engage with the life of the classroom

The same goals provide the focus for teachers' moment-to-moment engagements with children, with parents, with one another, and with the environment as they manage the classroom process throughout the day. These management actions include the following:

- Being available to listen, observe, and respond throughout the day
- Scaffolding children's learning
- Documenting children's learning
- Responding to upsets
- Coordinating the overall flow of activities and routines

Specifically, this chapter relates to how teachers carry out and integrate the above five actions. A key aspect of the answer lies in effective collaboration between the teachers in the classroom. Another aspect of the answer is the children themselves; that is, through learning the routines, procedures, principles, and processes of the classroom; through developing personal agency in taking initiatives; and by making reflective choices, the children become major allies in classroom management.

BACKGROUND INFORMATION

Two kinds of background information are useful for understanding processes of classroom management at Chicago Commons: the types of preschool programs that are offered and the place of in-depth studies in the life of the classroom.

Two Types of Preschool Programs

Chicago Commons preschool classrooms fall basically into two program categories:

- Half-day program: Two groups of children (e.g., 8:30–12:00 and 12:30–4:00), 4 days a week (Monday through Thursday). Classrooms are staffed with two teachers (head and assistant teacher). Teachers use Fridays for reflection, planning, and administrative work. This is typical of the Head Start model.
- Full-day program: One group of children (7:00–6:00), 5 days a week. Classes are staffed with three or four teachers with overlapping schedules so that two to three teachers are present at any one time. The morning schedule is like that of the half-day program. Meetings and administrative work take place primarily during children's 2-hour nap times.

In either program type, there are 17 to 20 children in a classroom, ranging in age from 3 to 5 years old. Children who stay for 2 years remain with the same teacher in the same classroom.

The Place of In-Depth Studies in the Life of the Classroom

On the average, one or two in-depth studies operate in a classroom at any one time. Children who are not participating in an in-depth study on a particular day are involved in focused play activities that involve many of the same learning processes as the in-depth study activities (see Chapter 6, Goal #1). A goal of the program is that all children be involved in one or two in-depth studies during the course of the year.

In-depth studies tend to take one of the following forms:

1. Mainly small-groups (two to five children). The study does not involve children beyond the small group except for occasional sharing with the whole class. The Chicken Community Study and Jazmin and the Ant (see Chapter 4) were in this category.
2. A small group, with the whole class engaging in inquiry at various points over time. For example, in the Dinosaur Study (see Chapter 5), the exploration started with a small group of boys but eventually involved the whole class, most notably in the trip to the museum and the grand finale.
3. Studies actively involving the whole class and carried out in small groups; for example, the Hands Study (see Chapter 5).

Note that all three forms emphasize small-group exploration. The small groups allow the children to collaborate and enable teachers to engage children effectively, offering them challenges, suggestions, and so on. The work on in-depth studies tends to take place at activity time (see later in this chapter) and during neighborhood explorations or field trips in the city.

A number of procedures and processes in the classroom support the in-depth studies:

- *Using the holding board*: This is a place where children's recent drawings, dictations, and dialogues, along with teachers' comments and photographs of children engaged in their work, are posted for revisiting and reflection by children, teachers, and parents. These documentations are an ongoing record of current in-depth studies and provide a reference point for planning from day to day. The items posted on the holding board frequently provide the source from which teachers select documentations to take to the weekly meeting (see "Collaborative Planning" later in this chapter; Chapter 10, "Documentation;" and Figure 7.1).

Figure 7.1.
A holding board with material from an ongoing study about painting, with references to van Gogh's paintings. The board holds transcripts from dialogues, discussion notes, dictations, paintings, and photographs as the children investigated and compared how they and the artist make their paintings.

- *Displaying children's work*, photos of children's work, or children's work plans in a learning area in which the work was done; for example, posting of children's blueprints, drawings, or photos of their block constructions in the block area to stimulate further constructions, drawings, interpretations, and revisions.
- *Children collaborating and teaching one another*, including elaborating, copying, critiquing, and helping.
- *Children sharing with the whole class*; for example, sharing their in-depth study work at circle time.

THE UNFOLDING OF A HALF DAY

In a morning half-day session, the following sequence usually takes place:

Arrival time
Snack time
Circle time
Activity time
Outdoor time or other large-motor activity
Story time
Lunch
Pick-up time

A Morning in Sharon and Yolanda's Room

The following, synoptic description of one morning in a Chicago Commons pre-school classroom is based on a videotaping done in June 1999. Its intent is to communicate ways in which the five classroom management actions can be carried out. Other classroom teams have somewhat different operating styles, and all teams are evolving over time.

The class was led by Sharon, the head teacher, and Yolanda, the assistant teacher. The children and their teachers were involved in two in-depth studies, one about the class *guinea pig* and the other about *communication*, including writing letters to people.

Arrival Time. Sharon sits near the door, exchanging greetings with parents and children. Sometimes a child reaches up to sit on her lap; to others she gives a hug, a smile, or a quick "good morning" as they run to join a friend. Two mothers come into the classroom and stay briefly to watch their children begin a puzzle together. Another mother waits on the bench while her toddler temporarily joins his brother and friends building in the small-block area. Yolanda checks on four girls playing the Boggle dice game that Sharon had set out earlier, along with a word card game. Two boys assemble flexiblocks on the light table. A girl sits chatting with Sharon before pushing the breakfast cart across the room to a table. She knows the routine well.

Snack. Sharon stays near the entrance door, while Yolanda checks to make sure that children wash their hands before breakfast. Some have already been to the bathroom to wash their hands, and three children use the sink by the painting table. Tommy mops the floor where water has spilled. Several boys help themselves to paper plates, muffins, and milk, and carry the open pineapple juice can over to the big table.

Sharon gets up from the snack table to assist young Delia at the computer. Two older girls join in and continue watching and occasionally helping Delia when Sharon leaves. Berenice and Maria, busy at the writing table, are using crayons, pencils, rulers, and paper they have selected from a nearby shelf. Yolanda asks them if they want to use the mailbox to send their letters to friends before they go to wash their hands.

It is Latoya and Kishanda's turn to clean the breakfast tables. Latoya likes spraying soap solution onto the tabletops, and Kishanda follows her, vigorously drying them with paper towels. Yolanda does the final checkup and pushes in the chairs around the table. Children finish brushing their teeth before making their way to the rug for circle time.

Circle Time. Yolanda, sitting among the children on the rug, responds affirmatively when Miguel brings a "hot potato" figure into the group. They all play the game until Yolanda starts the "good morning" song. Tommy leaves the circle and Sharon follows to talk with him. He agrees to return if he can sit next to Yolanda. Sharon endorses this. Yolanda begins a naming song that all the children know.

Sharon asks five children who, yesterday, had drawn houses for the class guinea pig, Guinea, to show their work to the others. Each child takes turns sitting on her lap, talking about the drawing as she holds it up for all to see. She also reads the dictations from the back of their drawings. Ulivo's drawing is of the outside view of a three-story house. Sharon suggests that today he might want to draw the inside of the house.

Tommy, upset again, withdraws from the circle. Yolanda follows him and listens closely. As they talk, he tells her he wants to make a house for Guinea out of wood. He then agrees to rejoin the group.

As children show their drawings, Sharon points out features that represent the things that Guinea needs (e.g., a bed and a blue door to the house). She also asks the group questions about colors, shapes, and how Guinea might use his house. The children show sustained interest in these presentations.

Sharon then turns to a basket of recently fired clay guinea pigs that five children had made the previous week. She identifies each child's clay guinea pig as they crowd around her. Some broke during firing so Sharon suggests mending them with glue.

As circle time ends, Sharon announces that she will put some clay and Guinea on the table again so children can make clay guinea pigs. Sharon also notifies the children that Yolanda will be there to help. The water table is also available today. Children quickly go to the areas in which they are most interested.

Activity Time. Tommy leaves the rug area for the writing table to draw his plan for Guinea's house. Yolanda informs Sharon of Tommy's ideas. Berenice asks Sharon where her "writing book" is. (The previous day they had made a red loose-leaf folder with her picture on the cover.) She finds it and begins making a new drawing for her book.

Laura and Miguel stay in the circle area, throwing the hot potato figure between them. Miguel pulls out his tiny flashlight to show Laura. Fabian joins them and the two boys begin to play with the hollow blocks, constructing a long tunnel structure. Laura joins Yolanda and three other girls at the table with the clay and Guinea. Sharon puts the fired clay guinea pigs on a shelf behind the table, then, holding a broken one, shows it to the girls, explaining that if they made a fat clay guinea pig it might break when it was fired in the kiln.

Guinea stayed on the table all during activity time. There were always at least two or three children at the table, looking closely at Guinea, petting her, and making clay figures while Yolanda offered support. Meanwhile, Sharon built on opportunities to challenge children and facilitate the extension of their understandings and representations. She documented children's work, using a camera or taking dictation. Some activities related to making a house for Guinea; for example, Ulivo constructed an intricate, large three-story house out of small blocks and architectural blocks. Like his drawing, he executed it on a grand scale with much elaboration and detail. He spent all morning on it, Sharon photographed it, and it was left standing after clean-up time.

A group of girls, including Berenice, are working at the writing table. They look happy as they talk, fold their completed work, and place it in envelopes, perhaps to post them in the class mailbox. Two girls leave for the water table where three girls are playing with containers. Berenice and Araceli remain at the writing table, with their writing books, drawing and talking about houses. Berenice gives Araceli advice about drawing houses.

Tommy approaches Sharon with his blueprint for the inside of Guinea's house. Sharon takes dictation as he tells her about it. He has drawn a door and stairs in the plan. Sharon asks: "How would Guinea get upstairs?" Tommy responds by moving his finger up the stairs, into the kitchen area, and across to a stove and refrigerator he has depicted. He explains how Guinea would use these appliances. Sharon continues to write down everything Tommy says as they converse. He creates a story about Guinea eating watermelon from the refrigerator and spitting out yellow seeds. He accompanies his story with gestures as he imagines Guinea enjoying the melon. Sharon then suggests that, since there is no wood for him to work with today, perhaps he could use blocks to build his plan for Guinea's house. Taking the blueprint, they go into the small-block area. Sharon tapes Tommy's plan onto the back of a shelf so he can see it easily as he builds. On the wall are photos and blueprints of previous block structures designed by Tommy and other children. Despite these visual references and Sharon's scaffolding, Tommy does not continue to use blocks to build Guinea's house. (The following day he would independently build the house from donut boxes that he found.)

Yolanda leaves the guinea pig table to observe Miguel and Fabian at their tunnel in the large-block area. Fabian climbs on top of the tunnel as she approaches. Yolanda asks him if she can tie his shoelace. He says "no." He and Miguel are absorbed with zooming metal cars through the upper level of the tunnel they have just finished constructing.

Yolanda returns to the clay table where more girls have joined the original group. Tommy comes over and they all pet Guinea. Tommy again talks with Yolanda about his idea of making a house for Guinea out of wood tomorrow. Meanwhile, he makes a clay rabbit figure. He takes the flat, two-legged figure to show Sharon, who invites him into the hallway to view the caged classroom rabbit. Together, they compare his clay figure with the real rabbit. Sharon gives him time and space to consider what changes he might want to make. She lets the rabbit out of the cage so Tommy can touch and observe it closely from different angles.

Berenice has been waiting patiently for Sharon's attention. In one hand she holds her writing book, and in the other her drawing of clothes hanging from hangers on a clothesline. She dictates a description of her drawing while Sharon writes under it in large print. Sharon shows her how to use the two-hole punch and they fit the new page into Berenice's book. As Sharon leaves, she asks Berenice if she wants to color her drawing. Berenice adds two people to her first drawing. Then she takes the initiative to begin a new drawing, this time focusing on color. She first uses a pencil to draw the outlines of five crayons and then colors each with a different-colored crayon.

Berenice finds Sharon observing Miguel and Fabian racing cars off a ramp. They sit on the floor beside the ramp while Berenice names the five colors in the same left to right sequence that she has drawn them. As Sharon writes Berenice's dictation, she uses her other hand, in a moment of double-tasking, to facilitate the boys' play by placing a block under one end of the ramp, raising it to a higher level. The boys, having been introduced to the idea of increasing the angle of the ramp, are delighted to find that this makes the metal cars go farther and faster.

Kishanda and Latoya are painting together at the triple easel. They copy each other as they paint sweeping red strokes and paint their own hands and arms red. Yolanda leaves the guinea table to inquire about their paintings. Kishanda says she is painting her mom; Latoya says her painting is Yolanda. Kishanda then declares that her painting is Sharon. Yolanda returns to the clay table where 3-year-old Lila is having difficulty connecting legs to a body. Yolanda shows her how to use water to make the clay stick together.

Raul and Lucas focus on creating various flexiblock constructions on the light table in the space under the loft. Their constructions are lit up and reflected back to them by the wall mirror, giving them an added perspective on their creations.

Throughout activity time, children were very engaged, both socially and/or with specific activities. Their collaborations were a natural ebb and flow. They did things in groups of twos, threes, and fours, with the exception of Tommy and Ulivo, who worked mainly on their own. Ulivo, however, at times incorporated and directed others when they wanted to help. The teachers frequently supported children's motivations and interests. Children took advantage of moving between areas to extend their play. There was never a moment when the teachers had to restrict the number of children in an area.

Clean-up time was signaled by turning overhead lights off and on, and singing a clean-up song. Two boys had built small-block structures in places where they could be left intact for the afternoon group to see. Yolanda photographed both structures. All the children helped until everything was back in place.

Outside Time. On this morning, activity time extended through outside time. Usually, teachers take the children across the street to the school's tree-lined playground. There, they enjoy tire swings, climbing structures, riding tricycles, playing in a boat, and balancing on rail ties.

Story Time. Sharon gathers the children on the rug and reads aloud the "Three Billy Goats Gruff" story as she intersperses questions and impromptu discussions with the children. She turns on a rock-and-roll CD and children begin to dance. Periodically, the music stops. Some children freeze, then dance on. Others leave to wash their hands before going to the lunch tables. Those who are especially enjoying themselves keep dancing until everyone is ready for lunch.

Lunch. Children are grouped at three tables. Yolanda sits with one group whose conversation is sometimes in English and sometimes in Spanish. Sharon sits with another group until children at the third table begin playing sliding-off-their-chairs. Shifting to that table, Sharon asks the children about activities they did that morning. Berenice talks about her story and how she put it in her book. Sharon asks who else has been writing stories and adding to their books. Some children do not have a book yet, and the conversation turns to figuring out which children have received their own writing book. Together, they name and count the seven children who already have books and the 10 who do not. Children clear their own plates and put the food containers on the cart. Two children then wheel it out into the hallway.

Pick-up Time. Sharon places a variety of children's books onto the writing table near the entrance door. Some children look at the books as they wait for their parents. Sharon responds to Javiar's request to read a dinosaur book to him, and Hilario and Juan join them. Other children play in the loft and small-block areas near the door, some with the small cars, others with puzzles, games, or flexiblocks. The small racing car play begins to extend back into the rest of the room.

Some parents arrive and children put the item they were playing with back in its place. Sharon talks briefly with Ulivo's father, and Ulivo shows his father the house he has built. Three girls show their mothers their writing books and drawings before they leave. On this day conversations between parents and teachers are brief.

Meanwhile, Yolanda begins imaginative and playful interactions with several children as they wait. She takes a magnifying glass and holds it to her eye, making it big, then holds up a mirror in front of the magnifying glass so she can see the effect on her own eye. She shares this trick with the children as they find other large magnifying glasses and mirrors. More children join in, surprised and laughing as they discover their big eyes. It is a spontaneous moment, enjoyable, experimental, and fun for all.

Yolanda takes Miguel and Juan downstairs to wait for their parents, who are late. She returns upstairs to have a quick planning meeting with Sharon during their lunch break before the afternoon class arrives.

Reflections and Comments

Using the above description, we invite you to think about the following questions:

> *What kinds of initiatives did children take?*
>
> *What range of teacher management actions did you notice?*
>
> *How did teachers collaborate?*
>
> *What did you learn from this example?*

Children as Partners in Management. During the course of the morning, the children showed initiative in assisting with snack and clean-up, suggesting a game at circle time, choosing and remaining focused on activities, assisting one another, and extending their own learning sequences. An example of the latter is the two boys who created flexiblock structures together. They frequently changed perspectives on their block creations by viewing them from different positions, constructing them in different locations, and moving them in concert with their own body movements. When they climbed into the loft, they experimented with length, gravity, and different structural forms.

Teacher Actions. While children took the initiative in choosing and then focusing on particular activities, the teachers were freed up to perform the five types of teacher actions outlined earlier in the chapter.

> *Listening/observing.* Throughout the morning, the teachers were able to observe and listen to the children. Even as they focused on a particular group or child, their "antennas" were tuned to the sounds and rhythms of the room, and they kept an eye on several sequences at once. Thus, Sharon was able to respond to Berenice and her drawing at the same time that she introduced a new element into the boys' racing cars and ramp activities.
>
> *Scaffolding children's learning.* Throughout the morning, small groups of children played the word and letter games that the teachers had set out in response to the children's growing interest in writing and using alphabet letters. On several occasions, children approached a teacher to show her their work. This opened up a dialogue between them that usually resulted in extending the activity. Sometimes children's dictations were added to their representations, and new perspectives or activities were offered, further challenging the child.
>
> After revisiting their guinea pig house drawings with the teacher at circle time, several children were inspired to go to the small-block area to build guinea pig houses or make plans for houses. Besides the types of scaffolding that involved challenges and extensions, sometimes teachers gave practical information to children.
>
> *Documentation.* Teachers documented children's activities that related to the two in-depth studies by taking photographs and writing down children's dictations.
>
> *Responding to upsets.* The teachers immediately responded to Tommy's upsets at circle time by careful listening, conversing, and planning with him.
>
> *Coordinating activities.* Both teachers were involved in coordinating the flow of activities during snack, circle, lunch, clean-up, arrival, and pick-up times.

Sharon and Yolanda frequently coordinated their activities with each other. For example, at arrival time, Sharon positioned herself to greet children and parents, while Yolanda circulated, greeting children as they chose activities or joined in with children who were already engaged in an area. Later, while Yolanda supervised work at the guinea pig/clay table and kept an eye on children at the nearby easel and large-block area, Sharon moved throughout the room, responding to individuals and small groups. Both were available when children approached them.

The activities of the morning followed a pre-established schedule, with the exception of outdoor time being replaced by an extended activity time. Teachers find schedules useful. They provide a general framework for the day, and they give both teachers and children a reliable set of patterns and expectations for action. However, schedules and other structures are altered to fit circumstances. In a classroom focused on responding to children's interests, there needs to be some flexibility in order to respond to intense levels of engagement. The adjustments are likely to be in the form of extending one period of time into the next. The adjustments ordinarily do not involve altering the order of the periods of the day.

Emotional Upsets

In general, emotional upsets fall into two categories. The first involves a child having a difficult day. Teachers respond by taking time to listen to the child in an unhurried and empathic manner. This kind of teacher response is facilitated when there is good communication between team members, enabling teachers to spontaneously and effectively coordinate their actions. Owing to the strong emphasis on responding to children's interests, we believe Tommy felt Yolanda was listening to his motives as well as to his feelings when she encouraged him to formulate his plans for making a guinea pig house.

The second type of upset is interpersonal conflict. When a conflict arises between two or more children, teachers support children in finding their voice and directly expressing their grievance to the child who has upset them. Teachers also encourage the other child to listen and respond. An example is the Missing Knife episode in Chapter 3. The scaffolding of this process by the teacher contributes to a classroom culture in which children learn to listen to, respect, negotiate, and appreciate different perspectives; make choices; resolve conflicts; and, in general, collaborate with one another.

The staff noticed over time that the more that children were actively engaged in experiences stemming from their own interests, the fewer the upsets that occurred. In addition, they noticed marked increases in the preschoolers' attention spans.

STARTING AT THE BEGINNING OF THE YEAR

If you are introducing a new group of children to a classroom process inspired by the Reggio Approach, here are some ideas that might be helpful:

- As usual, start the year with children learning the routines of the classroom and getting to know one another. Make sure that you have constructed the classroom environment to promote small-group, focused explorations (see Chapter 6).
- Introduce the exploration of one or two materials for doing representations (such as drawing materials and clay) and include experience in communicating with the use of those materials (see Chapter 4).
- Keep records on children's interests expressed during the course of the day. Provide possibilities for children to explore these interests by setting up areas in the room that respond to them.
- If there are some children who participated in an in-depth study the previous year, facilitate their moving into a new in-depth study so other children can join in and learn from the experience.

TEACHER COLLABORATION

The description of the morning in Sharon and Yolanda's classroom emphasizes the importance of communication and collaboration between teachers. Following are some Chicago Commons teachers' views on the subject.

What Do Teachers See as the Basic Principles Underlying Classroom Collaboration?

This discussion of teachers' ideas about classroom collaboration is based on individual interviews with 10 Chicago Commons preschool head teachers. All of the teachers, at the time of the interviews, had been exploring the Reggio Approach for 5 years or more. Each interview was organized around the question, "What's important in collaboration between you and your assistant teacher?" After an initial brainstorming phase, the interviewer read back the teacher's list of ideas and asked her to select the "three most important." The meanings of the three most important ideas then were discussed in depth, which included the interviewer asking "why" each idea was important. In the course of these discussions, the teachers not only discussed their ideals for a collaborative relationship with their co-worker, but also spontaneously mentioned obstacles, struggles, and difficulties encountered in establishing such relationships.

In response to the question "What's important in collaboration between you and your assistant teacher?", the word *communication* was always among the three most important ideas selected by the teacher. Further, in most cases, virtually everything else that the teachers included in their top three ideas connected in one way or another to the theme of communication. Here are some examples:

Sharing ideas

Teacher: It's important for your co-worker to share her ideas. A lot of times the title "head teacher" gets in the way. I think my co-worker is my partner and she has every right to share her ideas with me. If there's only one person that's giving ideas, that's not going to work because the other person has good ideas also.

Listening and responding to one another's ideas

Teacher: It's important to be able to have the feeling that you can go to another person and toss out your ideas or your thoughts, or even your misgivings, and see what they think about it. They may have another perspective on it, which may clarify what you're thinking.

Having common goals

Teacher: We both have the same ideas about the direction of the classroom. We both want to learn and study more about the Reggio Approach and implement more parts of it into our classroom.

Co-constructing understandings and plans through the interaction of ideas

Teacher: We can put our ideas together and come up with something better and work it out. Being able to share ideas makes your team stronger. It's a closer bond that you have with your teammate because she knows that I'm going to respect her ideas and we're going to try them out the same way that she'll respect mine and she'll accept mine. So I think that makes our relationship stronger and it makes us work closer together, which helps tremendously when you're working with someone the whole day.

Teachers see the above processes as made possible by several types of attitudes and actions:

- Being open to, valuing, and respecting one another's ideas
- Asking the other person for the reasons underlying her idea
- Being open to the other person's disagreements with your ideas
- Being willing to confront failures and mistakes

Finally, they view all of the above, taken together, as contributing to their professional development.

Teacher: It's a way of bouncing ideas back and forth. It's a way of growing together, and that's important, to be able to grow together. Your room cannot grow and you personally cannot grow unless you have those times and opportunities to communicate.

Teacher: By being able to communicate, and commit and share our ideas, we are able to grow together and be at the same level.

Teacher: This is a learning process. Without collaboration you wouldn't be learning.

The teachers' comments also focused on collaborative planning and spontaneous communication and collaboration in the process of classroom life.

Collaborative Planning

Teacher: You can't communicate *well* without taking the time to do it. I'm talking about serious communication here; serious collaboration where you really sit down and delve into what's happening for the week, or for the day.

A pivotal point in the planning process is the weekly meeting attended by teachers of two classrooms, the site director, a coordinator from the central office, and, frequently, the site's family worker. The weekly meeting is focused primarily on planning emergent curriculum processes in the two classrooms that are part of the weekly meeting team (see Chapter 10, "The Weekly Meeting," for details). The meeting focuses on four of the seven processes in the emergent curriculum cycle: interpreting, projecting/deciding, planning, and hypothesizing (see Chapter 5, "The Emergent Curriculum Cycle," and Chapter 10, "Goals for Teacher Professional Development"). These five processes also are carried out to some degree in the classroom team's meetings during the week (see below).

Teachers use an Emergent Curriculum Planning Form (developed in 1999–2000) to record, consolidate, and extend their planning from the weekly meeting. The form is printed horizontally on 8" × 14" paper. A collapsed version is presented in Figure 7.2.

Figure 7.2. Emergent curriculum planning form.

Classroom:		Week of			
Reflections on the past week (Summary and Interpretation of Documentation):					
Brainstorms and choice:	Planned activities:	Hypotheses (about children's responses):	Preparation:	Groupings of children:	Description of children's responses:
Learning outcomes (i.e., anticipated skill development):					

In addition to the weekly meeting, there are five types of planning that ideally are carried out by each classroom team:

1. Planning how to carry forward decisions made at the weekly meeting
2. Planning sessions before the children arrive
3. End-of-the-day reflection and documentation (e.g., "We tried this today. How did it work? Did it stimulate the children's ideas? What exactly did they get out of it?")
4. End-of-the-week evaluation (e.g., "On Friday, we make a list of where we want to work, where we want to be the next week. [If we didn't follow through on our plans for the week:] What happened?")
5. Preparation for the weekly meeting: Sorting through documentations and selecting examples to bring to the weekly meeting; brainstorming initial interpretations of potential plans for the following week (see Chapter 10, "Documentation"). The end-of-the-week evaluation (above) and this meeting sometimes are merged into one.

Spontaneous Communication and Collaboration in the Ebb and Flow of Classroom Life

Many teachers refer to the importance of spontaneous communication in the classroom, aided by the use of subtle signals that are a product of long-term habituation of working together.

> *Teacher:* The feeling that you don't have to say everything and explain everything in detail. A look or a nod, some kind of expression, and they catch it and know what you're saying and doing. By being together for so long and working together for so long, you kind of like get the feel of each other. . . . You have to *know your co-worker*, your partner. If you don't, there's *no collaboration*.

> *Teacher:* I think it's like a little dance. We pick up on each other. When we are in a circle, we pick up on what we are going to do. If I'm over here, the other one knows that she will be over there. . . . It's just like we have that kind of feel for each other.

The broad framework for the coordination of their efforts often has been established beforehand by planning. But the fine points of implementing the process, and dealing with contingencies, unfold as one goes along. For this to take place smoothly, it is essential that the teachers are in agreement on their purposes for specific actions and activities. One teacher refers to the consequences of co-teachers *not* being in good communication.

> *Teacher:* If there's *not* good communication, you feel stressed. It's stressful. It's a big burden. There's no sense of direction. The kids pick up on it quickly. They feel lost.

Obstacles to Collaboration

Achieving a collaborative relationship in the classroom is often not an easy task. Here are some of the difficulties that can occur.

Insufficient time can interfere with daily planning:

> *Teacher:* So much is going on that sometimes time gets away from you. You're rushing out to do other things, and you just don't take the time to sit down and say, okay, what's happening with you?

Some teachers have difficulty embracing the role of "partner" in the collaboration:

> *Teacher:* We started working together 3 years ago. It wasn't easy because she [the assistant teacher] was used to taking orders, not collaborating. I was ready to have that collaboration but it was difficult for her to share ideas. At times I had to really back off. She was still being an aide. She didn't want to share her ideas. She really didn't communicate. She had the rule of, "Okay, tell me what to do and I'll do it." After about a year and a half, she started to get the initiative of doing things on her own. It took her that long. I think I have made her a little assertive. I've helped her open up more. I think that she has been able to share more, at least with me. We're working really good together now.

Tension may occur when the head teacher has been exposed to Reggio ideas longer and is more committed to the Reggio Approach than her assistant teacher(s):

> *Teacher:* She [the assistant teacher] was very dependent on her traditional style of teaching. And it was kind of difficult for her to compromise between the way she was taught and Reggio because her traditional way of teaching was her safety zone. She was safe with that curriculum, because she knew it well. Our relationship in terms of collaboration was very rugged. We had to have a third person sometimes, to make us understand each other. . . . [In the long term, it got resolved by] basically looking at who we were. We really had to be honest with each other and tell each other how we were feeling and why we are feeling angry or frustrated or unhappy about something; because we weren't doing much talking, we weren't doing much relating.

The same kind of tension also has occurred in the reverse situation, when the assistant teacher is better versed in Reggio ideas than the head teacher.

Confusion can be experienced when both members of a classroom team experience a conflict between the Reggio Approach and their original training in preschool education:

> *Teacher:* We're still looking at Reggio in some ways as a separate educational process or tool for children. And it's not. There are times when I do that. We have to step back and say, "Wait a minute. We seem to be working on two things here, and really our goal is one." Once you stop that separation between "this is early childhood education and this is Reggio," the process will become easier—because Reggio in itself is about looking at children in a different way. A different way from what you were taught in school. So it's better not to have had that [the regular early childhood training] to be able to grasp the Reggio Emilia ideas.

Primary Care Attachment Groupings

How do you make sure that every child has a stable relationship with an adult in the room and is checked on regularly?

Each teacher is assigned half of the children in the class. It is a teacher's responsibility to keep a special eye on the well-being and learning needs of her charges and to meet at least once a day with small groups that include them. Sometimes a teacher sits with her special subgroup at lunchtime. The teacher's regular attentiveness to her group increases predictability for the children. Many children have a desire for other forms of predictability (e.g., where they eat or where their cot is placed at nap time). Predictability around these sorts of matters frees children from anxiety, permitting them to pay attention, socialize, and be productive.

RESPONDING TO MANDATED REQUIREMENTS

How can teachers who are pursuing the Reggio Approach manage their classrooms in a way that meets the requirements of the agencies governing education? Each classroom at Chicago Commons is accountable to a range of federal, state, and local government agencies that require teachers to follow specific practices in planning, assessment, record keeping, curriculum, the physical environment, health, and safety. This raises the question of potential incompatibility between Reggio Emilia ideals of teaching and the mindsets embedded in various external requirements.

The Chicago Department of Children and Youth Services, for example, requires formal weekly lesson plans. In response, Commons designed a lesson plan form, structured around day of the week and times of the day, that meets both their own administrative needs and the external requirement. This form works in a complementary way with the emergent curriculum form (described earlier in this chapter). The lesson plan focuses on setting out a weekly schedule of activities. The emergent curriculum form emphasizes observations, reflections, and general planning of activities emerging from children's interests rather than specific dates and times.

The Chicago Department of Children and Youth Services also requires comprehensive assessments of each child's development. They offer a choice among four different assessment instruments. Chicago Commons chose the "Work Sampling System" (Meisels, Dichtelmiller, Jablon, & Marsden, 2001) for two reasons.

First, the spirit of the assessment is compatible with Reggio ideals. For example, here are a few of the dimensions in the first half of the form for 4-year-olds:

- Shows eagerness and curiosity as a learner
- Demonstrates self-confidence
- Shows some self-direction
- Uses classroom materials carefully
- Interacts easily with one or more children
- Approaches tasks with flexibility and inventiveness

Second, most of the Work Sampling assessments can be made from the regular documentations of children's work that are stored in the portfolios, binders, and journals of the Commons preschool classrooms. Each classroom team has a *second* weekly meeting to deal with lesson plans, assessments, and various kinds of required record keeping.

Perhaps the most important aspect of Commons' response to the various requirements they encounter from outside the program is the underlying spirit in which they respond; namely, taking the requirement as a challenge and brainstorming creative responses that are compatible with the main focus of the program. In other words, the staff's response to such requirements is grouped with the many other challenges that they encounter in the process of exploring Reggio ideas. The entire Reggio-inspired enterprise at Commons is about responding to challenge.

Chapter 8

School Readiness

How does the Chicago Commons approach to preschool education, as described in this book, contribute to children's readiness for learning in kindergarten and beyond?

To our knowledge, no controlled studies have been done that examine the child development outcomes of the Reggio Approach. We propose that it is reasonable to assume certain outcomes based on the skills, motives, and orientations that we see children exercising and developing on a day-to-day basis as they participate in this program. We have organized the description of them, along with processes and experiences that foster them, into three major facets of school readiness:

1. Capacities for self-regulated, focused learning
2. Development in speaking, thinking, writing, reading, and mathematics
3. Social–emotional development

CAPACITIES FOR SELF-REGULATED, FOCUSED LEARNING

Two closely connected dynamics are at the heart of the Chicago Commons learning process for children:

1. Children engaging the world, individually and collaboratively, to construct interest-driven, personally meaningful understandings and to communicate those understandings to themselves and others
2. Teachers listening and responding to children with the intent of promoting the learning processes described above

The teachers' listening and responding are energized by their image of young children as being rich in interests, learning competencies, and ideas about the world, and as having deep motives to experience relationships with others and to communicate with others (see Chapter 1, "Image of the Child"). The teachers continually communicate that image in their interactions with the children (see Chapters 2 and 3).

We propose that the above-stated dynamics of teaching and learning result in the development of the following attributes in children: an orientation to focused, sustained learning; skills in observing, thinking, and representing; identities as actively engaged learners; and knowledge about the world.

An Orientation to Focused, Sustained Learning

An orientation to focused, sustained learning is fostered by the program's emphasis on interest-based learning sequences extending from one day to another, often lasting for weeks or months. Examples are the in-depth studies such as the Pipes Study, the Windows Study, the Chicken Community Study, and the Hands Study and Dinosaur Study described in Chapters 1, 2, 4, and 5, respectively. A major thread of continuity in these studies is provided by the children's drawings, dictations, and other representations that the children frequently revisit. They reflect on them, sometimes elaborate upon them, and experience them as an impetus to continue their inquiry and create new representations and understandings. This process of revisiting, reflecting, and extending is of great importance for the development of focused learning orientations, especially when the inquiry is interest-driven.

The development of this orientation to learning is strengthened further by the program's emphasis on representing while observing. For example, if a child is drawing an ant, a flower, or a dinosaur skeleton (see Chapters 4 and 5), the process of drawing while observing sustains children's focus for a longer period of time. It also encourages greater attention to details, relationships, patterns, structures, and forms than if the children simply were observing.

Skills in Observing, Thinking, and Representing

Children's observation skills are developing continually through the processes described above. The skills of observing, thinking, and representing develop in an integrated fashion through children's revisiting an object of inquiry to reconsider its elements and relations among them. The development of these three skills also is promoted by exchanges with teachers and peers in which children learn to construct and articulate types of relations, such as sequence, cause and effect, functional relations, and relations of similarity and difference (see Chapter 3). The program's emphasis on multiple modes of symbolization for representing ideas helps children to establish an understanding of symbolization as the vehicle for communication.

Through learning processes that connect observing, thinking, and representation in the service of constructing relations among elements, children develop capacities for holistic understanding (see Chapters 1, 3, and 4). That is, they learn to construct and understand something in terms of the relations among its elements and its relationship with the environment. For instance, in his shower drawing, Jonathon constructs relations among the various pieces of hardware in the shower system and, through drawing and verbal description, constructs relations between the configuration of hardware and the flow of water. He also connects the shower system to a wider water system (see Chapter 4, introductory section). In Chapter 3, Quincy, in response to the teacher's questions, demonstrates and describes the process of power generation in his Beetle Borg creation, and the flow of power through the Beetle Borg into the environment. He also describes the stimuli from the environment that cause the Beetle Borg to release its power. In the Chicken Community Study (Chapter 4), the children's representation implicitly expresses relations between the chicken's "needs" for particular household furnishings, a car, and stores, and the items responding to those needs that the children have incorporated into their construction. Further, their representation visually expresses spatial relations between house, yard (containing the car), and wider neighborhood. In these examples, children are learning to construct differentiated, integrated understandings evolved through interactions with the object of study, dialogue with teachers, and dialogue with one another.

Identities as Actively Engaged Learners

The children's identities as learners develop through their experiences in actively engaging the world to explore their interests in a focused way. They create understandings by gathering and integrating information, and through collaborating and communicating with others as part of the process. The term that describes this kind of identity is *sense of agency*, experiencing oneself as an active, self-directed agent of one's own learning, alone and in collaboration with others (see full definition in Chapter 5).

Children's sense of agency is developed and enhanced through teachers' openly and actively *valuing children's motivation and thinking* as the children engage in the above-described processes. The teacher embraces the child's motives and ideas by taking them into her own mind, thinking about them, valuing them, reflecting them back to the child, and challenging the child to extend, elaborate, and connect them (see Chapter 3). Examples are found in the Showers Study (see Chapter 1) and the first three episodes (see Chapter 3). In another vein, we see the teacher in the Janell and the Brick episode continually asking the children what they "think," thereby contributing to their developing awareness of their own thinking and their identity as thinkers (see Chapter 3). It is a very great service to children to ask them what they *think*, not in the spirit of assessing whether they have grasped an idea that is already in the teacher's head, but in the spirit of engaging their competence in a process of joint problem solving. These processes contribute immensely to the children's development of agency.

The dialogue between teacher and child in which the teacher is both listening to and valuing the child's ideas and engaging the child in co-constructing more extensive understandings is a model for children's overall interaction with the world; for example, listening and responding to each other and to the objects of their inquiry.

Knowledge About the World

The children's knowledge about the world includes knowledge constructed through books, school-based experiences such as interaction with a wide range of materials and media, trips to the neighborhood and beyond, and dialogues with one another, with the teacher, and with members of their families. Further, as described above, their knowledge often is organized in a holistic manner; that is, in terms of systems and configurations of interrelated elements. For example, in Figure 8.1, Linda's map shows her understanding of her neighborhood. She draws the mail truck, the post office, her

Figure 8.1.
A 5-year-old is capable of drawing a holistic representation of how the mail gets to her house. The drawing depicts relations, functions, connections, and processes. It includes the post office with its counter, the mail truck moving toward the house, and people within the different rooms.

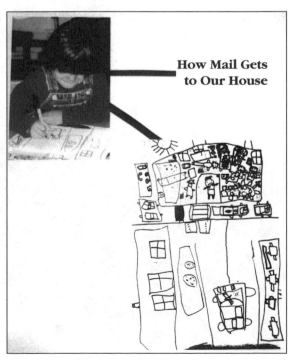

How Mail Gets to Our House

house, and another building, and indicates with a line that the mail truck is leaving the post office, taking letters to her house. Cars are parked outside the house, and inside she depicts an understanding of the different rooms in the house, how they are related, and how they are used. Another example is Janice's painting of a snake in the grass and her responses to her teacher's questions (see Figure 8.2).

DEVELOPMENT IN SPEAKING, THINKING, READING, WRITING, AND MATH

In our view, the development of the above-described combination of learning orientation, skills, identity, and understandings constitutes the foundations of *literacy in the broad sense*. This broad meaning of *literacy* is well expressed by Paulo Freire (1985) in his term "reading the world" (p. 15). Reading the world, as we interpret Freire's phrase, involves the processes described throughout this book: constructing and co-constructing understandings of the world through listening, observing, interpreting, reflecting, responding; then listening to and observing the world's responses to our responses; reflecting once more; and so on. It is about having a dialogue with the world. The understandings that emerge are about relations among elements in the world and about how to engage in dialogues with people and objects.

Dialogues result in transformations of the world and of our selves (Rinaldi, 2006). Having foundations in literacy in this broad sense of skills and orientations involved in reading the world provides sturdy foundations and contexts for the lifelong development of *literacy* as the term is most frequently used, namely, skills in speaking, listening, reading, writing, and mathematics. To return to Freire (1985) again, "There is a permanent movement back and forth between 'reading' reality and reading words" (p. 18). "The basic question in school is how not to separate reading the word and reading the world, reading the text and reading the context" (p. 20). We will see that Freire's observation applies to many of the examples that follow.

In this section, we build on the above perceptions by describing how children's processes of speaking, thinking, reading, writing, and mathematics take place in the Chicago Commons program. They develop through children's dialogues with one another and with the teachers, organized around shared dialogues with the world.

Figure 8.2. A snake that hides in the grass to catch a mouse.

Teacher: Janice, what are you painting?
Janice: I'm painting a picture.
Teacher: A picture of what?
Janice: My snake.
Teacher: What about your snake?
Janice: I'm making a picture of where he lives.
Teacher: Where does your snake live?
Janice: In the grass and the tree.
Teacher: Why does he live in the grass and the tree?
Janice: Because he can easily crawl in there and nobody can see him.
Teacher: Why can't we see him in the grass?
Janice: Because he go there to hide.
Teacher: To hide from what?
Janice: The mouse he trying to catch to eat him for dinner.

Development of Spoken Language

Much of the verbal language development that takes place in the Commons preschool classroom occurs in the context of *dialogue between teacher and child or among children*; that is, a process in which each listens in order to understand the meaning of the other and responds to it. Dialogue is of critical importance in the development of language (Halliday, 1994). It involves both listening and speaking, since one has to listen attentively to the other's meaning in order to respond to it coherently. Dialogue simultaneously involves the development of *thought,* since most dialogue is organized around constructing meaning in relation to a question, problem, or idea (Halliday, 1994). Thus, the development of language and the development of thought are deeply connected in the dialogue process. For example, in Chapter 3, the teacher facilitates the development of Vance's language and thought by framing her questions in a conditional form (see "How to Ride a Bike"). In the "What Can Babies Do?" episode (see Chapter 3), the teacher asks questions that challenge the children to make distinctions between small babies and other babies. The challenging atmosphere makes the connection between language and thought all the more profound.

Reading: An Authentic, Print-Rich Environment

The overall context for the development of both writing and reading is a print-rich environment in which children are surrounded by *authentic* print. By that we mean print that refers directly to children's experience in the world, including their relationships with others.

In the school environment, authentic print carries messages relating to four facets of the children's experience:

1. *Classroom activities*. Displays of children's work and activities are accompanied by typed children's dictations and teacher narratives. Children's dictations, handwritten by the teacher, also accompany children's work stored in binders, portfolios, and journals that children frequently revisit. Messages posted in the classroom are framed as invitations to action. For example, a "Restaurant" sign placed by an area outfitted with menus, dishes, silverware, and cooking equipment invites children to actively engage in a restaurant world. Menus, created by the children, containing drawings of food offerings along with the children's own writing, invite participants to place their orders for food.
2. *Home and family*. Typed statements by parents and/or their children accompany posted photographs or drawings of the children's families.
3. *Community*. Children's drawings of local stores are accompanied by the names of or signs on the store, written by the children (e.g., "Carpets"). This is augmented by a child's dictation about the store, such as "My tita works here."
4. *City*. Children's sketches (e.g., paintings of flowers from a trip to a park) are accompanied by their dictated commentaries on the experiences associated with them.

The examples above of authentic print express children's, parents', and teachers' own words. They are connected to actions, feelings, interests, and relationships. The words are presented against neutral backgrounds that encourage one to engage the message.

The widespread practice of teachers writing down and often typing up children's dictations to accompany their drawings provides children with frequent opportunities to revisit their drawing/dictation combinations and those of others. The display of these communications in the classroom and hallways, and their storage in available binders and portfolios, sends the message that *writing and reading are for communicating with others*.

Also, there is an extensive variety of story and informational books, invitingly displayed in several places in the classroom. The storybooks available to the children include stories that teachers read to them. The informational books (rich in images) often are connected to the children's in-depth studies driven by their interests. Art books may be placed in the painting area, and books on interior decorating in the housekeeping area. These books, which often stimulate children's interests, tend to be regular reference books in their field, not children's books. Sometimes the class visits the library, where the children are invited to choose books for the classroom. There are also books made by the teacher from documentations of the children's in-depth studies, and storybooks the children have made.

In addition to what we have said about the print-rich environment, there are further ways in which the learning process promotes the development of reading abilities:

- Teachers read and discuss stories with children at story time (see Chapter 7, "A Morning in Sharon and Yolanda's Room") and when children ask them to read a particular book
- Children "read" stories to classmates from picture books
- Children choose favorite books and tell classmates about them
- "Reading hunts" in the neighborhood in which children look for public signs that have significant meaning. For example, "stop" signs attract children, perhaps because stop signs control movement. The children identify words and letters within the words on the signs that interest them. All of this reinforces letter- and word-making activities in the classroom and extends the experience of a print-rich environment to engagements in the community.

A more subtle aspect of a print-rich environment is explicit *note taking* by the teachers. For example, as part of their documentation activities, teachers frequently move around the class taking notes. Children sometimes will emulate this process, carrying a notepad around the room, sitting for extended periods of time in one area, and writing scribble notes on other children's activities. Another example is the teacher who makes explicit to the children that she is writing notes to help her remember things.

Writing: Communicating Meaningful Messages to and About Meaningful People

The predominant forms of writing that we see in the classroom connect the children to their relationships with significant others and their own identities. Here are a number of examples.

Writing Letters to Other Children. Children are strongly motivated to communicate with their friends by writing letters or sending drawings. Teachers often scaffold the first stages in the development of this practice. For example, pairs of friends are seated side by side. Each child in a pair draws a picture of the other child or of something that he or she thinks will interest the other child and dictates an accompanying message that is written down by the teacher. The following example of a meaningful exchange shows how Eddie thinks and feels about his friendship with Julas, and that Julas is grateful for Eddie's present to him. Such writing conveys children's thoughtfulness and caring toward one another and demonstrates how friendship can create a powerful motive to communicate.

Eddie,
I make you a telephone. One that you chose. I maked the closed telephone for Eddie because that is what he likes. Thank you for making me a present.

—Julas

Julas,
Julas is my partner. I want to give him toys. I made this gift for him because he want it and he liked. Julas is my buddy. A buddy means holding your hand. I made a hippo for you because I love you. I play with the computer with him. I am your best friend. I hope you like the hippo. Take a picture for my eyes.

—your friend, Eddie

Many classrooms have mailboxes with a compartment for each child. The mailbox provides a major incentive for children to write letters to one another. Children frequently will write the name of the recipient as well as their own name on the letter.

Interclassroom letter writing is an exciting activity for children. In cases where there are windows or talking tubes between classrooms, or shared washrooms connecting two classrooms, the children are already in the habit of communicating with one another and are particularly interested in communicating on paper. For example, children from one classroom were playing in the playground when they spotted a fire taking place a block away. They saw the flames and the smoke and heard the response of the fire engines. They wanted to bring the children from the adjacent classroom down to the playground to see the fire. Their teachers suggested that instead they write letters to children in that classroom, telling them about the fire and enclosing their drawings of the fire. When they got back to the classroom, the teachers wrote down what the children wanted to communicate, and the children copied the dictations into their letters to children in the other class.

Some children write letters to their friends who have gone on to kindergarten in the Big School (see Figure 8.3). These letters may be a combination of invented spelling, dictations, and drawings.

Figure 8.3. Practicing writing by copying the teacher's printing of one's own dictation.

Dear Nevidian,

I'm getting ready to get out of this baby school to the big school. I miss you brother.

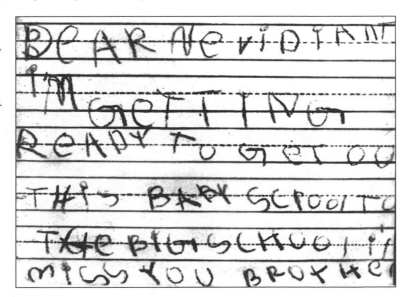

Writing Letters to the Teacher. A girl wanted to know her teacher's last name. At the top of a page she copied the name and at the bottom wrote her own ladybug signature symbol that she uses on the computer. She wrote these as the opening and closing parts of her letter to the teacher.

Writing Letters to Parents. In one class the children wrote letters to their parents, and the teacher addressed the envelopes. She enclosed her own letter, requesting that the parents bring their child's letter to school as soon as they received it in the mail. Each child drew a map of how the letter would get to his or her house (mailbox, post office, etc.; see Figure 8.1). When all the letters had been returned by the parents, the teacher and children made a graph of how long it took the letters to get back to the classroom (e.g., 5 letters in 4 days, 6 in 5 days, etc.).

Writing Letters to Outsiders. As part of a Pirates Study, children wrote a group letter to pirates. This communication was covered with scribbles that looked like words. The message was put in a bottle that was marked with an "X" (crossbones). The children carried the bottle with them when attending a play downtown about pirates. After the play, they presented the bottle to the actors.

Writing Public Messages. A boy's map and dictation showed others the location of rocks on the playground, information that he enthusiastically shared. The teacher posted his map and words and later placed them in his journal for him and others to read (see Figure 8.4).

As part of a Snake Study, one girl made a "pole snake" out of wire that she wrapped around the pole outside her classroom. With some spelling assistance from the teacher, she wrote a sign to explain her creation to all viewers. The sign read "A snake twisted," and included her name. A student in a morning class dictated a message to students in the afternoon class, asking them to please leave his block construction intact.

Figure 8.4.
Communication through a map. A boy's great interest in finding and
collecting rocks then leads to sharing the information with others.

This is a map to find the big rocks outside. We go this way and this way. When we get rocks, we put them in our pockets of our coats.

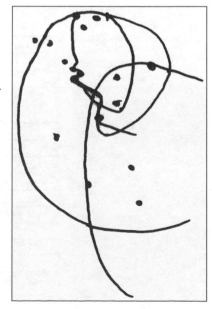

Writing Interview Questions to Ask Other People. During the Chicken Community Study (see Chapter 4), four children wrote their own questions about chickens to ask the manager of the farm zoo whom they then interviewed. Their teacher showed them how to write the words in their questions. Some examples were:

- Why do they want to sit on their eggs?
- Why do chickens eat food?
- Where do chickens go and eat?
- Who cracks the egg [that lets the chicken come out]?

One of the children's studies involved interviewing adults who work in the school building. Five children had a meeting with the assistant teacher to think up interview questions to ask the family worker. After the children decided what questions to ask, they were each given a clipboard and paper on which they wrote (in scribble writing) their questions. They took the clipboards with them to the interview.

In the Gifts Study, the children wrote questions to ask their friends (both in their own classroom and other classrooms) about the friends' likes, dislikes, and feelings in order to decide what kinds of gifts to make for their friends (see Chapter 4). Teachers assisted by taking children's dictations.

Writing About Relationships with Significant Others. Children like to write their own name and a friend's name and draw a picture of themselves and their friend together (see Figure 8.5).

Children draw pictures of their families and write their family members' names next to the persons in the picture. Some dictate the names to the teacher. Sometimes children draw pictures of themselves and a friend, and dictate explanations to go with the drawings (see Chapter 4, "Friends").

One teacher suggested to a child that she write about something she likes. She chose a book and wrote the title, explaining that it is a book her mother reads to her at night.

Another teacher engaged the class in planning the new housekeeping area. At home, children drew pictures of their kitchens, and family members helped them to label the items they drew. At circle time the teacher discussed the plan for the new area with the children, using their drawings as reference points (see Chapter 6).

Figure 8.5. Two friends. Their names and decorative, imaginative script on the sides show the ongoing connection between drawing and writing as skills develop.

A boy created a representation of his cat Rocky with wire, black marker, and wood-chip collage because he wanted others to know what Rocky looked like and that Rocky was his cat. He asked one of the teachers how to spell Rocky's name and included it on his picture. He then dictated a message about the cat, and the teacher posted the entire representation on the holding board (see Figure 8.6).

The child's involvement in this communication process was motivated by his relationship with his cat, his relationship with the teacher with whom he was communicating during his creation of the representation, and his relationships with his classmates and his parents, whom he knows are likely to see his communication about Rocky posted in the classroom. His communication exemplifies the main theme of this section on writing; namely, that the utilization and development of writing skills in these classrooms are motivated by the children's desire to express and communicate meaningful ideas and feelings to meaningful people. Through their literacy-related actions in the world, they intentionally connect themselves to others.

Writing About Oneself. Children have a widely shared interest in writing their own names. They try writing their names on their journals, on daily sign-in sheets, on their drawings, or as signatures on messages. In addition, they greatly enjoy making representations of themselves (in wire, clay, or natural materials, or on paper), writing their name on them, and dictating descriptions to accompany them. The descriptions invariably include reference to their relationships with others (see Figure 8.7).

Writing Letters of the Alphabet. Children frequently show a desire to learn how to write letters of the alphabet. They are especially attracted to alphabet activities that relate to their own identities and to significant others. Examples include learning the letter that begins one's name or a friend's name, searching for letters in the newspaper that correspond to the letters in one's name and copying them, and writing the entire alphabet in a letter to a friend or parent. Children also enjoy painting letters and making letters out of clay and wire. Often, they will spontaneously paint letters at the easel or add letters to a painting (see Figure 8.8).

Figure 8.6. Writing a pet's name and making a collage of him from wire, black marker, and woodchips.

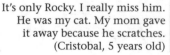
It's only Rocky. I really miss him. He was my cat. My mom gave it away because he scratches. (Cristobal, 5 years old)

Figure 8.7. Drawing and writing about oneself and what one likes.

I like the way my mommy puts me. That my papi gives me the headband, t-shirt, and the necklace. And I like my sister. In this picture I'm trying to get the flower and the wind was blowing and I was AHHHHHHHHH!
(Alyssa)

I like it when I'm beautiful. I like my earrings. I like myself when I come to school and when I go home and roller blade. I can do it all by Myself. I'm a big girl. I like when I get big Because I can be like my father, fixing doors, Windows. I can fix walls. I help my dad sometimes, but sometimes he doesn't let me.

[In this picture] I'm cooking. You see the pan. I wish I can be like my mom and cook. Look! I'm throwing the pancake up and catching it. My mom does that.

I have a long shirt. My shoes are high heels. My stripes on my shirt are pink. I need blue 'cause I have blue stripes too.
(Janette)

What I like about myself is I can walk. I can eat. I can grab and touch. When I make faces at the mirror, he [Miles] laughs. I can say "yes" or "no!" (Gena)

Figure 8.8. Children enjoy representing letters that are meaningful to them, using materials such as clay or paint.

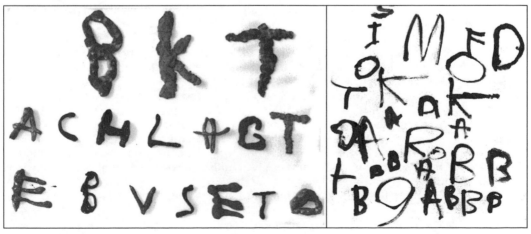

Figure 8.9. Kenneth's interest in cocoons and caterpillars was documented over several months in his journal. Entries included Kenneth's representations, his discussions with the teacher, and the teacher's comments.

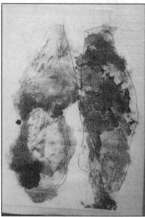

8/01: Kenneth is fascinated with insects. He loves to collect them. Here, he is looking through a large magnifying glass to get a closer look at a dead "roly poly" he found outside.

2/25/02:
Teacher: Kenneth, why did you choose this painting to copy and paste?
Kenneth: Those were the caterpillars. They were kind of goofy. I made another copy of more caterpillars for teachers.

3/21/02: Kenneth painted a cocoon.

Copying Other People's Writing. Children frequently copy other people's writings that are about meaningful things. Examples include copying their own dictations written by a teacher, a friend's name, the classroom rules, a question they intend to use in an interview, and words they see on trucks, shops, or traffic signs.

Contexts of Writing

While writing in the classroom happens at any place and time, the following contexts are specifically encouraging to the writing process: daily journals, writing tables, and making books.

Journals. Different classrooms have different approaches to journals, ranging from writing about anything one chooses to writing about what happened on a particular day. Some are journals about the whole class, written by the teacher and including children's work. Others are journals written by individual children. The children draw and write in their journals and have teachers write their dictations into their journals. They also paste photos and include collage items. Journals often reflect a child's sustained interest over time. For example, Kenneth's ongoing interest in nature is expressed in his journal through a communication to the teacher about his caterpillar drawing (see Figure 8.9).

Journals frequently have the student's picture on the front with the student's writing of his or her name accompanying it (see Figure 8.10).

The journals are always accessible to the children and parents. They are kept in open containers on low shelves. Most important, the collection of their ideas and the experiences recorded in their journals give children a chance to revisit them. There is a strong motivation to read what one has dictated, written, or drawn. Children enjoy looking at and talking about one another's journals (see Figure 8.11).

Writing Tables. As we saw in Chapter 6, a writing area, equipped with an ample writing surface, a rich supply of materials, and three to four seating places, is an ongoing

Figure 8.10. Journals are accessible for all to read and for children to add new items as often as they wish.

Figure 8.11. Looking, conversing, and "reading" journals together with a friend.

invitation for children to write and discuss their ideas as they write. The area includes a three-ring work storage binder for each child. In some rooms an antique writing desk for two or a desk under a loft provides special attraction for writers, who also have access to larger table surfaces. A well-designed writing area enables children's writing to be a permanent part of the classroom and makes a clear statement about its importance.

Making Books and Creating Stories. Children's enjoyment of books in the classroom, including those read aloud by teachers at story time, provides a strong impetus for children to make their own books. The children's books are usually narratives told through their drawings and dictations. One boy wrote a story, with two pictures, entitled "Tyrannosaurus Rex Wins the Race." Next to his first drawing he wrote: "Once upon a time there was two Tyrannosaurus Rex's and there was two other dinosaurs." In the second drawing he wrote, "They are fighting because they have a race." This was the beginning of his interest in writing and constructing stories.

Comments on Reading and Writing

Children are strongly motivated to write when their writing connects them to significant others. As they write, children re-experience the meanings, challenges, and pleasures in those relationships. The children's affirmation of their relationships is simultaneously an affirmation of their own identities. As Bakhtin proposes, our "selves" *exist* in relation to others (Bakhtin, 1984, 1990; Holquist, 1990).

In the many examples above of writing activities, we see reading and writing developing hand in hand. Through experiencing writing as a form of action that connects them to others, children are learning basic letter, word, and sentence identifications and are experiencing meaningful purposes for writing and reading. They are experiencing literacy skills as valuable tools that enhance their competence as active agents engaging the world. Kathryn Au (1997) aptly refers to this state of mind and accompanying patterns of action as children's "ownership of literacy." Neil Duke (2000) terms it "agency as print users."

Mathematics: Using Math Concepts and Operations to Learn About the World

This section sets out examples of children using mathematics concepts and operations to gather and organize information and then using the information to arrive at conclusions. The activities are grouped under the mathematics categories utilized in the Head Start Work Sampling form (Meisels et al., 2001).

Problem Solving. When children were setting the table for lunch, the teacher gave them six cups for an eight-person table and asked, "Do you have enough cups?"

A teacher asked the children to solve the problem of how to set up three lunch tables and accompanying chairs to accommodate the 17 children and 2 teachers in the classroom. Children drew floor plans and experimented with moving tables and chairs. After several attempts, together they drew a solution that provided everyone with a chair at a table. They then implemented their plan.

Number and Operations. Teachers invited children to do *number hunts* in different contexts, such as in the newspaper, the classroom, and the neighborhood. In the classroom, children found and named numbers, for example, on the telephone touch pad, computer keyboard, and the upper margins of computer screens. On walks in the neighborhood, children delighted in reading the numbers on house addresses, especially if it was their house or a friend's house.

Extending from their interest in traffic lights (see Chapter 1), children conducted a "truck tally" over a period of weeks. Children were showing an interest in the various kinds of trucks they were seeing from out the classroom window. Through further observation and dialogue with the teacher, they identified a range of types, such as fire truck, garbage truck, delivery truck, and so on. Next, the children assisted the teacher in finding examples of the trucks in magazines. The teacher then created two-column tally sheets. In the left columns she pasted the cutout pictures of the various types of trucks. In the right columns were spaces for children to place a check mark every time they spotted that type of truck from the window. The children made observations and entered check marks for over a month. The teacher and children counted the check marks and created a bar graph, showing the number of times each type of truck had been observed from the window. This led to discussions comparing the quantities of types of trucks they had seen.

Counting activities often are problem-solving activities that are very meaningful to the children involved. Teachers may ask children, "How many people are absent today?" Sometimes counting is combined with measuring; for example, "How many small blocks can you stack before the tower collapses?" In one classroom, children counted how many children in their class had received their writing books from the teacher (see Chapter 7).

Geometry and Spatial Sense. Children made shapes out of wire as they explored and experimented with the properties of different kinds of wire. They also used the light table and light projector to experiment with combining shapes and to create new shapes. Sometimes they used everyday items or shapes they created out of different materials. In one classroom, groups of children took turns lying on the floor and arranging their bodies into various shapes while others watched and made suggestions Teachers also invited children to go on *shape hunts* in the classroom, the school building, the community, and their own homes.

Geometric shapes often are explicitly integrated into other activities. For example, in the Hands Study (see Chapter 5) children used the concepts of "line," "triangle," and "circle" as aids in recognizing and drawing the contours of their hands and details in their hands. In a study of wood, children traced geometric shapes on pieces of wood, using pencils and stencil rulers, and verbally identified the shapes. A local carpenter then came to the classroom and cut the traced shapes for the children as they watched. The children used the shapes to construct houses.

Children sometimes created maps to lead other children to find something, such as the rocks shown in Figure 8.4, or to direct a friend to one's house. In one case, children drew maps of their school building to show others where they had hidden the life-sized monsters they had created. The other children chose whether to try to find the monsters or to avoid them. Commercial maps and aerial photographs sometimes are used as references in in-depth studies (see Chapter 4, "The Chicken Community").

Patterns. Amber noted the repetition of specific colors in the garden at the park and reproduced that repetition in her painting (see Chapter 4). Children sorted dinosaur figures by big and small, spiked and nonspiked, meat eaters and plant eaters (see Chapter 5, "The Dinosaur Study"). Children identified types of animals they had seen on a neighborhood walk and discussed where they live—squirrels in trees and dogs in yards with fences.

Measurement. Sometimes measurement is incorporated with exploring a material. For example, children made clay beads and used them to measure objects and distances. During an exploration of wire, children joined pieces to create a length that extended across the width of the classroom. They then determined its length by lying down beside it, measuring it in number of body lengths.

Children experimented with joining unit blocks or flexiblocks and using the strings of blocks to measure the circumference of their heads, the length of their bodies, and the width of the hallway. Teachers sometimes extended these activities by suggesting other materials, such as measuring the hallway with toilet paper. In one classroom, children made rulers out of wood, marked them with their names, hung them in the classroom, and used them for measuring.

SOCIAL–EMOTIONAL DEVELOPMENT

Four broad categories of social–emotional development contribute to school readiness:

1. *Creating and retaining relationships with other children:* Entering into co-activity with another child, listening to and attempting to understand the other's perspective
2. *Making and retaining relationships with teachers:* Listening to one another's ideas and suggestions, appreciating one another's perspectives, and negotiating differences
3. *Collaborating in small groups:* Voicing one's motives; sharing perspectives; negotiating a common goal; keeping focused on the goal; joining actions; co-constructing understandings; and acknowledging, discussing, and negotiating differences
4. *Acting as a member of the classroom community:* Following classroom rules, participating in the creation of rules, having empathy and consideration for others, standing up for oneself, participating in whole-class construction of understandings, recognizing a diversity of perspectives and feelings within the classroom

All four of the above categories involve *capacities for engaging in dialogue* with others (see Chapter 1, "The Significance of Dialogue for Human Development"). All four also involve a *sense of agency* as an active and effective participant in the world (see "Identities as Actively Engaged Learners," earlier in the chapter).

There are a number of features of the Chicago Commons program that foster the development of these social–emotional abilities and sensibilities.

The following features are especially emphasized in the Chicago Commons approach:

- *Listening and responding to children's interests* as the keystone of classroom life and the fulcrum of the teaching–learning process
- *The image of the child* as the governing ideal of teacher–child relationships and of classroom life in general
- *Co-constructing of understandings about the world*, based on shared interests and collaboration among children in small groups and between teachers and children
- *Extensive communication among children, both within and across classrooms*, characterized by collaboration in learning, writing letters, making gifts for one another, and so on
- *Relationships with friends* embraced as a value in itself and as a focus for inquiry among the children. For example, the Friends Study arose out of children being concerned about being separated from their preschool friends when moving on to kindergarten. This inquiry allowed the children to recognize their friendships and affirm the aspects of friendship that were meaningful to them (see Chapter 2, Child-Specific versus Universally Shared Interests, and Chapter 4, Friends).
- *Emphasis on dialogue in which multiple perspectives are expressed, compared, and connected.* Dialogue is the ideal that stands at the center of relationships between teachers and children, and among children (see definition in Chapter 1 and examples in Chapters 2–5).

Other features are similar to those of many preschool programs:

- Children are encouraged to work out their conflicts through communication and negotiation of perspectives, aided by appropriate scaffolding by the teacher.
- Imaginative play is encouraged and children explore a variety of roles (such as father, mother, child, older sibling, younger sibling, friend, doctor, nurse, police officer, lion, rabbit, etc). In such play, children enact these roles, practice them, and learn about reciprocal interactions between different roles.
- Teachers discuss aspects of fairness, mutual respect, and consideration both in small groups of children and with the whole class.
- Children engage in mixed-age activities (3–5 years old) in which older children serve as models and mentors to younger children.
- Teachers actively involve children in the creation of classroom rules.

CONCLUSION

This chapter had two purposes. First, it demonstrated how the Reggio-inspired approach to preschool education at Chicago Commons contributes to specific aspects of school readiness and to children's overall ability to create meaning in life. Second, it illustrated processes of literacy and math development that are grounded in children's own agency and experience as they explore their relationships with one another, their teachers, their families, and their world, both real and imagined. Returning to Freire (1985):

> Reading is more than a technical event for me. It is something that takes my conscious body into action. I must be the subject, with the teacher, of my act of reading and writing and not a mere object of the teaching of how to read and write. I must know! I must get into my hands the process of reading and writing. (p. 20)

Skill development is most meaningful and effective when it builds on children's motives to explore relationships and explore the world in the context of those relationships. Through these processes, children experience the pleasures of speaking, thinking, reading, writing, and mathematics as rewarding ways of pursuing their deep lying interests and their curiosities.

Chapter 9

Parent Partnership

The guiding question of this chapter is:

> *How can a preschool explore*
> *the Reggio Approach with parents?*

A turning point in the program's relationships with parents took place from 1997 to 1999 when staff began to systematically reflect on the relationship between the parents and the school. Before 1997, terms such as *parent involvement* and *parent participation* were used. The meanings of these terms were not well defined, and approaches to relationships with parents were not clearly conceived. Staff efforts had been focused on constructing the learning environment and exploring the teaching–learning process, and little attention had been given to thinking about parents.

Teachers and administrators wanted to move away from the traditional approach to school–parent relationships in which the school is designated as the expert and tells the parents what to do. The teachers were ready to try an approach that engaged the parents in a dialogue through which the parents' own perspectives, values, goals, interests, and strengths would emerge. They wanted to invite the parents to engage in that dialogue, rather than require them to do so. They began to think about the *image of the parent* as competent, rich in ideas, and interested in communicating with staff and other parents.

The result of those reflections was the development of an approach to parent–school relationships conceived of as a "parent partnership" in which teachers and parents collaborate to support the children. The perspectives of both parents and teachers were to be emphasized. We will describe how this ideal was explored in a number of contexts that involved staff interactions with parents from 1999 through 2003. In this approach the staff and program developed relationships with parents that were more consistent with and informed by Reggio principles.

THE HOME VISIT

The opening home visit of the school year is a meeting of one or both classroom teachers with one or both parents. There are three facets to this visit. The first is the Hopes and Dreams interview, in which parents are invited to share their hopes and dreams for their child as the teacher takes notes. The second is the teacher's explanation of the school's approach to education. The third includes questions that teachers ask to update the information required by the program.

In the *Hopes and Dreams interview*, the teacher asks the parent(s): "What are your hopes and dreams for your child in the future?" A variation of that question is, "What kind of person do you want your child to be when he/she grows up?" In the early years of this interview, teachers reported that sometimes parents were astounded by such a question, not expecting that the school would be interested in their point of view or their feelings about their child and their child's future. At the end of the visit, the teacher takes a photograph of the parent(s) and child together.

The advantages of the Hopes and Dreams interview are several:

- It starts the dialogue between teacher and parents in a way that is comfortable, thought provoking, and highly meaningful to the parent.
- The interview communicates the teacher's belief in the parents as partners in dialogue.
- It casts the discussion of goals for the child in a frame that is much broader than the ABCs.
- The parents' contribution to the dialogue broadens the teacher's framework for thinking about goals for the child.
- The exchanges that take place in the interview serve to strengthen both teachers' and parents' commitments to developmental goals for the child. Once, at a monthly meeting, a parent stood up and said something that has been etched in the minds of the staff ever since: "Now that I have said all those hopes and dreams for my child, I have to make them happen!"
- Finally, it provides teachers with a way to represent parents' voices in the school.

Sometimes other interview questions are used, especially when many of the children are in the class for a second year. Examples include: "What is your family's favorite activity?" "What was your favorite activity as a child?" or "What was your favorite story as a child?" Such questions stimulate rich conversations.

As soon as possible after the home visit, the parents' hopes and dreams statements, along with the parent–child photographs and children's drawings based on the photographs, are mounted for display in or near each classroom. The display encourages dialogues and further sharing among teachers, parents, and children, all of whom enjoy looking at the documentation. The display establishes the presence of each family in the school and is a way for parents' voices to be heard. Many parents have commented on how deeply touched they are that their hopeful feelings for their children are given attention and respect in the classroom (see Figure 9.1).

The home visit and teachers making parents' voices manifest in the classroom are a first step in the dialogue between parent and school.

THE MONTHLY MEETING

The monthly meeting is an important invention in the Chicago Commons Reggio initiative. The meeting brings together parents, teachers, site directors, and family workers from all the early childhood centers in the program, along with some central office staff. The purpose of the monthly meeting is to provide a place for parents and staff to come together, share perspectives, learn from one another, and deepen their understanding of the Reggio Approach as interpreted within the Chicago Commons context. Run by central office coordinators, each meeting focuses on a few topics. The following is a profile of how monthly meetings function.

- Meetings occur 10 months out of the year, September through June.
- Each month, two sessions are held on consecutive evenings. Parents and teachers who wish to attend can choose which evening is most convenient for them in any particular month. Having two sessions reduces the size of each group to about 40 attendees, allowing for greater participation in the discussion by each participant.

Figure 9.1. Part of a classroom display on parents' hopes and dreams for their children. This is a good way to include parents' voices in the school.

I hope Jason becomes successful and completes school. I want him to be athletic and to be able to get along with others. We want him to be happy in life and healthy, also stay out of trouble. We hope he develops his speaking skills because he talks fast.

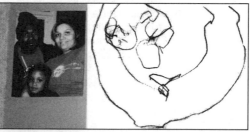

My hopes and dreams are that Javina have a successful future, to be able to make it on her own, be independent, and finish school.

I hope Benitta continues school, that she doesn't drop out. She study something she likes so she can get a good job. I want her to grow up to be somebody special, follow her own dreams, not someone elese's.

I hope Jamila will further her education, especially finish high school and go to college. I want her to utilize her skills and abilities to be the best she can be. I hope she's able to communicate to others, be a people person.

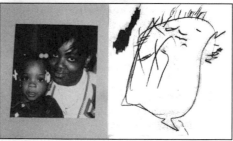

- Each month the meeting is held at a different Chicago Commons preschool center or at a city site that encourages exploration, such as the Garfield Conservatory or the Lincoln Park Nature Center.
- Parents usually constitute about half of the participants. One center on the South side of the city rented a bus to transport parents when the meetings were held on the North side.
- Simultaneous translation, English to Spanish and Spanish to English, is provided by a *professional translator* (rather than a staff member or parent) and is transmitted through headphone sets available to all the participants. This practice, which began in 2000, markedly increased the participation of Spanish-speaking parents. They feel more included and respected, and the dialogue is significantly enriched through their points of view (see Figure 9.2).
- A "parent liaison" from each center attends the monthly meetings, takes notes, and reports to the next parent meeting at his or her own center. Parent liaisons

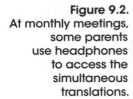

Figure 9.2.
At monthly meetings, some parents use headphones to access the simultaneous translations.

are paid a stipend for functioning in this role. At the beginning of the school year, they are given training for the role, including an overview of the elements of the Reggio Approach. One parent liaison described her experience as follows:

> It is very emotional when you do a presentation in front of the other parents from the center and they ask questions about what the children are doing, or why they do those things. It is very important and we never did it before. You think you are a very important person at this time, to carry all this that happened [at the monthly meeting] back to the parent meetings. It's nice. I like it.

- Notes are taken by staff at every meeting, to be revisited and discussed at the next monthly meeting. Audio recordings of each meeting provide backup for the notes.
- At the May meeting, participants are given a bound report on the year's meetings. It includes the agendas, notes on presentations, excerpts from dialogues that took place, colored photos of the participants, and some photos of the children's work that was shown and discussed at the meetings. Sometimes, outside educators are brought in to reflect on the report with the group.

The monthly meeting runs from 5:00 to 7:30 and usually unfolds as follows:

- *Buffet dinner.* Providing a dinner is an incentive to come on time and creates a congenial atmosphere in which people form or renew relationships. Children are included at the dinner, after which they may go to another room where child care is provided.
- *Tour of the building.* This includes the classrooms and common areas in which children's work is displayed. Parents and staff share a common interest and curiosity in seeing what is going on at each site, and learn from the experience. Staff members from the center lead the tour in three or four groups.
- *Discussion of highlights from notes* taken at the previous monthly meeting.
- *Presentation about children's learning.* A teacher classroom team, sometimes with a coordinator or a parent, gives a presentation about some aspect of the children's work; for example, an in-depth study or materials exploration (see Chapter 10, "Documentation"). A discussion of the presentation follows.

- *Whole-group dialogue.* One or two coordinators lead the group in a dialogue about an educational question of common interest. The dialogue sometimes moves into small-group discussions and then returns to the whole-group format.

Examples of Whole-Group Dialogues

While the spirit of dialogue runs throughout the entire monthly meeting, special emphasis is given to the dialogue process during the whole-group dialogues. The stimulus to a whole-group dialogue is one or more provocative *questions*. The questions always relate to some aspect of child development and tend to be of two types.

The first type is a general question regarding children and education. For example:

- What are the strongest influences on your children's lives? (October 1998)
- What does "school readiness" mean to you? What issues are connected with school readiness? (March 2000)
- What do you wonder about the care and education of young children? (December 2002)
- What is an interest? What do we mean when we say that a child or adult is *interested* in something? (March 2003)
- Do you remember something you were interested in as a child? How do you know when a child is interested in something? How do you support it? (April 2003)

The dialogues usually begin with the participants brainstorming responses to the question. Their ideas are recorded and some are discussed in detail.

The second type of question is posed in relation to visual stimuli, such as slides of children's drawings, transcripts of dialogues, or video clips of learning activities. Two examples follow.

Thinking About What Is on a Child's Mind

This example is from the monthly meeting of March 1999. It involved the group interpreting a set of slides showing children's drawings and accompanying dictations. The overarching question for this dialogue was "How do we discover what is on children's minds?" Below are excerpts from a video transcript of the group's response to three drawings.

First drawing (see Figure 9.3). This drawing was chosen for discussion because it lent itself to multiple interpretations. The group made several guesses before the coordinator revealed the child's words.

> *Coordinator 2*: With this drawing I see that the figures are telling more than the actual words. (She uncovers the child's dictation, which reads "My house and my cousin's house.")
>
> *Teacher 1*: I think these are cousins who live next door (to each other). I guess you could say that one house is here and the other house is there. The sun is shining on one of the houses.
>
> *Parent 1*: He could be describing distance. Because, as you can tell, one of the houses is much bigger than the other. The lines could be describing a street that divides the houses. It's that concept of distance.
>
> *Site Director 1*: To me the line looks like it could be a door. You know, the houses are close to each other and the two round black spots represent doorknobs. Somehow, he's connecting his cousin with the idea of going house to house. Evidently, the cousin's house must mean something to him in order for him to draw it.

Figure 9.3.
First drawing.

Site Director 2: I thought the size difference was interesting, too. One house has more shadow, shading, and detail. And I'm wondering which house is his? Is his the bigger one?

Parent 2: That's his house and that's his cousin's house and there is a happy face by his cousin's house. And that's because he has more fun at his cousin's house and that's why he put more detail into his cousin's house. They might live right next door, but he sees his house as being more smaller than his cousin's house. You know what I mean?

Coordinator 2: So, it sounds like it could be that all of these things are on the child's mind.

Parent 3: Also it could be that they live in apartments. And it could be that somebody could live in the front and somebody in the back. And it could be that somebody gets to see the sun before the other person does.

Teacher 1: I think that the line is a gate and the two dark dots are the boys, and they are separated by a gate, and the sun is making shadows on the house.

Participants: Oooooo (and laughter).

Coordinator 1: I think that it is fascinating that we are coming up with so many things that could be on this child's mind. It's just a simple drawing but it doesn't sound like it's just a simple drawing to me. So, I'd like to suggest that all those things that could be on the child's mind could be an opportunity to go and talk about it with the child. Because we don't know for sure and it sounds like you want to know, that you'd be curious to know.

Second drawing (see Figure 9.4)

Parent 1: I think that this is a field of grass and a storm is coming on and it's like clouds of lightning and the grass, it's like it is down to their level of seeing. Just the world around them because they are at a lower level.

Teacher 4: I'm thinking about, one part looks like an airplane representing maybe the air and water show.

Parent 3: It's water and the sky and maybe ducks flying in the sky.

Parent 1: Could be that this picture represents people. And he could be at the air and water show and this time it started to rain (laughter). It could be that.

Coordinator 1: We do have some of the child's thoughts about it.

Parent 1: Yeah, I may be wrong.

Coordinator 1: What does the child think? We have some ideas about what was on this child's mind. (The coordinator reveals the child's words, which read "It's raining and thundering and the mud is turning into mud. And the grass is wet and fresh.")

Figure 9.4.
Second drawing.

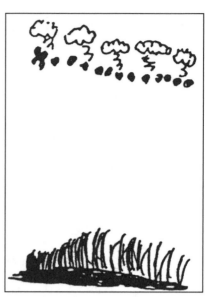

Participants: Ooh!

Parent 1: I did say a field of grass with rain (laughter). So, I was right. What do I get?

Coordinator 2: I find it fascinating because we can guess what's on a child's mind. We're curious to know.

Teacher 4: Children have a different way of thinking than us. You know, children have a different way of making sense of things than how we make sense. We all have our own opinions. You know, we're looking at this picture, but we don't know exactly what the child is saying, we're looking at it in our eyes and they're looking at it in their eyes.

Coordinator 1: I was also thinking that from everything that everyone is saying, that we can take these drawings as an indication that the child really does have something on his mind. These are some possibilities, and we might want to go and find out: What could that be?

Third drawing (see Figure 9.5)

Coordinator 1: There's one more. (She covers the child's words that go with the drawing.)

Parent 1: Maybe he's in the tub. You know how kids are when they get in the tub they think, Oh, let's go swimming. So, he's picturing that, he's picturing that he's in the tub.

Coordinator 2: So, let's see what additional thoughts the child has with his drawing. So, these are his words: "This is the man who lives outside, behind the school and sleeps in the trees."

Participants: Ooohhhh.

Coordinator 2: So, it seems that sometimes we're surprised at what children are thinking about. Is this the larger context for this child? I don't know. Is this really the man who is in the neighborhood near the center? It could very well be. Is this someone who the child sees on the way to school or to the store? I don't know the specific context or situation. But, it seems that this child's expression, and the words, are telling us that this child is noticing something that we might not realize. So, think about that question: What might this drawing and this child's words tell us about *what might be on this child's mind*?

Teacher 1: I would also say that this is a child who is beginning to observe his surroundings, and what is going on in the environment he is exposed to, and

Figure 9.5.
Third drawing.

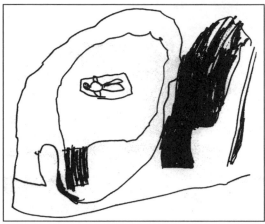

paying attention. And that's really good at this young age to know what's different and what's going on. He recognizes that there is a person who is sleeping
outside as opposed to sleeping inside of a house.

Site Director 1: I think that sometimes we're surprised at what children notice. Children hear and see so much more than we could ever imagine. Because I know
a little bit about this child, I know that this child was very concerned about the
homeless people that live on this block because we were doing a study on the
city. Where you live became a part of this study, and so he was very concerned
about the people who live in the park. It looks like he created a little entryway
down here at the bottom, and then he also enclosed the person and made
him appear to be very safe. Because he's not just exposed, he's in the middle of
something. And what he has him enclosed with is protecting him and then he
has him laying on something, some kind of blanket I guess.

After discussing the third drawing, one of the parents spontaneously shifted the
conversation to reflecting on her interactions with her own child.

Parent 4: Sometimes we don't recognize how capable children are of drawing
what they see and how much they take in and the value they give everything
they see. And how they build upon what they know. Sometimes we have to
provide help for that to happen. Children are very intelligent and we don't take
the time to realize their capabilities. We don't build upon what we think they
need to know in order to grow. Sometimes it's easy, when the child hands you a
picture, to say, "Wow this is a wonderful picture," and then you put it away. But,
you should take time to look at that picture as we are doing right now and look
beyond that one picture and save it. And give it the significance that the child
has given it. Do that with everything the child gives you.

Parent 2: You know, she's absolutely right because just the other day my son drew
me a picture of my family and I just threw it in a drawer without giving any
thought to what he was really trying to say.

Parent 4: The children always try to be the center of attention, but as a parent
sometimes you're just too busy, you're just trying to redirect them to do something else.

Parent 3: I would like to thank everybody for being here. First, I really like what the
other parents said and that's why we're here as parents and educators to have
an orientation of how to work with the children. Five minutes is not too much

of your time to come work with a child who gives you a picture; 5 minutes to actually explain, and understand, and to take that time to ask, "What were you thinking?" "What are your ideas and why did you draw this?"

Teacher 4: Or just ask your children questions. I ask my daughter questions all of the time and it's just amazing the things that she's thinking or the things that she says. They take in a lot. There are things that she'll remember from when she was 2 or 3. I'm like: "You remember that?"

Site Director 1: You know, this is really amazing to me, and every staff member. What has begun to happen is that we have become very comfortable and are able to speak up. What has happened to both parents and teachers is that we have also given each other insight into our children. I really think that this is fantastic. When we are able to ask our kids questions, and we wonder what they are wondering about, this is really good. Then, when you go and talk with your child's teacher in the future, you will know some different things about how children learn, especially your own.

Parent 1: My statement isn't going to be a grand statement like that. It's just a basic statement about how important documentation is, because as a parent, when a child gives you a picture, I think it's important to document yourself, what your child said to you and what they felt and what that represented [to them] and write that on the picture. Because once that child has given it to you and you have placed it away, they might not remember it again and then that moment is gone.

Coordinator 2: My goodness, thank you all very much. These were some wonderful ideas to share.

Reflecting on How to Respond to a Child's Theory

Nine months after the Pipes Study took place, staff gave a presentation at a monthly meeting about the final phase of that study in which a number of children made drawings of how showers worked (see Chapters 1, 4, and 5). The presentation included the dialogue between Jonathon and the teacher about Jonathon's drawing of a shower. At one point in that conversation, the teacher asks, "And then where does it [the water] go?" (i.e., when it leaves the tub). Jonathon responds, "Out here [draws a line from the bottom of the tub to a cup]. It goes in this cup. Then they put it in bottles and sell it to people." (See Chapter 1, "The Showers Study.")

After the presentation, the coordinators posed the following question to the participants at the meeting: "Should the teacher have given Jonathon the correct information at the end?"

Parents played a major role in the ensuing dialogue, with great diversity among their points of view. Some of the perspectives voiced by parents were as follows:

Parent 1: Find a bathtub [with the child], or a house being built, to see if it drains and if there is a cup or what.

Parent 2: You could describe to them that yes, if the water coming from the faucet is clean, yes, you can drink it, put it into a cup or into a bottle. But if it's used to shower your body, then, no, we can't use that to drink. That obviously can't be used for anything else.

Parent 3: You know what, I think it's good for you to let him know [that the water does not go into a cup and get sold] because when he makes a mistake, the other one is going to rat on him, you know what I mean? "It don't go into a cup!" So I think it's good for the adult to at least let the younger person know reality. Because the younger person won't feel so bad when the older person says, "You must be stupid! The water don't go into a cup!"

Parent 4: I felt that he had this concept, that after the water leaves our house that we use it as drinking water. In a way he was right. He knows that water doesn't just disappear. He has that theory and it's somewhat right.

The discussion raised important issues about the purpose of education: How important is it to give children the right answers when they come to conclusions that are different from those of adults? Conversely, how important is it to give children an opportunity to discuss their ideas with one another, to hear others' perspectives, to carry out further inquiry and revisit their own theories?

DROP-OFF AND PICK-UP TIMES

In every classroom there are a few parents who spontaneously engage the teachers in conversation. These tend to be the same parents who, at the beginning of the year, are most likely to volunteer to participate in school activities. The large majority of parents, initially at least, are inclined to drop off their child with as few words as possible and are equally as eager to leave when they pick the child up in the afternoon. What do teachers do in such cases?

A first step is to construct the classroom entry area in ways that communicate, "We want you to stay and be a part of what is going on" (see Chapter 6, "The Classroom Environment"). Examples are benches for parents to sit on; a basket that contains the children's journals, or teachers' journals on the children's competencies and accomplishments with notes and photos; a display panel with recent photos of children's families; and the holding board that contains children's work in progress (see Chapter 7, "Background Information," and Chapter 10, "Documentation").

A further step is to engage parents in conversation as much as possible. Sometimes it begins with a simple "Hello" and then goes beyond that; for example, "How are things going?" Many parents will respond to that question in ways that lead into a dialogue about the parent's life, the family's life, or the child. Thus, the foundations for a relationship of trust begin to get established.

Once some degree of relationship with a parent has been established, teachers find it relatively easy to focus their communications with the parent on the activities, interests, and accomplishments of the child. For example, the teacher may show the parent a drawing by the child that has been posted on the holding board along with the child's dictation about the drawing. The child often will join into this type of conversation, explaining some of the details of the drawing to the parent. When, on repeated occasions, the parent sees these concrete works of the child along with the child's dictations, and hears the child's further explanation, the parent's perception of the child often is transformed.

During spontaneous exchanges with parents, teachers may report on something interesting that their children said or did, or report on a specific accomplishment of the child, or mention a strong interest that the child is pursuing. Eventually, in response, many parents will start to report their observations of the child's expressions of interests at home. After learning of such an interest, the teacher becomes more attuned to the child's potential expression of that interest in school.

Conversely, parents, on occasion, when learning about the child's expression of interests at school, will look for opportunities to foster activities or conversations at home that extend those interests into the home setting. Teachers also look for opportunities to give examples of children's development, activities, interests, and behaviors that directly relate to the hopes and dreams that the parent has shared with them. Thus, in the long run, the teacher's proactive and ongoing engagements with the parent often grow into a dialogue that reflects and guides their shared investment in the child.

PORTFOLIO NIGHTS

Once a year each classroom holds a portfolio night. Three to four families are scheduled in each time slot to come to the classroom and explore the child's portfolio with the child and the teachers. The parents take time to notice the ways in which their child's work develops over time. At some sites, parents are given a clipboard and paper on which to write their comments and observations after looking at their child's work and before discussing it with the teacher (see Figure 9.6).

The children's binders and/or journals are included along with the portfolios. These opportunities result in three-way conversations among parent, teacher, and child in which the child and the teacher explain the child's work to the parent. Their explanations reveal the strengths and interests of the child as reflected in drawings, photos, and so on, and as reflected in the child's commentaries about them.

Portfolio night has replaced one of the two traditional parent–teacher conferences. The focus on children's strengths and accomplishments, seen through the portfolios and other sources, puts parents at ease. Many parents anticipate, based on their experiences at other schools, that meetings with the teacher will focus on the child's deficits and behavior issues. The portfolio session contributes to a teacher–parent dialogue about the child's interests and competencies, and how adults can respond to them at school and at home. This is part of a pattern that we have seen emerging elsewhere in this chapter; for example, the discussion of slide presentations at the monthly meetings, and the day-to-day dialogues with parents about their children's interests and accomplishments. On one portfolio night, families drew collective pictures of themselves after exploring the children's portfolios. The pictures then were combined to form a classroom family quilt.

INVOLVING PARENTS IN CHILDREN'S IN-DEPTH STUDIES

As part of a Shadows Study, the teachers sent disposable cameras home with a letter, asking parents to find interesting shadows with their child and to photograph them. Since the children had been engaged in a Shadows Study at school, they were quite prepared to enter into this exploration with their parents at home. Parents also were asked in the letter to take photos of their child's shadow as it moved throughout the day.

Figure 9.6. A parent thoughtfully makes notes on her child's work at portfolio night.

Along with the camera and letter, the teacher sent a "Shadow Questionnaire" for the parent to fill out after exploring the shadows with their child and taking the photos. Questions included:

- What did you learn about this experience?
- What did you notice about your child's thoughts?
- What do you think your child is learning from the experience?
- Have you changed any of your ideas or theories about shadows after viewing them through the eyes of your child?

The parents returned the disposable cameras and questionnaires to the teacher. The photos were developed and the exploration was turned into a display panel that included the photographs and examples of parent responses to the questionnaire.

At the end of the Hands Study, in which children did an extended series of drawings of their own and one another's hands (see Chapter 5), the children invited their parents to attend an evening workshop. A Polaroid camera was used to photograph parents' hands. The children hosted and guided the parents. The children, building on their own experience in the study, suggested to the parents that they trace their own hands and use the photographs as well as their actual hands to help them draw in the details. Parents enjoyed these activities and compared their drawings. They noticed details of their hands that they had never noticed before. At the end of the workshop, the photographs of the children's hands were spread over the light table so parents could try to identify their own children's hands (an idea previously suggested by one of the parents). The parents were easily able to identify their children's hands, recognizing tiny details and telling stories that related to many of the details that they had identified. It was an evening of friendship, exploration, and collaboration, with everyone sharing the pleasures of working with their children in a new way and appreciating the uniqueness of each person.

PARENTS COLLABORATING WITH TEACHERS IN THE CLASSROOM AND ON FIELD TRIPS

Classrooms often have parents who participate in the room or on field trips. These collaborations tend to emerge from the various kinds of engagements mentioned in this chapter. The challenge for the teacher in these situations is to engage parents in ways that encourage them to foster the children's sense of agency (see Chapter 5, "The Developmental Goal for Children). Such parent collaborations include:

- Documenting children's activities by taking photos or videotaping.
- Reading books with children.
- Participating with the teachers in the planning and construction of display panels (see "Documentation" in Chapters 1 and 10). In a number of the centers, groups of parents, facilitated by the center's family worker, have created display panels about their communities.

The parents' presence in the classroom during the school day gives the teacher an opportunity to model and explain teacher interactions with children. The following two teachers' accounts give us examples of how that can take place:

I see parents [volunteering in the classroom] now standing back and asking questions like, "Well, why did you ask it that way?" or "But he told you the wrong answer!" And it gives me an opportunity to explain or to show them the next step that we would do with children. I can see them stopping themselves from giving an answer or making a suggestion [to the child] and waiting to see what the child does, before they jump in totally. So it's kind of like they really want to see what's in the child's mind, instead of planting their information or their ideas into the child.

A lot of parents are beginning to use our ways of talking to children and disciplining the children and they are using some of our activities at home. They've been able to work with their child better in a way where they're not disputing a lot with them but are working with them. They learn a lot of things by watching us work inside the classroom or from how we talk to children in the hallway. Like when they're coming in and the children say "Hi" to us, they see how we get down to their eye level and really listen to what they're saying and try to find out more about what they are saying. I think that many parents are able to see that and they are using that. I've seen a lot of parents trying to find out more about what their child is trying to say to them by asking more questions. Some of the parents pick it up and some of the parents don't.

Parent classes in the same building as the preschool centers, such as job training, literacy, or ESL classes, may contribute to parent participation in the classroom in an interesting way. Often, these classes let out before pick-up time. In such cases, some parents find it convenient and meaningful to help in the classroom until it is time for their child to go home.

CONCLUSION

We have examined a variety of ways in which the program has learned to promote relationships with parents that are built on dialogue, co-exploration, and collaboration. Many of these interactions involve teachers and parents together observing, recognizing, reflecting on, and responding to the strengths and interests of children, or reflecting on children in general.

These exchanges are life affirming to parents because through them, the parents' thoughts, ideas, motives, and strengths are valued and incorporated into their relationships with the school. We saw this process occurring during the home visits, in the practice of displaying parents' words in the classroom, in dialogues at the monthly meetings, in casual encounters with parents at drop-off and pick-up times, and in the general spirit that teachers bring to school–parent interactions. The exchanges with parents are satisfying to teachers as well, because they involve mutual openness, the sharing of perspectives, and engaging the parent as a collaborator in the development of the child.

Often, the key to parents becoming interested in engaging with their child's learning in the school is when they start to see the complexity in their children's thinking and experiences as revealed in the documentations of their children's work and dialogues about those documentations.

The school–parent relationship that we have described is likely to have several major results. First, the teacher's interest in the parent's motives, feelings, ideas, and strengths provides a model for parent's valuing and responding to the inner life and competencies of the child. Second, dialogues in which teachers and parents co-construct understandings about children provide a model for parents to have dialogues with their children in which they co-construct understandings about the world. Third, the dialogues between teachers and parents provide an avenue through which the teachers' perspectives on teaching and learning can be shared with the parents.

The processes described above are further augmented by hands-on experiences that parents have in exploring materials, such as clay or wire, at site-based parent workshops. These experiences parallel the kinds of exploratory experiences that teachers are fostering with the children. Once these explorations are experienced, enjoyed, understood, and internalized by the parents through direct participation, the parents are more likely to incorporate them into their relationship with the children. They also are more likely to understand the educational approaches taken in the classroom.

When teachers speak about developing parent partnership activities in the various contexts described above, they frequently comment that the activities result in the parent feeling "part of" the school and part of the children's learning. This idea fits into an implicit theory of parent–school relationships. The more that parents feel part of the children's lives in school, the more they will want to participate in a broader range of the school's activities and to extend the spirit of the school into their interactions with their children at home.

Chapter 10

Professional Development and Support of Teachers

> *We haven't learned how to be learners.*
> *We've learned how to be teachers, and it is different.*
> —Amelia Gambetti, Reggio Emilia educator,
> in a dialogue with Chicago Commons staff

In the Reggio Approach as practiced in Italy and at Chicago Commons, teachers are given the opportunity to be reflective and curious and to learn new ways of learning that redefine their roles as teachers. Underlying this emphasis is an image of the teacher that parallels the image of the child as capable, interested, rich in ideas, wanting to grow, and wanting to communicate (see Chapter 1 and the conclusion to Chapter 2). In the various professional development processes at Commons, teachers are respected for their ability to think and contribute to the co-construction of understandings.

The key question in this chapter is: What kinds of professional developmental experiences and supports empower Chicago Commons teachers to embody Reggio principles in their teaching and learning? The chapter is organized into four parts:

1. *Goals for teacher professional development:* What were the goals underlying the Chicago Commons approach to teacher development?
2. *Professional development and support of teachers through day-to-day work:* How do teachers' engagement in the ongoing processes of teaching, documenting, and collaborating contribute to their professional development?
3. *Provision of special professional development experiences:* How do specially planned professional development events such as in-service experiences and participation in conferences contribute to teachers' abilities to explore the Reggio Approach?
4. *Parallel process:* When Reggio principles are incorporated into the processes of teacher collaboration and learning, do they strengthen the implementation of those same principles by teachers in their relationships with children?

GOALS FOR TEACHER PROFESSIONAL DEVELOPMENT

The fundamental goal for teachers' professional development is teachers growing into a new relationship with children based on listening, observing, valuing, and responding to children's expression of interests, feelings, and ideas. This relationship is informed by an *image of the child* as competent, keenly interested in the world, rich in ideas, able to think and make connections, wanting to grow, and wanting to communicate with peers and adults (see Chapter 1, "Image of the Child"). Teachers and children are *partners in dialogue*. Through that dialogue, they co-construct understandings about the world and their relationships with it.

Growing into this relationship with children involves deep levels of learning by the teacher. It involves experiencing and valuing children as a separate source of consciousness with their own motives, ideas, and perspectives.

Seven Teacher Development Goals

The above relationship with children, based on listening/observing, valuing, and responding, is the reference point for seven, more specific goals of teacher professional development:

1. Learning to engage in moment-to-moment dialogues with children that build on their interests and involve the co-construction of understandings (see Chapters 1–3).
2. Learning the skills and understandings involved in carrying out emergent curriculum cycles, involving listening/observing, documenting, interpreting, projecting/deciding, planning, hypothesizing, and implementing (see Chapter 5, "The Emergent Curriculum Cycle").
3. Learning to design and construct classroom environments that promote small-group learning, communicate the children's identities, invite children to take multiple perspectives, promote a sense of well-being, and encourage parents to engage with the life of the classroom community (see Chapter 6, "The Classroom Environment").
4. Learning to participate in collaborative dialogues with other staff to co-construct understandings and teaching strategies (see Chapter 7, "Teacher Collaboration").
5. Learning to engage in dialogues with parents that connect the perspectives of parents and teachers to support the development of the child (see Chapter 9, "Drop-off and Pick-up Times" and "Portfolio Nights").
6. Learning to be a researcher. The idea of teacher as researcher is akin to the notion of teacher as "learner" in Amelia Gambetti's quote at the beginning of this chapter. Being a *researcher* means infusing a research perspective into all that one does as a teacher: experiencing curiosity and engaging the object of one's curiosity, formulating questions, hypothesizing, gathering and analyzing pertinent data with one's questions in mind, coming to conclusions, reflecting on the application of the conclusions, and pondering next steps in the research. Teachers usually do not think of themselves as "researchers," yet this aspect of their role is vital in the Reggio Approach.
7. Developing a sense of agency. In Chapters 5 and 8, we proposed that the development of a sense of agency in the child is a key child development goal underlying our interpretation of the Reggio Approach. For the convenience of the reader, we repeat the main part of the definition here.

> Experiencing oneself as an active, self-directed agent who can, individually and in collaboration with others, formulate personally meaningful learning goals, figure out strategies to achieve them, engage the world to pursue them, construct understandings, and communicate the newly developed understandings to others. (See full definition in Chapter 5, "The Developmental Goal for Children.")

This definition of *agency* applies to the teacher as well. A sense of agency underlies every facet of teacher development that we have outlined above. Further, a sense of agency in the teacher is a prerequisite to the teacher being able to promote the development of a sense of agency in children. Without experiencing it oneself, one cannot imagine the processes that would support its development in another person.

Potential Conflicts Between the Reggio Approach and Teachers' Previous Experience

Since most teachers have been taught traditional preschool approaches, their development toward Reggio ideals requires them to undergo a major "paradigm shift" regarding the nature of teaching and learning. In the traditional paradigm, the main focus is on the child's acquisition of pre-established knowledge in which there are clearly right and wrong answers. In the Reggio paradigm, the primary emphasis is on children *learning how to construct their own knowledge and understandings*. The rightness or wrongness of the answers that they generate is less important than their engagement in learning strategies and processes through which they construct, re-examine, critique, and communicate their ideas about the world.

Broadly speaking, the difference is between a predominantly *content* emphasis in traditional methods and a predominantly *process* emphasis in the Reggio-inspired methods. In the former, the teacher's primary role is to be disseminator of knowledge. In the latter, the teacher's primary role is to be a facilitator and researcher of the children's construction and co-construction of understanding stemming from the children's own interests. It is often difficult for teachers to make this shift in emphasis. It requires an accompanying shift in their identities as teachers.

While the predominant emphasis in Reggio-inspired methods is on process, there is still a concern with content. However, the content of learning is *realized through the Reggio process* described above. Thus, for example, as we saw in Chapter 8, children are engaged in developing reading, writing, and math skills through engaging the world in pursuit of their interests, co-constructing knowledge and/or communicating with significant others. Similarly, children learn science and social studies content through pursuing their interests in the world around them, representing their discoveries, and revisiting their representations on the way to further understandings and inquiries.

PROFESSIONAL DEVELOPMENT AND SUPPORT OF TEACHERS IN DAY-TO-DAY WORK

> *What was different to me was to be able to notice a child's or a group of children's interest, and follow that interest and really work with the children to investigate, and explore, about what they wanted to know, or learn, or explore.*
> —Teacher, Chicago Commons

While teacher professional development often is thought of as taking place through specially designed training events, a major part of the teachers' learning in the Chicago Commons program occurs through their active participation in the ongoing processes associated with their teaching. This section examines teacher learning in the context of those day-to-day processes. They include the weekly meeting, the ongoing experience of teaching and learning, documentation, classroom collaboration, teacher research studies, and monthly meetings.

The Weekly Meeting

Each classroom team (head teacher and one or two assistant teachers) is part of a weekly meeting team, usually made up of two classroom teams, the site director, a coordinator from the central office, and sometimes the center's family worker (see Chapters 5 and 7). The team meets once a week for 1½ or 2 hours and discusses the work of each classroom. The discussion of a classroom usually involves two phases.

The first phase includes descriptions, documentation, and interpretation. The teacher and assistant teacher(s) describe the past week's activities and present documentation of children's work. The group responds to the documentation by interpreting the interests and ideas that are being expressed through it.

The second phase includes projecting/deciding, planning, and hypothesizing. The teachers, with the help of the whole group, brainstorm possible responses to the children and choose one or two to pursue. Next they make plans and hypothesize the children's responses to the implementation of the plan. The latter was often difficult for the teachers.

The program requires that these meetings occur every week and that teachers bring documentation to the meetings to provide a reference point for the team's reflection and planning. The following are excerpts from a weekly meeting taped in May 1998. In reading it, you might want to consider the following questions:

> *How might a teacher value this meeting?*
>
> *In what important ways did the coordinator facilitate the group's task?*

Descriptions, Documentation, and Interpretations. A team of two teachers, both relatively new to the Reggio Approach, reported on their early explorations with the children on the topic of the City. They laid out some drawings made by children following a walk in the neighborhood and read the accompanying dictations.

> That's the people. This is a cat. There is a big boy with his little brother, a lot of flowers, and a big dog. It stink.

> There were a lot of flowers. These are cars. This one is bigger. These are people on the street and they have a coat of the Chicago Bulls.

Teacher 1 then read some dialogue from a discussion with Henrietta and Candace (the questions were adapted from those used in a City Study at Reggio Emilia). Here are a few of the questions and responses.

> *Teacher*: What is a city for?
> *Candace*: For people working.
> *Henrietta*: So we could go to the store.
> *Teacher*: Why were cities constructed?
> *Candace*: So they can do some stuff, build a train.
> *Teacher*: Is it possible for a city to have a beginning and an end?
> *Candace*: It ends downtown, because we went downtown; daddy, mommy, my
>   brother, and me.
> *Teacher*: Do you live in a city?
> *Candace*: No, in a family.
> *Henrietta*: Candace's house is close to my house. Her house is small.

Coordinator (to the group): What are your reactions?
Teacher 3: It seems like they don't have a lot of experience with the city and what it is.
Site director: I don't think they don't have the experience. They just don't have the
    vocabulary to express it.
Teacher 1: I think they haven't yet grasped or understood the concept of what a
    city is.

> *Coordinator*: It seems like they are talking about things that are close to their own experience, in their own lives, rather than how we think of the city as a sort of abstract concept.
>
> *Teacher 1*: The next day we had a whole-class discussion to revisit the drawings.
>
> *Coordinator*: Can you read some of that dialogue, please. And can the rest of us, as we are listening to the words, think about what you are interested in finding out about some of the ideas that are coming up.

Teacher 2 read the following dialogue from the whole-class discussion:

> *Teacher*: Does the city start somewhere?
>
> *Paolo*: In Chicago.
>
> *Teacher*: And where does it end?
>
> *Candace*: Where the people work.
>
> *Teacher*: Is there something you like about the city of Chicago?
>
> *Jerardo*: Mexico. Only Puerto Rico, Mexico, and Chicago.
>
> *Teacher* (trying to re-focus on the question, by modeling some possible answers): I like the stores, the zoo, and the lake.
>
> *Letti*: I like the dresses. I like the songs and the Chicago Bulls.

Projecting and Planning.

> *Coordinator*: These are some *new ideas*. What more do you want to know about them?
>
> *Teacher 2*: Me, personally? I think that asking them about what they *like* is going to be a good step toward their knowing what the city is. One of the children says she likes dresses. Next I think we can ask them, "Where do you get these dresses?"
>
> *Coordinator*: That's a great question!
>
> *Teacher 3*: Candace mentioned "people working" in the city. So we could ask, "What kind of work do the people do?"
>
> *Coordinator*: And we could ask, "What is downtown?"
>
> *Site director*: I would want to know *why* they think the city ends downtown.
>
> *Coordinator*: Let's think about the drawings as we think about this. Can we put the drawings out on the table again?
>
> *Teacher 2*: If we ask, "Where do you get dresses?" they are going to say, "Store." So let's ask them to *compare types of stores*. "Can you get it at a grocery store?"
>
> *Teacher 3*: We could ask, "Are there different kinds of stores in Chicago?"
>
> *Coordinator*: I'm looking at this drawing of a crow. Other children mentioned dogs or cats. So children are noticing little animals that live in the city. I'm wondering "What other kinds of creatures they think live in the city?" And then, specifically, "Where does that crow live?" "Where does it get its food?" "Where do each of the other creatures live and find food?"
>
> *Teacher 3*: A lot of children drew various types of *people*. So we can ask, "What kinds of people live in the city?"
>
> *Coordinator*: Let's see. How many drawings have people in them?
>
> *Teacher 1*: They also mentioned cars and trains.
>
> *Site director*: Yes, lots of transportation.
>
> *Others*: "How do you get around the city?" "How do you get to the store?" "How do people get to work?"

The coordinator (who had been taking notes) read the group's brainstorms back to them.

> *Teacher 2*: We could start with that idea about the Chicago Bulls and ask, "What sport do the Chicago Bulls play?" "Have you seen any other sports in Chicago?"
>
> *Teacher 1*: And maybe, "Where do you think they play at?" Then go back to the parks and other places.
>
> *Coordinator*: I'm wondering where do you think would be the next place to take

what is happening here? We have to keep in our minds that we want to provide experiences for children that *extend the ideas in their minds.* They have some beautiful, rich ideas already.

Site family worker: When we ask what city they live in, they say they live in their "family" instead of a city. What if you extend that and say, "Where does your family live?" Maybe they would say "In a house," but it would lead toward something.

Teacher 3: We could connect this to the stores thing and say: "What kind of stores do you go to with your family?"

Teacher 2: And then there are things you can get at one store and not at other stores.

Teacher 1: I know they would be able to say what you can buy at Jewel that you can't buy at Venture or K-Mart or Sears.

Coordinator: So it sounds like we are dealing with two main things: *places,* like downtown or stores, and *people.* So what if we pursue these two things and, based on the information we already have from the children's drawings and dialogues, continue with those lines of thought, revisit the children's ideas with them and help them, extend those ideas.

Teacher 1: I have this thought of calling the local store, Bodella, and asking them if we could just go in the store with the children and walk around the store and make a visit.

Coordinator: To actually go to a store. I think that is a great idea! How would you prepare the children to do that?

Teacher 2: I think by going back to the question, "What stores do you visit with your family?" I know a majority of them are going to say, "Bodella" because it is the closest grocery store.

Coordinator: What about first asking your questions, "What stores do you go to with your family?" to find out what they are thinking about. They will have a lot of ideas, I am sure, and it honors the connection with their family.

Teacher 2: Another thing that Maria [site family worker] just brought up to me, the sewing machine store that one of our parents owns. It's right across from Bodella.

Coordinator: Is there a way we could connect that to your previous experience with children thinking about sounds in the city?

Others: Sewing machine sounds! Meat grinder sounds! The sounds of cash registers!

Teacher 1: Show them the photos [from the walk] again and ask them if there are any stores in the photos.

Coordinator: Another question, to sort of go along with this, is the question, "Where do people work?"

The coordinator asked Teacher 1 to sum up the plan so far and she did.

Coordinator: I want to encourage you to work with the children both in the large group, like you've been doing, and also to work in small groups, with perhaps no more than two children. You could start by meeting with them in small groups and ask them to share a little bit more about their drawings. Let's try also to tape-record your discussions about the stores and where people work, so we can have a typed dialogue to work with next week. I'd be happy to help you transcribe that if you need it.

> *What do you see are the various roles that the coordinator played in the meeting?*
>
> *Did you see any major turning points in the conversation?*

Comments on the Meeting. The group constructed a useful schema for promoting the first stages of an emergent curriculum based on eliciting children's ideas and helping them to extend and connect those ideas into initial understandings of a topic. This sets the stage for further explorations. The schema consisted of a sequence with four strategies (see Figure 10.1).

The schema is related to the questions posed to children by the teacher in the How to Ride a Bike and Going Downtown episodes (see Chapter 3). In those episodes the teacher continually draws on knowledge that the children possess and then asks them to connect elements of what they have said to additional knowledge that they have.

The processes through which the group examined the documentation and constructed the schema helped move the emergent curriculum forward. As the teachers began to see the potential in the children's ideas and to imagine the children's responses to various types of questions, they became increasingly appreciative of the richness of the children's minds.

The success of *creating a promising teaching schema*, combined with a high *quality of dialogue*, no doubt moved the participants forward in their sense of being able to collaborate successfully with others. Repeated experiences such as this enhance teachers' collaborative abilities and sense of agency.

Figure 10.1. Linked teaching strategies developed at the weekly meeting.

Strategy 1:
Ask open-ended questions that elicit children's initial ideas about a topic.
For example, ask, "What are things you like about (the object of study)?"
Give them direct experience in some facet of the topic (e.g., the neighborhood walk). Ask them to make drawings based on the experience, and take dictations about their drawings.

Strategy 2:
Ask questions that encourage the children
to extend the ideas they expressed in response to Strategy 1.
For example, building on "dresses," ask, "Where do you get those dresses?"
Building on "crows," ask, "Where do crows live? What do crows eat?"

Strategy 3:
Pose questions that help children to fill out and further extend the categories
suggested by the ideas elicited through Strategies 1 and 2.
For example, ask, "What other types of animals live in the city?" If the child answers, "squirrels,"
ask, "Where do squirrels live?" "Where do they hide their food?"

Strategy 4:
Ask questions that lead to making connections across categories.
For example, ask, "How do you get to that store?" (This links transportation
with stores.) "How do people get to that kind of work?"
(This links transportation with types of work.)

In our estimation, the coordinator played a vital role in the meeting. She kept the group on track and moved them forward by

- Asking questions that challenged the participants' thinking and encouraged them to offer a variety of responses
- Scaffolding the thinking process
- Giving directives
- Valuing the teachers' minds by reinforcing and building on their ideas
- Contributing ideas
- Summing up and offering practical support

The teachers began the session stumped by the documentation, stumbling into a mode of noticing children's deficits rather than their interests and ideas (see Chapter 1, "Image of the Child," and the Appendix, "Year 4"). With the help of the coordinator, they subsequently were able to recognize the rich potential in the children's responses. Their successful co-construction of strategies empowered them and made their next steps possible.

The Ongoing Experience of Teaching and Learning

At the center of teachers' development is their *direct experience* in interacting with children; that is, their observations, interpretations, feelings, and reflections in response to how the children are responding to their actions and initiatives. The weekly meetings and the many other sources of support make important contributions to teachers constructing strategies and to the conceptual frames through which they observe and interpret the children's responses. The ultimate nexus of their learning, however, lies in the direct experience of trying things out, observing, reflecting, adjusting, reframing, responding, and observing once more.

The professional development process, then, is usefully conceived as a *loop* between classroom experience and external sources of support. For example, there is an ongoing loop between classroom experience and the weekly meeting. The strategies for extending children's ideas that were developed in the weekly meeting that we described above most likely were explored by the teachers in subsequent weeks and the results brought back to weekly meetings for collective reflection. The schema also may have been tried by the two other teachers in the group. As we advance through this chapter, it is instructive to reflect on how the various sources of teacher support work in tandem, forming more complex loops with the classroom. For example, an idea generated at an in-service event might be reviewed in a subsequent weekly meeting and tried out in the classroom.

Documentation

We owe much of the inspiration for the following discussion of documentation to the work of Lella Gandini (1998, 2001) and Carlina Rinaldi (1998, 2001).

In 1997–98, there was a virtual explosion in the program's emphasis on documentation, as Karen and the staff began to fully realize the indispensable role that documentation plays in the process of listening/observing–reflecting–responding.

Documentation is an integral part of *listening* and *observing*. It carries listening and observing forward to enable in-depth *reflection*. It holds observations still in order to interpret children's interests, feelings, and ideas. It provides reference points that can be revisited and reflected on by more than one person, allowing co-construction of children's meanings to emerge. Hence, documentation makes *reflecting* and informed *responding* fully possible. Documentation is also an essential factor in children's learning, since it makes it possible for children to revisit and reflect on the ideas expressed through their work. Finally, as we learned in Chapter 9, documentation provides a major reference point for dialogue with parents.

Documentation activities fall broadly into three categories: *collecting*, *organizing*, and *formal communication*. In all of these practices, teachers' ongoing reflection on the intentions behind their acts of documentation is of major importance.

Collecting. Teachers selectively record children's actions and words through notes, audio recordings, video recordings, photographs, and dictations, and by collecting children's representations.

When teachers first start collecting documentation, some tend to overdocument; for example, taking many more photos than they can use. They also pass up important documentation opportunities. With time, they become more refined in their choices of what to document and how to document it. What kinds of judgments underlie this increasing refinement and how do those judgments develop?

As teachers grow professionally, they increasingly experience listening, observing, reflecting, and responding as part of a single process (see Chapter 2). Correspondingly, they come to understand the critical role that documentation plays in that process. The most important factor in bringing about this understanding, is their participation in the *uses* of documentation for interpreting children's meanings and for extending those interpretations into planning responses to children. For example, in the weekly meeting described in this chapter, the participants experienced that by having a rich supply of carefully gathered documentation before them, they were able to collaborate in the interpretation process and move forward in planning meaningful responses to the children. This no doubt helped them to grasp the relationship between listening, observing, and documenting, on the one hand, and reflecting/responding on the other. Further, the sharpening of teachers' conceptual and perceptual lenses for interpreting children's meanings from documentation that occurs in the weekly meetings carries back into promoting greater refinement in their judgment about what to document and how to document it. In other words, they bring an interpretive frame of mind to the collection process itself, selecting those things that show promise for further interpretation.

The use of documentation in the weekly meetings also helps teachers to see the importance of collecting *multiple forms* of documentation on the same learning sequence. For example, in the weekly meeting reported earlier, the teachers brought in four forms of documentation of the children's ideas about the city: drawings, dictations, interviews, and whole-class dialogue. The group's interpretation and planning benefited from *combining* the four.

Collection of documentation also requires learning the basic operation of equipment and learning a variety of ways that a piece of equipment can be used; for example, understanding the value of taking a close-up photograph versus a whole-group photograph in relation to a particular purpose that one has in mind. Effective collection of documentation also rests on teachers learning to organize their tools of documentation, so that they have pads, pencils, as well as loaded cameras and tape recorders available for spontaneous use. Workshops on documentation help to promote these kinds of learning.

Organizing. *Organizing* refers to selecting and grouping the documentation in order to reflect on them. By "grouping" we mean positioning various items in relation to one another in ways that assist the process of interpretation. One example is the juxtaposition of a drawing with the corresponding dictation. A further example is grouping documentation in ways that facilitate noticing patterns among them.

Organizing documentation often involves posting informal arrangements of selected photographs, drawings, dictation, and so on, on the classroom holding board for children and teachers to revisit; for parents to explore, learn from, and wonder about; and as a focal point for dialogues among children, teachers, and parents (see Chapters 7 and 9). Organizing also includes preparation of documentation to take to the weekly meeting and reflecting on how to present it. Arranging items on the holding board may be an interim step in this preparation process. Ideally, organizing documentation is carried out by the classroom team. This allows for more than one perspective to come into play when deciding how to present the children's work.

As is the case with collecting skills, organizing skills develop both through exercising them and through teachers' participation in the weekly meetings. For example, at the weekly meeting described in this chapter, the participants searched for *patterns* in the documentation. Teacher 3 noted that "a lot of children drew various types of people." The coordinator then searched to see how many of the drawings had people in them. Another example of pattern finding occurred in the Windows Study where the participants of the weekly meetings noted that windows and stairs frequently appeared in the children's drawings and that references to "windows" occurred frequently in their dialogue (see Chapter 2, "The Windows Study").

The practice of searching for patterns when interpreting documentation during the weekly meetings is likely to feed back into the teachers' organizing of documentation. For example, in selecting what items to place on the holding board or to bring to the weekly meeting, teachers are sensitized to include items that show patterning across them. Teacher awareness of the potential of pattern finding also has implications for the *collecting* of documentation. Knowing that patterns in the documentation help them to interpret shared interests among the children, teachers pay attention to potential patterns when deciding what to document.

In sum, when listening/observing–documenting–reflecting–responding is experienced by the teacher as a single process, the skills and motivations applied in one aspect of the process encourage and strengthen the application of related skills and motivations in the other aspects of the process.

Formal Communication. Formal communication includes *display panels*, *presentations*, and *publications* such as booklets, postcards, and posters used to publicize the program or give to children and parents at the end of the year.

Display panels integrate photos, drawings, dictation, dialogues, and three-dimensional representations (in wood, clay, wire, etc.) to tell a story of children's thinking and learning in a particular area of investigation. A primary purpose of the panels is to stimulate the viewer's thinking about the learning process.

A panel has a title and often has an introductory statement written by the teachers, explaining the background of the children's investigation. The photos and children's representations may be organized in a temporal sequence to show the unfolding of a learning process or they may be organized around different perspectives on the subject. Often, panels include the teachers' account of what was happening in the learning sequence. Figure 10.2 shows a display about children's explorations of light and shadows. The teachers created four panels. The first panel describes an experiment in which children experienced changes in the position, shape, and size of a shadow by visiting the site twice during a 2-hour period. The panel includes photos of the experiment and the teachers' account of the initial challenge they gave the children in asking them, "Do you think the shadow will stay in the same place?" After the children saw that the shadow had moved, the teachers asked them, "What happened to the shadow?" The panel presents many of the children's answers to the second question. It also includes four of the children's drawings depicting the experiment.

In the second panel, they relied on photographs to tell the story of the different ways that the children explored, created, and experimented with light and shadows. The teachers used captions sparingly to guide or deepen the viewer's appreciation for

Figure 10.2. Four panels from the Light and Shadows display.

The first panel

At the beginning of our study, we arranged a situation to challenge the children about their theories on the movement of shadows. We set up a chair for one child to stand on so the children could see his shadow cast upon the snow. We outlined the child's shadow with blue powder paint and asked, "I wonder what will happen to the shadow later? Do you think the shadow will stay in the same place?" After 2 hours, we went back to the same spot, allowed the child to stand on the chair again, and traced the new shadow with red powder paint. Here are some of the children's theories as to why the shadow had changed:

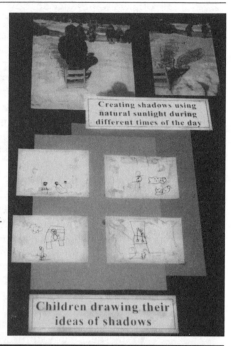

Cristobal: You moved the chair.
Irvin: The sun moved.
Giovani: The sun moved the chair.
Frisco: One is red and the other is blue and Irvin moved the chair.
Ramon: A guy took the chair and my dad took the shadow.
Josie: The shadow moved.
Darryl: Lucila moved the shadow.
Lea: Lucila took her shadow home.
Lina: God moved the shadow.
Edmond: One is big and the other is small.
Jena: The blue shadow is big and the red shadow is little and fat. You moved the chair.

The second panel

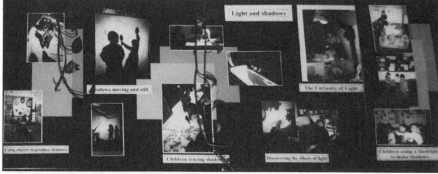

The third panel

The fourth panel

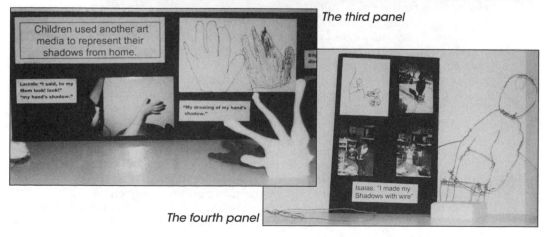

what the photographs showed regarding the children's capabilities, for example, "Using objects to produce shadows," "Shadows moving and still," "The curiosity of light," "Discovering the effects of light."

The third panel emphasizes the connection between learning at home and learning at school, using different media to represent and provoke understandings. It documents a three-stage learning progression showing Lucinda's growing understanding of shadows as she uses different media, and it explores different perspectives on the relationship between her hand and its shadow. The panel begins with Lucinda's comment to her mother as they explore hand shadows at home. It includes her mother's photograph of Lucinda making a shadow with her hand. The photograph was taken with a disposable camera provided by the school (see Chapter 9, "Involving Parents in Children's In-Depth Studies"). Beside this documentation is an example of the second stage in Lucinda's exploration, drawing her hand and her hand's shadow side by side. She colored the shadow with a black marker, placing it to the right of a slightly larger but similarly shaped drawing of her hand. Included on the panel are quotes from Lucinda that convey her excitement when exploring shadows and her sense of agency as she draws her hand and her hand's shadow. In the third stage, she used clay to represent her hand and its shadow. As in her drawing, she represented the shadow of her hand in a color that is considerably darker than the color she used for her hand. In this three-dimensional medium she no longer represents her hand and its shadow as parallel to each other, but shows *how the shadow is joined at right angles to the hand*, indicating that she is thinking more deeply about the relationship between her hand and its shadow. In this panel, the viewer can see how changing the medium can enable a child to express a clearer understanding of the phenomenon being explored.

An overhead light shining on the display creates an actual shadow from the white clay hand onto the clay shadow behind it. The provision of a flashlight near the display would give viewers the opportunity to create a variety of shadows cast by the clay hand sculpture and the wire figure on the adjacent shelf.

In the fourth panel, the teachers presented an example of how children's exploration of an interest can be extended and deepened through the use of another medium; in this case, wire. The panel includes a photograph of Irvin casting his shadow on the snow as he stood on a chair and Irvin's drawing based on the photo. Beneath these pictures, two photographs of Irvin show how he used his drawing and the photograph as reference points to create a wire replica of himself on a chair and a wire shadow stretching alongside it, enabling the viewer to see the relationship between them. Irvin's sense of agency is expressed by his quotation, "I made my shadows with wire."

Over time, teachers learn *not* to try to convey too much in one panel and to be careful in organizing its layout so the viewer is clear about how to read it (e.g., from left to right or starting at a central point from which other points radiate). The relatively simple panel layouts used in the four panels of the Light and Shadows display, taken together, convey a range of learning processes. When looked at closely, each panel conveys a set of rich learning experiences that draw the viewer into a deeper understanding of children's capacity to construct and express knowledge.

Teacher presentations are usually about children's in-depth studies or other classroom experiences, such as materials exploration. Like the display panels, presentations usually tell a story of children's learning. The presentations utilize slides or video clips, accompanied by a commentary that details the learning process and tells how teachers' interpretations of documentation guided the direction of the children's inquiry. The commentary also may include the presenters' reflections on what they learned from the experience. Presentations are given at monthly meetings, in-service events, learning tours (discussed later in the chapter), and outside conferences.

When teachers prepare a panel or presentation, they receive feedback from the site director, coordinator, and other teachers at the center regarding the content and organization of the communication in relation to the message they want to convey and the audience they want to reach. This openness to other perspectives and willingness to contribute them is a general principle of the program. It applies to virtually every facet of staff activity. In this case, it contributes to the quality of the panel or presentation and to teachers' overall ability to create them. In many cases, presentations are created and delivered jointly with a coordinator, site director, parent, or family worker.

The creation of display panels and presentations provides teachers with major opportunities for professional growth since these activities require them to think retrospectively and systematically about children's learning and their role in promoting it. The processes of re-creating a teaching–learning sequence, articulating the intentions behind it, reviewing the scaffolding process, identifying significant kinds of learning that took place, and documenting the role of children's interests, ideas, and initiatives in driving the learning process promote teacher development. These processes etch a particular experience in the teacher's mind for further use in facilitating children's learning. They also give the teacher a chance to reflect on dead ends and missed teaching opportunities. Further, the creation of a display panel or the planning and delivery of a presentation are likely to result in an enhanced *sense of agency* in the teacher. This comes from having facilitated an in-depth study or other exploration and from having competently created a communication about it. Both are guided by a clear sense of purpose (see discussion of teacher agency at beginning of this chapter, Seven Teacher Development Goals).

A periodic revisiting of past display panels is a useful professional development strategy that over time creates a store of knowledge about the best ways to create panels. In revisiting the best of the old panels, teachers can reflect on ways in which panels can be created to clearly communicate intended messages. At one monthly meeting, teacher teams took turns showing their panels. Participants responded by saying what the panel meant to them. Then the panel creators explained what they had in mind when they created it. Teachers also get guidance in panel making through workshops and printed guidelines.

Further, teachers learn from listening to and observing children and/or parents as they interact with display panels. Their comments and emotional responses give teachers insights into the meaning of the panel's contents to children and parents. This, in turn, can be a stimulus to on-the-spot dialogue with the children or food for thought regarding both future panel making and future learning activities for children.

Final Thoughts on Documentation. The practice of documentation changes teachers' ways of seeing and interpreting. It provides opportunities to look closely and think deeply about children and their learning. It leads to collaborative learning processes for teachers that are stimulated and enriched by the sharing of perspectives. As teachers' documentation skills develop within this ongoing collaborative, reflective framework, teachers feel they are becoming researchers and producers of knowledge.

Classroom Collaboration

In Chapter 7, we looked at the nature of teacher collaboration in the classroom and the difficulties that teachers sometimes experience in trying to achieve it. The teachers pointed out that the smooth and satisfying flow of classroom life and the ability to keep up with their many tasks require ongoing dialogue between them.

Teachers had to work on improving their communication and negotiating skills in order to collaborate well with each other in the classroom. For some, the learning process was more uphill than for others; for example, when it was complicated by one teacher being more committed to Reggio principles than the other, or by an assistant teacher feeling uncomfortable with taking initiative (see Chapter 7, "Teacher Collaboration").

Sometimes improvements in team relationships occurred after teachers were offered opportunities to engage in negotiation and compromise during workshop experiences. Teachers also gave one another advice informally based on their own experience. Coordinators and site directors facilitated communication within some teams or offered specific suggestions.

Teacher Research Studies

A facet of the teacher's role as researcher is her involvement in the design and implementation of teacher research studies in the classroom. Several times a year teachers were asked to conduct a somewhat formal research study on an aspect of classroom life. The focus of these research studies was to understand something about children in a direction determined by the teachers' interest and curiosity. Teachers typically were given a set of suggestions to stimulate their thinking about possible studies. For example:

- How do children use the dramatic play area?
- What is arrival time like for children?
- What is boy/girl play like in the block area?
- Study the results of a change in the classroom environment.
- How could you ask children questions and have dialogues with them?
- Follow a child, observe/interpret what the child is trying to pursue, and suggest ways to support the child in that process.

Teachers used photographs, videotapes, classroom observation notes, and children's dialogues to reflect on their study topic. They frequently shared their research studies at weekly meetings and monthly meetings. The studies strengthened the teachers' observation and listening skills, led to new avenues in facilitating children's learning, and more firmly established the teacher as a researcher.

Monthly Meetings

The monthly meetings were described in Chapter 9. We will focus here on some facets of those meetings that have particular impact on the professional development of teachers.

Visiting One Another's Classrooms and Centers. Since between 30 and 40 teachers attend a monthly meeting in any particular month, a large proportion of them have the opportunity to visit many classrooms in the program during the course of the year. The host teachers, coordinators, and site director are available at the time of the visit to converse with the visitors. The classroom tours expose the visiting staff to new ideas and strengthen relationships among staff across centers.

Teacher Presentations. Professional development associated with teachers creating and delivering presentations has been described in the Documentation section above. For the teachers in the *audience* who are viewing and responding to the presentations, the benefits are also substantial. Each time teachers witness and discuss the unfolding of an emergent curriculum process, they are exposed to new possibilities for working with children and new perspectives on children's interests and capacities.

Whole-Group Dialogues. The dialogues involving staff's and parents' responses to challenging questions about the slides, video clips, and transcripts presented at the monthly meetings provide teachers with ongoing opportunities to develop their ability to interpret children's meanings and reflect on children's learning.

PROVISION OF SPECIAL PROFESSIONAL DEVELOPMENT EXPERIENCES

So far, we have looked at professional development and support of teachers in the context of their day-to-day work. The program also provides special contexts in which teacher professional development takes place: in-service experiences, learning tours, outside conferences, visits from Reggio Emilia educators, and visits by Chicago Commons staff to Reggio Emilia.

Portrait of an Annual In-Service Event

Two types of in-service experiences for teachers typically are provided by the program. The first is the annual August in-service, lasting 2 to 3 days. It launches the new school year and provides professional development in targeted areas. These events are attended by teachers, site directors, and family workers, and are run by Karen and the coordinators. The second type are half-day workshops given as the need arises during the year, focusing on particular content; for example, core versus surface interests of children, emergent curriculum, or classroom environment. We will focus here on the August in-service events because of their comprehensive nature. Figure 10.3 shows the topics engaged at annual in-service events from 1993 to 2001.

The following are excerpts from the August 1998 annual in-service event. The topics, covered over 2.5 days, were

- Day 1: Reflections on the Past Year, Hopes and Dreams for the Future, the Meaning of Words
- Day 2: Emergent Curriculum, Advice to New Teachers, Parent Participation, Materials
- Day 3: Documentation, Challenges, and Expectations for the Coming Year

Figure 10.3. Topics at annual in-service events, 1993–2001.

Topics at Annual In-Services	1993	1994	1995	1996	1997	1998	1999	2000	2001
Image of the child	X	X			X				
Observation			X				X		X
Documentation	X			X		X			X
Interpretation of children's ideas, interests, and feelings from documentation			X		X	X			X
Projecting responses to interpretations						X			
Emergent curriculum					X	X	X		X
Dialogue with children						X	X		
Participants exploring materials			X	X	X	X			X
Children's use of materials	X	X			X	X	X		X
Exploring light/shadows		X			X				
The learning environment	X	X	X		X		X		
Parent involvement				X	X	X		X	
Teacher as researcher					X				
Portfolios				X					
Emergent curriculum planning form					X				
Letters and numbers							X		
Reggio process throughout the day								X	

Accomplishments of the Past and Hopes for the Future. The in-service opened with participants creating a list together of what they had accomplished in the previous year. The discussion then turned to brainstorming about where they wanted the program to go in the next year. Both sets of ideas were recorded at the easel and retained.

Meanings of Words. A coordinator read a list of terms connected with the Reggio Approach that frequently are used in the program. She invited everyone to think about "what the words mean to us."

- project
- learn and educate
- teacher and child points of view
- core and surface interests
- observing/listening
- to be an explorer

Participants were organized into six groups corresponding to the six terms. Excerpts from the "observing/listening" group follow. The discussion began with reading the following quote from Sergio Spagiari (director of the program at Reggio Emilia):

> The importance of listening is the key. Listening gives value to the person who is speaking. Unfortunately few people listen to the children. . . . To listen is to go through the adventure of research that leads us to a new road. We have to be willing to discover something new. We have to be ready to notice a signal, a change taking place. We have to be ready for the unpredictable.

The group then created an initial list of meanings associated with listening/observing. Here is part of the discussion that gave rise to the list.

Family worker: I think listening is a reflective process.
Coordinator 2 (writing the idea on the easel): How so?
Family worker: Because when you are listening you are asking questions and you are questioning yourself. The more you listen, the more intrigued you get and the more questions you can ask.
Teacher 1: When you are asking questions you are getting into a dialogue.
Family worker: Yes, listening is like a prelude, or an open door, to an exchange.
Teacher 1: Listening gives value to the other person, but what do *you* get from listening? I guess it's the way you learn about other people.
Family worker: Yes, and the way you grow yourself.

The six groups came together and a dialogue ensued around each group's associations with their word or phrase. Here is a piece of the dialogue following the presentation of the "listening/observing" group's list.

Teacher 2: Can you elaborate more on "to be able to really listen, you need to be willing to change"?
Family worker: You need to be able to change because a lot of times when you get new ideas it will cause you to evolve.
Coordinator 4: You are holding on to what you want to hear and therefore you are not really letting the outside in. You can't listen openly unless you are willing to be open to what you hear.
Coordinator 5: I am interested in those who thought, "Listening/observing has a

purpose and invites you to go into unknown territory." I would be interested in how you got into talking about that.

Teacher 3: When you are listening you are doing it for a reason. It is like an unknown flight plan because you don't know which direction it is going to take. But you are listening to children with a purpose; it could be to further a study [in-depth study] or to get to know a child better, or it may be to get ideas for making changes within your classroom [environment].

Coordinator 5: Are you saying that keeping the purpose in mind helps you become a better listener?

Teacher 3: You are just not listening as an aimless thing to do. It has a purpose. It's going to be used somewhere within your classroom, or as a way to change or a way to grow.

After the ideas from the various groups had been shared and discussed, the session moved into exploring words and phrases that the teachers had not explored in previous workshops: *identity, culture, team collaboration, sense of time, language,* and *pleasure/ joy in learning.* As before, each group discussed one of the terms and brought their ideas back to the whole group. These inquiries challenged teachers to think deeply, drawing on knowledge from their own experience.

Emergent Curriculum.

Exercises in Listening/Observing: Participants discussed some of their experience thus far with emergent curriculum, including the obstacles they experienced and how they dealt with them. Karen and the coordinators sometimes suggested solutions to problems, raised issues, or posed challenging questions intended to stimulate additional perspectives.

Karen: The issue of how to converse with children is not how to ask them questions. It's how to have a dialogue. Conversation comes with relationship. It's more like a dance. You validate and recognize what the child says and you build on it. It helps the children when you respond. It validates them and helps them say more. You don't ask a series of questions. They may say something, then you say something. It's not all questions. How can we have more conversations?

Teacher: It's different than responding to a peer.

Karen: Although it's different we can still be curious and wanting to know. We can pick up on their vocabulary and gestures.

Coordinator: It's about having a relationship.

Karen: You have to watch in a relationship to see what's inside of the other person. It's not about giving children information. We are listening to children, looking inside the children to support their learning and growth.

Everyone was given a two-page transcript of a conversation with children about the Big School. The coordinator asked the participants to pair up, read the transcript and "look for moments when a child is trying to pursue something or expressing an idea, interest or feeling." The coordinator and Karen encouraged everyone to go beyond surface interpretations; "a child's interest can be deep."

As people responded, Karen clarified the purpose of the assignment.

We are *not* trying to find out if the children have the correct information about the Big School. We are *using the dialogue to find out about their interests in life.* What can I learn about you to support your interests in life? It's not about what can I learn about you to prepare you for the Big School.

All of the interpretations were entered on chart paper and discussed. Coordinators encouraged the participants to look for patterns in the children's responses. The teachers then were asked to project beyond their interpretations of the transcript and discuss, "What would you do next?"

The exercise was repeated with a second transcript, working with the same partners. Then the exercise was done once again, with a nonverbal episode shown through a set of slides.

Presentation of an In-Depth Study: The teacher team that had done the Windows Study with their children (see Chapter 2) gave a slide presentation on it. They ended with a question that emphasized their learning from the study: "Is this something I'm interested in or is this something the child is interested in?"

Defining Emergent Curriculum: Karen read aloud parts of an interview with Carlina Rinaldi (Reggio Emilia educator). As she read, the text was projected onto a screen for all to see. A coordinator summed up Rinaldi's statement by saying:

> Emergent curriculum is valuing children for their thoughts, ideas, feelings, and using these to construct new meanings. In the traditional way children are not seen as capable, nor as naturally curious. In the traditional approach teachers are not constantly discovering and building understanding.

The group then discussed two questions: "What is the purpose of emergent curriculum?" and "What would be the outcomes and consequences of emergent curriculum?"

Advice to New Teachers. Everyone received a three-page handout containing advice one might give to new teachers. They reflected on these then added five more suggestions:

1. Take time to observe the children and look for things they are interested in.
2. Take good notes.
3. You need to be open-minded. Things won't always go the way you expect.
4. Don't be afraid to explore.
5. It's okay to feel overwhelmed.

Parent Participation. The group recalled experiences from the past year when they sought to establish a partnership with parents. A slide was projected containing 15 strategies, which had been suggested at a recent monthly meeting, for developing partnerships with parents. People were asked to add their ideas to this list. At the end, the coordinator offered the proposition that "documentation is the key to parent partnership," referring to the role that documentation plays as a focus for dialogues with parents (see Chapter 9, "Examples of Whoe-Group Dialogues," "Drop-off and Pick-up Times," and "Portfolio Nights").

Materials. The materials activities began with a video clip showing a child exploring shells with the teacher in the Carmen and the Teacher episode (see Chapter 2). The question posed for discussion was: "When did the teacher enter the child's world?"

The participants then explored materials in relation to their own identities. They were divided into three groups, each of which did the following three activities:

- Write down a list of emotions. Then use one of the hand mirrors to explore facially expressing each emotion on your list. Next, select one of the emotions and, in clay, represent your face expressing that emotion.
- Write two or three sentences about your favorite place in your classroom.

Construct a representation of that place, portraying yourself and possibly others within it.
• Create an image of yourself in wire. (Each participant was given a photo of him- or herself, taken earlier in the day, to use as a visual reference.)

The three groups came together to share their experiences and creations. The teachers enjoyed the exercises. They felt comfortable in using the materials and were eager to try similar activities with their children.

Documentation. Coordinator 1 noted that documentation is a powerful tool for emergent curriculum, for research, and for engaging parents. He asked the group, "What in your experience connects to these three aspects of documentation?"

> *Teacher 1:* Documentation is listening. Listening legitimizes the other's point of view. If we don't listen, then we are only valuing our own point of view.
> *Coordinator 2:* If you've documented a child's experience and put it in the hallway, then you are giving it back to the community. At first, parents are only interested in their own child. Then they start connecting to other children and the whole classroom community.
> *Coordinator 3:* We are not just consuming knowledge, we are producing knowledge.
> *Teacher 2:* When parents look at a panel together that starts conversation, it opens a door. Documentation isn't something just to do. It's fundamental to the process of learning.
> *Coordinator 1:* When you write something down, you're wondering about it. As adults, we're still learning and documentation is always going to raise new questions. Everyone is going to be learning. It's opening up a learning community.
> *Teacher 1:* There's not just one way to do it.

The in-service ended with a whole-group discussion on "challenges and expectations for the coming year." Finally, the participants filled out an evaluation form.

The format and spirit of the in-service activities provided a platform for teachers to have ideas and express them. Emphasis was placed on hearing many voices. There was a spirit of openness and nonpressure in the exchanges. People contributed their experiences to the discussions. There was not a race to get everyone to the same place. Instead, it was recognized that each participant was at a different level in the process of learning about and trying out Reggio ideas. The in-service experience is part of a continuous process of development.

Scaffolding of the exercises frequently involved a combination of stimulus and challenge. For example, the group was presented with a children's dialogue and asked to "look for moments when a child is trying to pursue something or is expressing an idea, interest, or feeling."

There was a balance between whole-group discussion and small-group work. The small groups reported back to the whole-group session, they shared ideas, and dialogue ensued. There was a continual building of community, not only through sharing ideas, but also through joining the ideas of the group with the ideas generated at other meetings.

Inspiring quotations along with a variety of visual, verbal, and tactile stimuli elicited comments as people reflected and shared experiences. The wide range of media retained people's interest and attention throughout the in-service.

Learning Tours

A learning tour is a 2-day event covering aspects of Chicago Commons Reggio Exploration work and is attended by people outside of the program, often from other cities. Nine such tours took place from 1999 to 2003. The tours were staffed by teachers, coordinators, site directors, and the program director. Teachers participated by preparing for and hosting visits to their classrooms and by serving as presenters and coordinators along with other staff.

The purpose of learning tours is to help others reflect on how the experience of the Chicago Commons program might be instructive to their own situations. A further purpose is to help the Commons staff think through their teaching practice by presenting their ideas and responding to questions. In addition, the learning tours provide revenue, establish recognition for the program, and create connections across the country with educators pursuing similar interests. Both the Chicago Commons staff and the visitors benefit from sharing their ideas and reflecting on their work.

Each tour focuses on a topic; for example, "On Creating Parent Partnerships" (March 2001) and "The Challenge of Following Children's and Teachers' Interests for Learning" (March 2003). Figure 10.4 shows the agenda from the August 2001 learning tour.

The professional development benefits of the tours for Chicago Commons staff occurred through preparing for the event, giving presentations, having discussions with the visitors during classroom visits and small-group engagements, hearing outside perspectives, and experiencing professional recognition for their accomplishments.

Outside Conferences

Teachers frequently attended national and regional conferences in early child development, and smaller conferences across the country as *presenters* and *audience*. Often, the conferences were devoted wholly or in part to the Reggio Approach; presenters included educators from Reggio Emilia and teachers from the United States who were exploring Reggio ideas.

Figure 10.4. Schedule for the learning tour on children, identity, and community.

Day One	Day Two
Reflection, journal writing, and discussion.	Tour of New City Center.
Overview of Chicago Commons Child Development Program.	Tour of Guadalupano Center.
	Dialogue with coordinators.
Elements of the Reggio Emilia Approach that have inspired Chicago Commons.	Write reflections in journals.
	Discovering the community.
Revisiting children and identity.	Interactions with Butch the Dog (a children's study).
Presentations: Exploring Identity Through Hair; Seeing Traces of Identity When Exploring Light and Shadows.	Working with wood (presentation).
	Small-group discussions.
	Think of three amazing dreams for your program and write them in your journal.
Tour of Nia Family Center.	Think of three realistic changes that you can act upon immediately after you return to your program—write them in your journal.
Dialogue with staff and parents from Nia.	
	Evaluations and sharing.
	Closing.

Once or twice during the course of a conference, Karen or another leader from the program met with the Chicago Commons participants at the end of the day and facilitated a dialogue in which people shared and built on their reflections about the sessions they had attended. Sometimes people from other programs joined in. In these discussions each person was listened to, and nobody was hurried. Some people were challenged to think more deeply and to draw more on their own knowledge and experience. The spirit was to listen, extend, and go deeper.

The staff were encouraged to take notes on the presentations they attended and write in their journals. After their return, these notes were assembled into a book and shared with other staff, stimulating further thought, discussion, and action within the various centers.

Visits from Reggio Emilia Educators

Since the late 1980s, the municipal preschools of Reggio Emilia have made a concerted effort to reach out to the rest of the world. This began, and still continues, with hosting delegations from other countries for 1- or 2-week seminars at Reggio Emilia. Karen and Dan attended such seminars in 1991 and 1994, and Karen has attended many others since.

Another point of contact with Reggio Emilia educators has been through the periodic visits to the program by Lella Gandini, liaison from Reggio Children to the United States, and Amelia Gambetti, also of Reggio Children. Reggio Children is an organization devoted to the support of the early childhood program of Reggio Emilia and to the dissemination of the practical and theoretical knowledge gained through a half century of experience.

From 1993 to 2003, Lella made eight visits to the program and Amelia made four. A typical engagement lasted 3 days and included visits to classrooms, feedback to teachers, large-group dialogues, and meetings with Karen and the coordinators. In a November 1999 visit, Amelia praised the Chicago Commons staff for interpreting Reggio ideas from their *own perspectives* and, through that, *exercising their own agency.*

> I have incredible memories of all the times I have been here. Because your experience is touching to me, and it reminds me of many experiences I had in my life that I am proud of. So you should be very proud of what you have done. Visiting the centers I had an encounter with a lot of joy that was a strong presence everywhere—the joy of your living your daily life in the classroom with your children. . . . I saw a great deal of dignity in your work. I could notice how much you've worked and how much you have tried to use the experience of Reggio as an inspiration, in terms of making connections with other ways of thinking. *My respect for what you have done is maybe more because you have given your own interpretation to what Reggio offered and can offer.*

In a later statement the same evening, Amelia returned to the theme of *agency*, this time as it applies to children.

> I have to tell you that in the beginning [at Reggio Emilia] it was not easy to get the attention of the parents. It was because of the way we learned how to include them in what we did, that the parents started to build a sense of confidence, and they started to understand that their children were learning many things. I think the key point was when the parents started to realize that the children were *learning to own their life.*

Lella, in her March 1998 visit, touched on the theme of seeking and valuing multiple perspectives in relationships with parents:

> You could *add the voice of the parents to the display panel.* You could open it up with a little *notepad* attached to the panel for the parent to write on.
>
> One of the beliefs that teachers mentioned to me is that parents and teachers might have different points of view and they might not want to agree completely. I think it's important to *really hear the different points of view, to have an exchange,* keeping this reciprocal trust and saying, "We are looking at this together; we don't have the perfect answer for everything, but we can talk."

During their visits, both Lella and Amelia promoted dialogue among the Commons staff rather than expounding their own points of view. Their general posture was to build on what other people were saying and to help the group build on one another's ideas. For instance, when Lella asked a question, it was meant as a stimulus for thought. Her questions do not come from a land of absolutes but rather encourage a spectrum of possibilities and perspectives. Once they are asked and received, their impact begins. Staff members have learned from Lella how to ask questions in ways that are caring, focused, and concerned, yet, at the same time, are not limited by expecting a particular answer or response. Her questions and suggestions have been great gifts to this program.

Visits to Reggio Emilia

> One thing I know that really touched me was Sergio's [the Reggio Emilia director's] speech about the journey, that you can't just pocket Reggio and bring it back. It's like a journey. You go down one road and you find out that that's not it, so you go back up and take another one. If you have to take a hundred roads 'til you find the one for you, that's what you have to do. There's not a right one or a wrong one. That made me feel a whole lot better. I'm not scared to try anymore. (Assistant teacher, after returning from the 1998 visit to Reggio Emilia)

From 1995 to 2003, the program sent six groups to Reggio Emilia to listen to presentations by Reggio teachers and leaders, participate in discussions, and visit schools. The May 1998 contingent to Reggio totaled 16 people from Chicago Commons: three head teachers, five assistant teachers, two coordinators, two family workers, three site directors, and Karen. During the visit, many of the Reggio Emilia staff and visitors expressed their appreciation for the Chicago Commons staff's comments and questions. Karen realized how much more professional her staff had become.

Shortly after returning to Chicago, the group shared their impressions with others. Here are a few examples:

> *Assistant teacher:* One of the things that impressed me most was listening to others, not just with your ears, but with all your senses and your heart. To listen to others shows that that person has values and a point of view that are important to you. Listening also means being open to differences. I'm not always open to differences. Recognizing differences requires change, and when you change it doesn't necessarily mean you lose your power for being whatever you are in the classroom. Listening to the child is putting yourself together with what the child knows and what he sees or hears, to help him understand his environments. They see things in parts or pieces and sometimes they can't put it together.
>
> *Site director:* There are some things that impressed me a lot. It was about the voices

of the children being displayed. How important it is that children's voices are heard and seen. I was amazed at the amount of documentation that you can see in every school and how important they made the parents feel.

Family worker. I saw a lot of documentation on parents and families. We have a good relationship with our parents, and parents want to stick around, but we really don't have that much for them to do. Maybe more workshops. I think we would involve them more if they saw more of themselves on the panels.

Each time Chicago Commons staff visited Reggio Emilia, they came back inspired and invigorated. It is a powerful and meaningful way to strengthen people's commitment to teaching and learning and to the partnerships and collaborations that they entail.

PARALLEL PROCESS

You may have noted some interesting parallels between the learning processes that teachers are engaged in and the learning processes in which children are engaged. You also may have noted parallels between the ways in which the coordinators and Karen scaffold teachers' development and ways in which teachers scaffold the children's activities. The scaffolding can be characterized as follows: creating an open, inviting climate in which everyone's point of view is sought and valued; offering challenging questions that stimulate reflection; emphasizing careful observation and documentation/representation; fostering dialogue with and among participants; and urging everyone to think more deeply by extending their ideas and exploring the reasons underlying them.

There are at least two ways of viewing these parallels. The first is that they are pursued in order to *promote the cultural unity of the program*. Thus, for example, image of the child as capable, interested, rich in ideas, wanting to grow, and wanting to communicate is paralleled by a similar image of the teacher. Children's co-construction of understandings with one another and with the teacher is parallel to teachers' co-construction of interpretations, projections, and plans with one another. Children's creations of representations are parallel to teachers' documentations, and children revisiting their representations are parallel to teachers revisiting their documentations.

The second way of interpreting these parallels is that they *promote experiences and types of development in the teachers that enable and motivate them to promote similar experiences and types of development in the children*. For example, when teachers are listened to, they are more likely to listen to children. When teachers are related to as people who can think, they will be more likely to relate to children as people who can think. When teachers experience themselves as researchers, they are more likely to embrace the children as researchers. When teachers learn to dialogue with one another, they extend that spirit and capacity for dialogue into their interactions with children and to their facilitation of children's interactions with one another. The chart in Figure 10.5, as an example, hypothesizes causal connections between the teachers' experiences of collaborative dialogue with one another, the coordinators, and the administrators on the one hand, and their relationships with children on the other. The chart suggests that the engagement of teachers in collaborative dialogue across many contexts of the program contributes to teachers *growing into a relationship with children based on listening, observing, responding, image of the child, and the child as a partner in dialogue*.

While we are suggesting that teacher development through collaborative dialogue is a major contributor to the development of teachers' relationships with children, we are not suggesting that it is the *only* contributor. Rather, it works in tandem with other experiences, such as the emphasis on listening, observing, reflecting, and responding that pervades every aspect of professional development and support in the program.

Figure 10.5. Parallel Process.

Dimensions of Collaborative Dialogue ⇨	Resulting Development in the Teacher ⇨	Consequent Development of Teacher Relationship with Children ⇨
Sharing ideas in relation to achieving a commonly held goal.	⇨ Experiencing oneself as a source of ideas. ⇩ ⇨ Enhanced sense of personal agency as creator of useful ideas, both individually and within a collaboration.	⇨ Greater propensity to view and relate to children as sources of ideas and to encourage idea sharing among children. ⇨ Greater propensity to take initiatives with children.
Listening, respecting, and responding to the ideas being shared by others.	⇨ Strengthens one's skills for listening and interpreting meaning. ⇨ Develops overall capacity for viewing/experiencing others as a separate source of motives and ideas. ⇨ Develops a value for taking/entertaining multiple perspectives.	⇨ Greater capacity to listen and respond to children. ⇨ Greater propensity to view child as a separate source of motives and ideas. ⇨ Greater propensity to encourage multiple perspectives in dialogues with and among children. Better observing of children (because one takes a wider range of perspectives when observing). ⇨ Greater propensity to wonder about children and to encourage children to wonder.
Building on the other's idea(s).	⇨ Enhances sense of collaborative dialogue.	⇨ Greater propensity to engage in collaborative relationships with children and to foster collaborative relationships among children.
Stating reasons for one's own ideas, or for one's agreement or disagreement with another's ideas.	⇨ Strengthens reasoning abilities, reasoning motives, and ability to express reasoning. ⇨ Strengthens awareness of and commitment to commonly held goals. ⇨ Strengthens sense of agency/selectivity, owning one's own ideas and reasons. ⇨ Strengthens sense of self as source of ideas.	⇨ Greater propensity to encourage reasoning in and among children. ⇨ Greater propensity to keep commonly held goals in mind when interacting with and planning for children. ⇨ Greater propensity to encourage children to voice their ideas and reasons. More likely to take initiative in planning for and interacting with children. ⇨ Greater propensity to recognize children as sources of ideas.
Asking others for clarification or reasons underlying their ideas.	⇨ Strengthens both parties' propensity to justify ideas with reasons.	⇨ Greater propensity to ask children for the reasons underlying their statements and to model reasoning for children.
Being open to others' disagreement with one's ideas.	⇨ Develops sense of the other as a separate source of motives and ideas. ⇨ Enhances one's overall openness to a wide range of perspectives. ⇨ Reduces propensity to equate one's self with one's ideas. Self-esteem becomes less dependent on agreement from others.	⇨ Greater openness to children as separate sources of motives and ideas. ⇨ Great propensity to encourage children to challenge one another and take alternative perspectives. ⇨ Greater flexibility in interacting with and responding to children. Less personal need for children to embrace one's plan or idea. More space to understand why they are not accepting one's plan or idea.
Co-constructing connections, understandings, and plans with others.	⇨ A sense of accomplishment in co-constructing ideas with others through dialogue and actions. ⇨ Enhanced sense of personal agency ⇩ ⇨ Internalization of dialogue as a mode of relating to others.	⇨ Greater propensity to co-construct ideas with children and to encourage children to co-construct ideas with one another. ⇨ More likely to take initiative in planning for and interacting with children. ⇨ Greater capacity and propensity to engage children in dialogue and to foster dialogues among children.

CONCLUSION

In the professional development opportunities offered at Chicago Commons, teachers are being asked to think and to collaborate. They are encouraged to use multiple perspectives as a way to develop their own thinking and understanding. They are encouraged to act upon their ideas and theories. Their own cultures and histories are respected and influence their thinking as they create a new culture together. Dialogue and exchange of ideas occur among all sites and all staff members, regardless of whether they are officially designated as Head Start, child care, infant–toddler, or after-school programs. The organizational structure facilitates professional development. The structure itself and the roles people play change over time in response to the many levels of dialogue among staff, parents, and children, and with external colleagues and organizations. Various processes of professional development are well documented by administrative staff so that the learning that takes place can be built on authentically and can stimulate further discoveries. In this sense, all are researchers in an evolving creative learning process that serves all the participants. This takes both commitment and time.

In the next chapter, we will extend the description of the professional development processes offered to teachers by looking at the organizational structures and processes that generate and support them.

Chapter 11

Organization of the Program

This chapter examines the organizational structures and processes that support everything we have described in Chapters 1–10. It addresses four questions:

1. Who guides, supports, and inspires the activities of the coordinators and the site directors? How is it done?
2. What is the role of the program director in these processes?
3. What is the administrative structure of the Child Development Program?
4. How are the teachers, coordinators, site directors, and others integrated into a learning community? How do children and parents participate in that learning community?

COORDINATOR MEETINGS

In Chapter 10, we saw the role of the coordinators in leading weekly meetings, monthly meetings, and in-service events. We also saw their one-to-one collaboration with teachers in creating display panels and presentations. The question is, where do the coordinators get their direction and support? Much of the answer lies in the weekly coordinator meetings.

The coordinator meetings are a major context for reflection and planning in the program. The principal participants are Karen and the coordinators. The meetings take place weekly for 2 to 4 hours. The range of functions served by the coordinator meetings touches on virtually every aspect of the Reggio Exploration. For example, plans are made for the weekly meetings, monthly meetings, in-service events, conference presentations, learning tours (in conjunction with the coordinator of professional development), and courses for new teachers and interested outsiders. The coordinators' work with teachers and site directors is reflected on and advanced in these meetings.

A look at excerpts from coordinator meetings will give us a sense of the kinds of issues that were discussed, some strategies projected to address those issues, Karen's role in promoting the dialogue, and the professional development of the coordinators that takes place through their participation.

An Example of a Coordinator Meeting

We begin by looking at a meeting held in September 1997. The agenda for the meeting included three items:

1. Creating a schema for guiding the coordinators' work with teacher teams
2. Discussing general issues in working with teachers
3. Planning work with the classroom teams at one center

Creating a Schema for Guiding Work with Teacher Teams. Several coordinators shared ideas that they had prepared for developing a conceptual framework to guide their work with the weekly meeting teams (see Chapter 10, "The Weekly Meeting"). Karen summed up the group's ideas as follows:

1. In the beginning we support the staff by helping people be comfortable in exploring the unknown. We are getting to know the staff, how they think, their interests, and their strengths. We are helping them to make initial connections with Reggio principles. We are giving direction and leadership in all of this.
2. The members of the team are now developing a more complex understanding of Reggio and its principles, and are planning more complex explorations. We are challenging them to stretch their understandings.
3. The team has arrived at a high level of collaboration. Everyone can challenge another member's thinking. There are ongoing dialogues and collaboration in planning. We are no longer the only ones asking challenging questions.

Confronting Issues in Working with Teachers. The following are two of the many issues raised during the meeting, along with excerpts from the ensuing discussions. The first issue is about the coordinator's role with the teachers.

Coordinator 1: I'm getting more comfortable with this but it's confusing how to be an explorer and a leader at the same time; it's hard to resolve these two roles.
Coordinator 2: Being a leader doesn't mean you have to understand all the answers.
Karen: It's a comfort [for teachers] knowing that someone is leading the team. Explorers [in history] had to do that.
Coordinator 2: People have been trying to figure out these things forever. Why wouldn't you want to learn? What is scary about learning and teaching at the same time?
Coordinator 3: You don't lose your identity. You focus on a new identity.
Coordinator 1: Do teachers also feel this? It's hard to give up some of your old identity to become an explorer.
Coordinator 3: This is connected with the parallel process idea. We see ourselves as researchers and model the research role for the teachers. If we have our own agendas and curiosities, it's okay for us to lead and do our research. Teachers can [then] see us doing that.

The second issue concerns getting stuck.

Karen: What do you do when you don't see a way to go, when you get stuck?
Coordinator 2: [I ask myself] what was I exploring that led me to this fork in the road, or to this darkness? What was the inspiration? You may lose direction, but you can remember the inspiration, the initial reasons you started out. Then it becomes calm. Otherwise you worry about, "Where am I going?"
Karen: You can always buy time. You have to be willing to look back on something as well as forward, and be under no pressure. We can enjoy being stuck!
Coordinator 2: It's best to do something, though.
Coordinator 3: Getting stuck can be fuel. If you are frustrated then you take a fresh look. It's part of the learning process. Then you go forward. Otherwise, if you're satisfied where you are, then you don't go forward.
Coordinator 3: If we get stuck, we can go back to Reggio principles.
Coordinator 4: We can use certain reference points of the year as a grounding— like the Reggio in-service or the monthly meetings.
Karen: When I've gotten stuck I've read things, like articles and books. I've also consulted with people. Three heads are better than one.

Planning Work with the Classroom Teams at One Center. In the last hour of the meeting, the New City site director joined the group to participate in a discussion about working with classroom teams at her center. The discussion of each team was structured around three topics:

1. Accomplishments of the team
2. What the team needs to work on to move forward
3. Goals for the coming year

The following are some excerpts from the discussion covering one classroom team. The speakers are the classroom team's site director and the two coordinators who work regularly with the team.

> *Site director:* They are still in the process of becoming a team. They are being more introspective and they are working together on ideas they have gotten from the children. They are beginning to really listen to the children and talk with them. And they are talking about the weekly meetings.
> *Coordinator 2:* They are often participating with the children in explorations.
> *Coordinator 1:* They are more observant of the children. Sylvia has been using her observations from the block area to challenge herself about the way she has been thinking about children.
> *Karen:* Where do they need to grow?
> *Coordinator 2:* I'd like to see them document more of their explorations with the children.
> *Coordinator 1:* And they need to communicate key parts of their observations back to the children and to the parents; for example, put their documentations up in the room. Use them in an ongoing way and not just as a summary of their own learning experience to use for themselves.
> *Karen:* There seem to be two goals.
> *Coordinator 2:* To do observations, documentations, and reflections on a daily basis, so it's not just a special activity.
> *Coordinator 1:* To go back to the children and reflect their ideas back to them.

Examples of Issues Raised at Other Coordinator Meetings

During coordinator meetings over the 2 years, a number of other issues were raised that reveal other challenges that the program was encountering during that period. *Most of the issues related to the coordinators' work with the weekly meeting teams, as reflected in the examples below.*

1997–98 School Year

- How to keep the weekly meeting discussions on track
- How to encourage teachers to bring documentation to the meetings
- How to help teachers to think more deeply about children's interests
- Teachers staying with their first interpretation of a child's interest rather than letting their understanding evolve through further interaction with the child
- Some teachers not understanding how to share perspectives with children

1998–99 School Year

- *Karen:* We're missing having regular team meetings. Two weeks between team meetings is too long a gap. Backsliding happens when there are not regular meetings. We can't let other things bump that weekly meeting. From now on, any time a meeting doesn't happen within the week, then I want to know.

- Teachers are finally all collecting documentation, but not always knowing what to do with it.
- Teachers are having difficulty knowing what to do after they identify children's interests.
- Many teachers are still thinking of Reggio as being just a time of day; that is, confined to activity time (see Chapter 7) rather than applying to the whole school day.
- How to facilitate teachers' wondering and imagining.

It takes time to deal with the types of issues mentioned above. For example, two of the issues in the 1997–98 school year were about teachers collecting and bringing documentations to weekly meetings and thinking more deeply about children's interests. By the following year, those issues had been somewhat resolved. The emphasis then turned to helping teachers learn to interpret the documentation and build on children's interests.

Being Aware of Intentions

Running through these 2 years of coordinator meetings we find repeated references to the importance of everyone in the program being aware of the *intentions* underlying their actions. By "intention" we mean the purpose or aim(s) of an action or set of actions. Here are a few examples:

I think that the teachers don't always understand why they do something. The coordinator might suggest something to do, but it is hard for them to build on something if they don't understand why they are doing it. (Coordinator)

I need to be more explicit and direct with the teachers about *why* we're exploring with materials or why we start the year with focusing on how children get to know each other. (Coordinator)

I think some teachers are thinking that there's a magical, right question [to ask a child] that the teacher just hasn't yet figured out how to ask. We're trying to get them to think about *what they want to know* when they ask a child a question, and they are not always understanding the relationship between what you *ask* and what you *want to know*. (Karen)

Our goal is to help teachers establish a better sense of what the *purpose* is when they collect dialogues and capture observations. (Coordinator)

For next week I want you to think about, "What's the *purpose* of the weekly meetings?" (Karen, to the coordinators)

Later in this chapter we discuss why and how staff's awareness of their intentionality plays an important part in the Reggio Exploration (see "How Does Learning Occur in Their Community?").

Professional Development of the Coordinators

Much of the coordinators' professional development takes place through the regular discourse at coordinator meetings where issues are analyzed and strategies are considered. In addition, Karen introduced activities to foster coordinators' development.

Reflecting on Video Clips and Transcripts from Weekly Meetings. Each coordinator videotapes a weekly meeting in which he/she is playing a leading role. The coordinator then selects two clips from the video for discussion at the coordinator meeting: one from a section of the meeting "that went really well," and one from a section "that was really hard." In a variation of this activity, the coordinator brings in a transcript from a portion of a weekly meeting where he/she exercised leadership, and the group discusses it.

Imagining Emergent Curricula. Each coordinator is paired with a site director for this exercise. Karen gives each pair a topic for a children's in-depth study. They are given a week to prepare their responses. The task is to:

1. Design opening activities. What kinds of experiences would you set up that children might be interested in?
2. Imagine children's responses and interpret them in terms of interests and ideas.
3. Imagine next steps. Where can you go with it once you find out what they are interested in?
4. Imagine possible directions that the study might take after that.

The following is a sketch of the types of thinking that a coordinator/site director pair might have included in a response to the topic "animals that live in the city."

1. *Opening activities*: Tell the children that they are going to take a walk in the neighborhood to discover different kinds of animals, and invite them to draw pictures of the animals that they think they might find. Take children's dictations about their drawings. In the whole-class discussion of the drawings, help the children become aware of the full breadth of the term *animals* to include insects, birds, mammals, and so on. Take them on an animals walk. Equip them with disposable cameras, magnifying glasses, binoculars, drawing materials. Audio record and take notes on their ongoing comments. After the walk invite children to draw and discuss the animals that they saw or heard. Tape the conversations. Conduct and tape further discussions in response to the drawings, transcripts, and developed photographs. Place a selection of drawings made before the walk and after the walk on different parts of the holding board.
2. *Children's responses*: Children most noticed and remembered animals that they saw moving and often commented on how fast or slow they moved. The older children did more detailed drawings after the walk than before the walk. These drawings showed how they noticed animal legs and wings in relation to their bodies, perhaps indicating attention to how animals move.
3. *Next steps:* Teachers invite children to do a study of "how animals move." Children make comparisons of how different animals move and experiment with acting out the comparisons. The teachers document the children's responses and invite them to revisit the neighborhood to observe how animals move. They encourage the children to observe the classroom pets and bring additional animals (such as caterpillars, worms, ladybugs) into the classroom for them to observe.
4. *Subsequent directions*: Children discover that many animals have four body parts that help them to move (e.g., four legs, or two legs and two wings). Some notice that insects have more than four, that some insects have more than others, or that some insects have both legs and wings and some have wiggle muscles. One child observes that birds use their tails to move as well as their legs and wings. Children spontaneously act out the movement of different animals, and "guess the animal" (from its acted-out movements) becomes a favorite circle time activity. A group of children compare their drawings of animals they observed with the fish in the fish tank, the classroom guinea pig, dinosaurs, and people. This raises the question of whether people are animals, too. Teachers take numerous opportunities to incorporate math concepts of number, counting, shape, pattern, and measurement.

This exercise opens up and develops the coordinators' and site directors' abilities to imagine teaching strategies designed to elicit and facilitate the extension of children's interests and ideas. Having to imagine an entire emergent curriculum process frees the coordinators and site directors to be more creative in their thinking and to think more clearly about how one stage of a children's in-depth study connects with subsequent stages. It also helps them to appreciate the value of dialogue with colleagues in hypothesizing possible directions of a children's study. The overall purpose of the exercise is to advance the coordinators' and site directors' abilities to help teachers develop the same set of capabilities.

COLLABORATION WITH SITE DIRECTORS

In Chapter 10 we noted that site directors participate in weekly meetings, engage in dialogues with teachers about their display panels, and attend the monthly meetings and in-service events. In this section we look further at the site directors' participation in the Reggio Exploration.

The site directors are administrative specialists rather than education specialists. Their role is to hire and supervise staff, administer the classrooms, provide for other Commons programs in the building, deal with parent issues, handle physical plant problems, provide substitutes for absent teachers, and compile reports on finances, enrollment, attendance, health, and social services. Frequently, site directors feel overwhelmed in their job. Given these pressures, the question is what role are they able to play in an exploration of Reggio principles?

The site director meeting takes place twice a month. Karen, the site directors, the coordinators, and other central office staff, such as the coordinators of health and parent involvement, attend these meetings (see Figure 11.1 later in this chapter). Up until Year 6 (see Appendix), the site director meeting dealt only with administrative issues. Starting in Fall 1996, as part of an overall effort to bring the site directors more directly into the Reggio Exploration, Karen added an "education hour" to the meeting and began to bring Reggio ideas into the discussion. By this time, an average of two classrooms at each site were involved in exploring Reggio principles. Thus, there was ample reason for the site directors to become more directly engaged.

In many of the coordinator meetings between 1997 and 1998, there were recurrent discussions about how to increase collaboration between the coordinators and the site directors. A precipitating factor was the coordinators' concern with "follow-up" after the weekly meetings (see above). Someone at each site was needed to touch base with teachers about implementing plans made at the weekly meeting and about bringing documentation to the next meeting. Follow-up was particularly needed in the case of teachers who were in their first few years of exploring Reggio ideas. Karen and the coordinators proposed to the site directors that they and the coordinators have *planning sessions* prior to weekly meetings and *debriefing sessions* after meetings to reflect on the meeting and plan follow-up to support the teachers. One or two site directors, because of their career experience and interest, were in a position to step easily into this expanded role. In fact, they were already playing it to some extent. For others, it involved a steeper learning curve.

Karen also began to make requests to the site directors aimed at increasing their greater involvement in the teacher development process. An example follows:

> One of the things to think of is if you could ask the teachers to discuss the purposes of the documentation that they have pulled together. Ask them to really think about what they are trying to communicate [through the documentation], why, and to whom.

ADMINISTRATIVE STRUCTURE OF THE CHILD DEVELOPMENT PROGRAM

The chart in Figure 11.1 is a structural–functional view of the program's organization as it looked from 2001 through 2003. Within the program, five types of meetings took place among various combinations of personnel:

- *Coordinator meetings* (weekly; see details above)
- *Site director meetings* (twice a month; see details above)
- *Administrator meetings* (weekly). All of the administrative staff shown in Figure 11.1, except the site directors, participate in the administrator meetings. These meetings include sharing of goals and activities, coordinating activities, dealing with issues of accountability and reporting, sharing future plans, promoting the overall integration of the program, and avoiding the disintegrative "silo effect" of departments working in isolation.

Figure 11.1. Administrative structure of the child development program from 2001–2003.

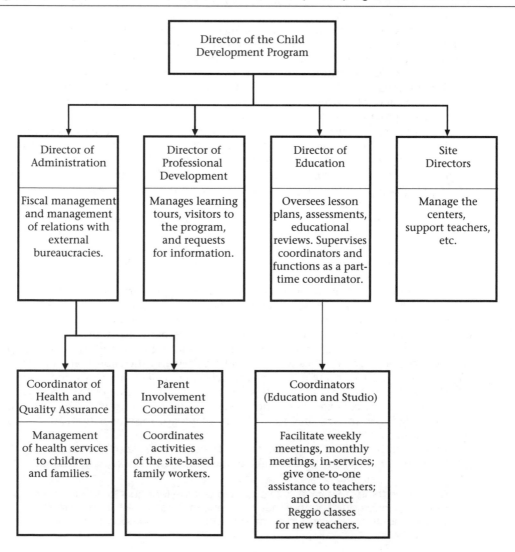

- *The annual retreat* (yearly). This 2-day August event involves all of the staff listed on Figure 11.1. Its function is to reflect on the past year and plan for the coming year. A quarter of the meeting time is devoted to the Reggio Exploration.
- *Close down day* (yearly). At this annual 1-day event, all the employees of the Child Development Program gather in one place. All the centers are closed down for the day. The gathering includes teachers, coordinators, site directors, other administrative staff, family workers, and Karen, as well as the kitchen staffs, maintenance people, and clerks. The emphasis at these meetings is on sharing aspects of the Reggio Exploration: reflecting on the past and future, introducing a special focus for the year ahead, and hearing everyone's voice.

CONNECTIONS AMONG CONTEXTS OF COMMUNICATION

In this and previous chapters, we have looked at 11 contexts of staff dialogue and collaboration within the program: weekly meetings, one-to-one engagements between teachers and coordinators or site directors, classroom collaboration, monthly meetings, in-service events, coordinator meetings, site director meetings, planning/debriefing meetings of coordinators with site directors, administrator meetings, annual retreats, and close down day. The following sections describe ways in which these 11 contexts of communication connect with one another to promote the ongoing functioning and development of the program.

Multiple Roles Represented in Each Context

Each context of communication brings together staff whose roles are functionally related to one another. Thus, for example, teachers, coordinators, the site director, and the family worker come together in weekly meetings. Teachers, parents, site directors, coordinators, family workers, and the director of the program come together in monthly meetings. The purpose and structure of each communication context encourage the participants to enter into collaborative dialogue.

Multicontext Participation

Each staff person participates in *multiple* communication contexts. Consequently, the participants of any one context also participate in a variety of other contexts. Figure 11.2 shows the multiple role composition of each context and the multicontext participation of each type of staff member.

Flow of Ideas from One Context to Another

Because people participate in multiple communication contexts, there is a natural flow of ideas carried by participants from one context to another. Thus, ideas and information flow back and forth between classrooms and weekly meetings, between weekly meetings and coordinator meetings, between coordinator meetings and monthly meetings, between monthly meetings and weekly meetings. For example, a team at the New City Center developed and implemented the idea of children exchanging clay gifts across classrooms (see Chapter 4, "Gifts"). The coordinators who were part of that team described the clay gifts idea at a coordinator meeting. From there, it was transmitted to many of the teams in the program via other coordinators

Figure 11.2. Communication contexts for each staff role.

Communication Context	Teachers	Coordinators	Site Directors	Family Worker	Director of Program	Director of Education	Other Administrators	Other Staff
Classrooms	X							
Weekly meetings	X	X	X	X	X*	X*		
One-to-ones	X	X	X					
Monthly meetings	X	X	X	X	X	X		
In-services	X	X	X	X	X	X		
Coordinator meetings		X	X*		X			
Planning/debriefing meetings		X	X					
Site director meetings		X	X	X	X	X	X	
Administrative meetings		X			X	X	X	
Annual retreat		X	X		X	X	X	
Closedown day	X	X	X	X	X	X	X	X

* Attends some meetings.

who were present at the meeting. Further, at that meeting, Karen and the coordinators decided to ask the NIA team to give a slide presentation on the clay gifts activity at the next monthly meeting. As a result of the monthly meeting presentation, teachers of many sites saw the details of the implementation and brought the ideas back to their weekly meetings. As the idea went through the process of deliberation in the weekly meetings, it took on a variety of forms and adaptations.

Cross-Site Communication

The monthly meetings (see Chapters 9 and 10) and the in-service events (see Chapter 10) bring together staff from all of the sites in the program. Since the monthly meetings occur at a different site each time, the participants get ideas from visiting one another's classrooms, from observing the display panels, and from seeing the particular ways in which the studio and common areas engage children, parents, and visitors.

Cultural Continuity

A common set of Reggio principles provides shared reference points for learning across all of the contexts. Since communication in each of the contexts involves co-constructing ideas, understandings, strategies, and solutions in relation to provocative questions, and since many of those questions are shared across the various contexts, the participants in the program have the collective experience of being a learning community.

A LEARNING COMMUNITY, A LEARNING CULTURE

> *We need to see ourselves as explorers of learning.*
> *We are all trying to understand and learn together. . . .*
> *While we are talking about all this, we are creating our own culture.*
> —Karen Haigh, coordinator meeting, February 2, 1998

A *learning community* is a group of people who collaboratively pursue answers to shared questions. The question that provides the focus for the Reggio Exploration as a learning community is:

> How can we implement Reggio principles in our own context?

In previous sections we outlined the program as a *structure* and as a *process*, made up of a variety of players collaborating in a variety of organized and regularly occurring communication contexts. We now turn our attention to the *culture* of this learning community; the set of ideals and beliefs that guide action, thought, feeling, and intention.

The *ideals* of this culture include *actions* such as listening, collaboration, dialogue, co-construction of understanding, challenging, documenting, revisiting, reflecting, and projecting. A prominent *belief* in this culture is the image of the child; that is, the belief that children are competent, rich in ideas, and so on. It is a belief about the way children actually are. Another belief is that the staff is *capable* of seeing children in this way. It is part of the image of the teacher (see Chapter 10, introductory paragraph). The ideals and beliefs of the culture are articulated through its *language*, as well as through the actions of its participants. Hence, the program often engages the staff in reflecting on the meanings of key terms (see Chapter 10, "Portrait of an Annual In-Service Event").

How Does Learning Occur in This Community?

The ideal learning process in this community is a reflection–action–reflection cycle. It is an ideal often stated by Karen to the staff. The following is a formalized conception of the process, subject to many adaptations.

The reflection–action–reflection process starts with reflecting on a situation that is seen either as an *opportunity for action* (e.g., these children are really interested in animals that live underground) or as a *problem* to be dealt with (e.g., the weekly meetings are falling apart, or the children have lost interest in the caterpillars). Reflection then moves into thinking about contextual information concerning the opportunity or problem, framing an aim (intention) for action, and brainstorming possible actions to take toward achieving the aim. The aim and potential actions become increasingly refined as they are considered in relation to one another. Finally, the reflection process moves to making a decision about which action to pursue and how to pursue it; that is, a plan for action is constructed.

Next, the *action* is implemented and accompanied by observations on how it was implemented and what immediate results occurred. *Reflection* occurs once more. This time it involves evaluating the action, interpreting the results of the action (often with the aid of documentation), and trying to derive what one has learned from the whole sequence. The reflection then proceeds to considering subsequent aims and strategies of action, moving the process into another reflection–action–reflection cycle.

The participants' awareness of their *intentions* plays a critical role in the reflection–action–reflection process. In a well-developed planning and learning sequence, one has a clear sense of the *aim* that an action is designed to achieve (see Chapter 2, introductory section, and "Being Aware of Intentions" earlier in this chapter). Learning takes place when comparing the results of the action to the aim.

When a teacher's sense of agency is well developed (see Chapter 10, "Seven Teacher Development Goals"), the teacher is able to articulate the aims behind the actions she/he takes and to learn by reflecting on the relationship between aim, actions, and results.

The reflection–action–reflection process involves both thinking about what did happen and what can happen, taking the time to talk about it and brainstorm with colleagues. At Commons, time is provided for these processes in the 11 contexts of communication (reviewed in Figure 11.2). In these contexts, staff interpret documentation and observations, bringing to bear past experience. They brainstorm and plan strategies for action, and they acknowledge their accomplishments and generate new understandings.

In the Reggio Exploration, reflection processes occur mainly through *collaboration*. The action part of the cycle also is likely to be collaborative, as in teachers jointly carrying out a preplanned strategy in the classroom, or Karen and the coordinators jointly running a monthly meeting.

Where Does the Collaborative Learning Take Place?

In the Reggio Exploration, the reflection–action–reflection learning cycle often takes place in the *pairing of work contexts*. One of the most prominent of these pairings is between the weekly meeting and the classroom. A major part of the reflection for classroom planning is carried out in the weekly meeting; for example, reflecting on the documentation of the past week and on the planning for the next week. The action, and additional reflection, is carried out in the classroom or in some other children's learning context, such as a walk in the neighborhood. Teachers document and reflect on the children's responses and bring the documentations to the next weekly meeting for further reflection.

Another major pairing is between the coordinator meeting and the weekly meeting. For example, strategies for working with teachers are generated in the coordinator meetings and tried out in the weekly meeting. Then the coordinators bring observations of the actions and outcomes back to the coordinator meeting for collaborative reflection.

There are also important pairings between the coordinator meeting on the one hand, and the monthly meetings and in-service events on the other. In each case, Karen and the coordinators create a plan in the coordinator meeting, implement and observe its results in the other context, and bring back their observations and reflections for discussion at a subsequent coordinator meeting.

Very often, the learning process is more diffused and does not follow the simple learning cycle suggested by the examples above. Let's revisit the coordinator meeting of September 23, 1997 (see "Coordinator Meetings" earlier in this chapter). Karen posed the question, "What do you do when you don't see a way to go, when you get stuck?" Four different strategies were brainstormed in response. None of the strategies actually was turned into a plan of action during the meeting. However, everyone's awareness of the potential strategies was heightened. Staff frequently hear the same strategy brainstormed several times before they act on it.

Learning also may take place *within* the process of reflection itself, prior to the action phase. For example, in Chapter 10 ("The Weekly Meeting"), we described how the weekly meeting team evolved a strategy for extending children's initial ideas about the city. Three types of learning appear to have taken place in that situation. First, the participants created a viable teaching strategy that they could carry forward. Second, they learned about the process of developing a strategy through collaborative dialogue. Third, they learned that it was possible to construct such strategies and that they clearly benefited from doing it collaboratively. The above three types of learning took place within the reflection process itself. But that reflection was made meaningful by the realization that it was taking place within the broader context of a reflection–action–reflection framework that is part of this culture.

Where Is the Learning Documented?

Much of the learning is documented in *display panels* and in *presentations* given at monthly meetings, in-service events, close down day, learning tours, and conferences (see Chapter 10, "Documentation"). Another vehicle for documenting learning is publications put out by the program (e.g., Chicago Commons, 2002). Finally, learning is recorded and disseminated through journals or book chapters written by staff (Alexander & Cecil, 2003; Haigh, 1997, 2004, 2007). The publications are often extensions of the thinking done in presentations.

Extending the Concept of the Learning Community

So far we have considered the learning community as made up of the program's staff. Does it extend to the parents and the children?

Parents. Contexts in which the program engages parents are home visits, the classroom at drop-off and pick-up times, parent conferences, collaboration in the classroom, special events such as the parent–children's workshop at the end of the Hands Study, and monthly meetings (see Chapter 9). Dialogues in all of these contexts highlight the many ways that parents are part of this learning community. For example, in the monthly meetings, parents, teachers, coordinators, site directors, and others engage in dialogues responding to children's drawings, presentations about classroom learning, and questions about early childhood education. The emphasis at these meetings is on eliciting as many parent voices as possible and as frequently as possible in exchanges with one another and with staff (see Chapter 9). Another example is the ad hoc learning that occurs when a parent, a child, and the teacher engage in dialogue about the child's work that is posted on the holding board or when relating to the child's portfolio on portfolio night (see Chapter 9).

Children. The classroom itself is a learning community. This is especially evident when in-depth studies are carried out, since the studies in one way or another engage the whole classroom (see Chapters 5 and 7). The classroom is also a learning community in that children are constantly moving around, visiting, and often joining in with others' activities. Nearby classes observe each other's activities (especially when connected through windows) and engage in collaborative projects such as the Gift Study described in Chapter 4.

In what ways are the children part of the learning community involving staff and parents? Clearly, the documentation of children's learning plays a huge role in the dialogues of the staff–parent learning community. Even more dramatically, the children participate in this wider learning community through their eager expression of interests, their focused engagement in collaborative learning activities, their many learning initiatives, and their imaginative representations. Their contributions make the learning community come to life and its purpose visible.

Relationships

Everything we have discussed regarding the program as a learning community is made possible through the human relationships among the participants that have continuity over time. The relationships are formed gradually through collaboration and dialogue that encourage reciprocal listening to, valuing, and responding to the expressed motives, feelings, and ideas of the participants. Because the people in the program are actively exploring and hence living out the Reggio ideals, they form relationships that embody those ideals, based on the pleasure and productive power of reflective dialogue. These relationships emerge from the exploration and in turn create a context that makes the exploration possible. It is a spiraling phenomenon.

Dialogue with Other Learning Communities

The Reggio Exploration is an open system in that its members enter into a wide variety of purposeful exchanges with others outside this learning community on the very issues that it is exploring. Major examples are the learning tours, participation in outside conferences, consultations to other programs, visits to Reggio Emilia, and visits from Reggio Emilia educators (see Chapter 10). In all of these settings, the staff present their ideas and actions to others and eagerly pursue the perspectives of others as they respond. These exchanges are inspiring and result in the continual vitalization of the program and in making contributions to other learning communities.

CONCLUSION

In this chapter we have presented the organizational structures and processes in the Chicago Commons early child development program and how they shape and support classroom teaching and learning, and the professional development of teachers that we described in the preceding chapters. In the final section of this chapter, we brought the many strands of the program together and showed how they connect through paths of communication and are unified by the cultural ideals and beliefs that infuse and guide them. By analyzing the program as a learning community, we have tried to capture the structural and cultural dynamics and integrity of the program as a whole. In the final chapter, we will look at some of the most important insights that we believe have been gained through the experience of exploring the Reggio Approach.

Chapter 12

Lessons Learned

Reggio is not something that you do exactly in one way. It is a way of thinking and a way of working with children. Once you change the way you think about children, you start working with them using the Reggio ideas.
—Chicago Commons teacher

We want to share with you our view of some of the important lessons learned in the Chicago Commons Reggio Exploration from 1991 to 2003. The lessons include our thoughts about the spirit of the Reggio Approach, the recognition of realities relevant to exploring this approach in the Chicago context, and the development of effective strategies.

Toward the end of the chapter, we draw on some of these lessons, as well as lessons from other parts of the book, to suggest a set of considerations for educational leaders who plan to explore the Reggio Approach in their own setting. Finally, we have a few words to say about why we think the Reggio Approach to education is of great value.

THE SPIRIT OF THE REGGIO APPROACH

In our view, the Reggio Approach is first and foremost about a *process of learning*. The process is the co-construction of understandings through dialogue, motivated by the learners' shared interests and curiosities. This collaborative process values and builds on the protagonists' own knowledge and capacities. The process of learning is the goal, the key reference point. The goal applies to the involvement of all of the participants: children, teachers, other staff, and parents. In the case of children, the strong emphasis on a process of learning that is grounded in their interests enables them to easily accomplish the learning standards in areas such as reading, writing, math, and social–emotional development (see Chapter 8 and Chapter 10, "Potential Conflicts Between the Reggio Approach and Teachers' Previous Experience").

In Chapters 1 through 11, we described a variety of useful structures that have served to facilitate the pursuit of that process of learning in the Chicago Commons context. They include organizational structures such as the weekly meetings (which support teachers in the reflection and planning process) and monthly meetings (which join teachers and parents in dialogues about children's learning) and conceptual structures such as the emergent curriculum cycle (which guides teachers' facilitation of children's in-depth studies). The structures, however, are simply strategies created to promote the process of learning in children and teachers. The strategies evolve and may even change radically over time, but the goal remains the same. Finally, because the goal is about continuous learning on the part of children, teachers, other staff, and parents, the ongoing evolution of a Reggio-inspired program is built into its very conception. This applies equally to Reggio Emilia where the municipal preschools themselves are involved in a process of gradual but continual transformation.

Looking Closely

There is a vital component in the above-described process of learning that tends to remain implicit in descriptions of the Reggio Approach. To our knowledge, it does not have a name. We call it "looking closely at something" or "looking at something with great care." It is reflected in Reggio principles such as revisiting, multiple perspectives, and documentation. Looking closely characterizes virtually everything that one undertakes in the Reggio Approach. Children and teachers look closely at objects of inquiry. Coordinators and administrators look carefully at strategies for supporting teachers and their development. Teachers and other staff look with great care and respect at children's deeper lying interests, their strategies for learning, their modes of problem solving, and how they initiate activities.

Dialogues with the World

Looking closely at something can be characterized as having a *dialogue with the object of inquiry*, whatever it may be (see Chapter 4, "Jazmin and the Ant"). As we engage the object of inquiry, it speaks to us in some way, through our senses and interpretive frameworks. We ask questions of it and it gives us some answers, usually incomplete. We ask the question again or ask new questions and it speaks to us again. And so the process continues, as we investigate it. We find a reference to this idea of a dialogue with the object in the Reggio Children publication, "Children, Spaces, and Relations" (Ceppi & Zini, 1998).

> The concepts of interaction and interface suggest a parallel between interpersonal relations (based on dialogue) and the relation between people and the object world (also based, if you will, on dialogue, comprehension, and identity). (p. 13)

The concept of dialogue with the object suggests a concise view of the Reggio learning process as *dialogues with each other about shared dialogues with the world*. The dialogues are open, inclusive, and evolving processes.

How Does Feeling/Emotion Fit into All This?

It might appear that everything we have said above about the process of learning falls into the realm of pure cognition. This is definitely not the case. To begin with, the concept of children's interests is meaningless without reference to the feelings that infuse those interests. One of the main ways that teachers discover children's interests is by observing and connecting with the children's expressions of joy and other emotions that accompany their actions, reactions, and experiences. Witness, for example, the joy that the teachers noticed when children were spontaneously making charcoal prints of the palms of their hands (see Chapter 5, The Hands Study) or the pleasurable excitement that the children expressed when the teachers suggested that they might draw pictures of their favorite windows in small groups (see Chapter 2, The Windows Study). Children's widely shared interests in relationships with friends and family are deeply infused with feelings connected to their evolving sense of identity.

Further, feelings are a major part of the thought processes involved in making connections among the elements of one's experience. We propose that emotions underlie the making of connections and construction of wholes in our minds. Emotions integrate and give unity to our experience (Dewey, 1934/1958). Further, the very processes of making connections and constructing wholes are inherently satisfying.

There are many implications of the above comments about the role of emotion in learning. One implication is that teachers create space in their minds and hearts for the emotions underlying and associated with children's interests and thought processes, as well as for the cognitive aspects. They can then reflect back to the child a fuller grasp of what the child is experiencing. This in turn opens up in children a broader awareness of and openness to the richness of their experience. An example is when Carmen's exploration of shells leads to the point where she and the teacher share the experience of creating unexpected sounds by blowing through a hole in a shell (see Chapter 2).

A REVISIT TO REFLECTION–ACTION–REFLECTION

In Chapter 11, we described the learning process of program staff as *reflection–action–reflection* and elaborated on its meanings. In this chapter, we would like to extend that concept further. The reflection–action–reflection process applies to two types of learning: "how to" and "what is."

- *How to* learning is the constructing of understandings about how to achieve particular aims; for example, learning how to engage children in ways that facilitate their thinking.
- *What is* learning is the constructing of understandings about the nature of things in the world; for example, learning the interests, feelings, and ideas of the children as expressed through their drawings and dictations.

"What is" learning often is pursued in the service of "how to" learning; for example, one observes how children are using the classroom environment as part of learning how to construct that environment in more effective ways. Conversely, "how to" learning often is pursued in the service of "what is" learning, as in children learning clay-working techniques from their peers in order to participate in representing what chickens need (see Chapter 4, "Chicken Community"). In any particular context, one of the two types of learning usually characterizes the overall focus while the other nests within it.

We propose that the reflection–action–reflection process applies to children's learning as well as to staff's learning. The Chicken Community Study (see Chapter 4) is an example.

- *Reflection*: The teacher asks, "What do chickens need outside their house?" In the discussion that follows, the children decide to make a car that will accommodate a family of chickens.
- *Action*: The teacher takes the children out to look at cars in the neighborhood as potential models.
- *Reflection*: The children discuss their observations of cars with the teacher and they make a plan.
- *Action*: The children construct a clay car together.

The process involves a continual moving back and forth between action (constructing the car) and reflection (recalling observations and plans).

The application of this concept both to teacher learning and children's learning suggests another form of parallel process (see Chapter 10). To the extent that teachers experience and internalize the reflection–action–reflection process in their own learning, they have a well-grounded framework for scaffolding the reflection–action–reflection process with and among children.

FACILITATING AND SUPPORTING TEACHER THINKING AND ACTION

The term *reflection*, as used above, has the meaning of pausing, standing back, taking one's time, and considering many aspects of something that has occurred or that one is intending. The term *thinking*, also used frequently by program staff, has a more specialized meaning; namely, energized, concerted mental action focused on arriving at some specific conclusion; for example, thinking about the precise aim of an activity one is planning and whether there is a good fit between the aim and the planned activity. This particular type of thinking is essential to teacher learning (see Chapter 11, "How Does Learning Occur in This Community?").

In addition to thinking about the relation between aim and action, there are two other types of teacher thinking that have been crucial to the program: thinking involved in interpreting children's interests and ideas from documentation, and thinking in projecting and planning activities that build on those interpretations.

Interpreting Children's Interests and Ideas from Documentation

Some teachers experience difficulty interpreting children's interests and ideas from documentation. There seem to be several contributors to the difficulty. First, teachers who are new to the Reggio Approach are accustomed to regarding documentation as assessment (to determine what children can or cannot do) rather than as sources of information about children's curiosities, interests, and ideas to be cherished and built on. Second, they often have difficulty perceiving the child as a separate source of consciousness, independent of their own consciousness and independent of cultural ideals that say what children should embrace. Third (and related to the second), the process requires *empathic imagination*—the ability to imagine the inner experience of another human being. Empathic imagination is often more difficult when applied to a child than to someone closer in age to the adult.

The program found the following supports to be effective in promoting teachers' development in interpreting documentation:

- In the weekly meetings, participating in group dialogues devoted to interpreting documentation (see Chapter 10, "The Weekly Meeting").
- Group analyses of documentation at monthly meetings (see Chapter 9) and in-service events (see Chapter 10).
- Frequent reminders that documentation and interpretation of children's actions and representations are forms of active listening.
- Encouraging teachers to reflect on their own childhood experience as an aid to taking the perspectives of children.
- Teacher research studies; for example, following a particular child and supporting what he/she is trying to do. The teacher documents the child's actions and the processes that take place. This includes processes between herself and the child as she tries to support what the child is pursuing. Later, she reflects on the documentation, discusses it with others, and infers what might be learned from it (see Chapter 10, "Teacher Research Studies").
- Teachers' preparation of presentations and panels that include references to how children's interests and ideas were interpreted (see Chapter 10).

- Karen and the coordinators actively listening to teachers' thoughts, motives, and ideas, and encouraging teachers to listen to one another. This suggests a form of parallel process (see Chapter 10); namely, that when teachers are listened to, they are more likely to listen to children.

Projecting and Planning

Teachers sometimes have difficulty figuring out how to build on children's interests and ideas once they have identified them. There are several factors that contribute to this problem. The process requires the imaginative projection of possible activities. The projection process depends on teachers first making their own connections within the subject matter as a basis for figuring out how to help children make connections. Finally, the process of flexibly projecting ideas can be inhibited by the great amount of *uncertainty* that is inherent in this type of teaching (Malaguzzi, 1998). In more traditional approaches to teaching, learning sequences are laid out in advance, often created by other people. In the Reggio Approach, very little can be laid out in advance because it is an emergent process. There are no recipes or formulas to follow. Even when a plan for the following week is designed in a weekly meeting, there is still uncertainty about how to build on children's responses to the implementation of the plan. Once teachers come to accept uncertainty, they are better able to free up their imaginations and try possibilities.

The program offered several contexts in which teachers received support for projecting and planning. Three examples follow.

Weekly meetings are a consistent support for teachers in the process of projecting and planning; for example, in Chapter 10, we described how the group constructed a set of strategies for extending children's thinking about the city. The weekly meetings also assist in reducing teachers' discomfort with the uncertainty associated with pursuing emergent curricula. First, through their participation in the group, teachers realize that they are not alone in experiencing uncertainty. Second, they know that there will be another meeting the following week to help them with the continuity of their work with the children. Third, the process of generating hypotheses about children's responses to the planned activity reduces uncertainty because it enables teachers to imagine some of the outcomes that might occur (see Chapter 10, "The Weekly Meeting").

Presentations and display panels by other teachers about emergent curricula help a teacher to get a better grasp on how one can respond to children's interests and ideas (see Chapter 10, "Documentation" and "Monthly Meetings"). Thus, teachers learn from one another as knowledge is acquired and shared.

In-service activities often give teachers experience in brainstorming responses to interpretations of children's interests (see Chapter 10, "Portrait of an Annual In-Service Event").

OTHER SUPPORTS FOR TEACHERS

The overall spirit of everyone being a learner helps to reduce teachers' concerns about taking risks. Karen often makes statements to staff such as "It's good to have a goal and it's okay if you don't meet it. What is important is that you are moving forward."

The coordinators seek a balance between challenging teachers to grow and supporting them in their response to the challenge. The balance is delicate, individualized, and important.

The program maintains a "can do" attitude in response to extra challenges that inevitably surface; for example, teachers being transferred from one center to another or classroom teams broken up due to the closing or opening of centers, limitations imposed by city ordinances, reduction in funds, or increased demands for record keeping and assessment by funding agencies (see Chapter 7). In response to these various challenges, Karen's message has been:

> In each situation ask, "What can we do?" not, "Why can't we do anything?" You need to adopt a stance in which you don't see changes as negative limitations that prevent other possibilities. Rather, ask, "What can we do, given the changes and the limitations?"

The major emphasis in the program on hearing everyone's voice, and accepting everyone where they are in their development, encourages teachers to take an active posture and move forward.

Finally, general messages to staff endorse them as learners and encourage them to pursue their learning in a relaxed, reflective manner. Karen tells them:

> Take time to reflect, go slow, pay attention to details that you've never seen before, build a foundation, and then build on that.

SUGGESTIONS TO LEADERS WHO PLAN TO INTRODUCE REGGIO IDEAS TO TEACHERS

Here are a few ideas for educational leaders who are beginning Reggio explorations in a preschool setting. *These ideas are offered as a set of possibilities* rather than as a formula, since each program is different and will undergo its own emergent process.

When exploring Reggio ideas, keep in mind the processes of *reflection–action–reflection*, *collaboration*, and *looking closely*. The following suggestions are made through those lenses.

After becoming acquainted with readings on Reggio Emilia and visiting some settings that are exploring Reggio ideas, take some time to look at your teachers. What are they interested in? Are they curious about other approaches to teaching and learning? What is on their minds?

Consider how best to present Reggio ideas in your own situation. When presenting, use a variety of media and engage staff in discussions that follow up on their thoughts and questions. Invite the participants to think about the image of the child and how other Reggio principles relate to it. The ensuing questions and dialogue will reveal how people are thinking. By recording, transcribing, and then revisiting such dialogues, ideas for planning the next steps can be generated.

Continue the ongoing dialogue with staff. Create structures that support the staff in talking about children and learning, and in talking about themselves. Invite interested staff to visit programs where explorations of Reggio ideas are taking place. Take time to discuss with them, during and after the visits, the ideas and elements that they respond to. Which things would they like to try in their own contexts? These discussions can inform the teachers' first steps.

It is important to document the ideas that teachers mention after visiting another program. This allows staff as a whole to revisit their thoughts at a later date. As staff progress, some ideas that initially seemed impossible will seem within reach.

While doing all of this, have an ongoing dialogue with someone *outside* of your setting with whom you can reflect; for example, a preschool director who is starting to explore Reggio principles or a collaborator who is experienced in applying Reggio ideas. It is vital to have additional perspectives.

Then work with a group of volunteer teachers who are attracted to the Reggio ideas. Consider which staff members might be able to facilitate the teachers' development. If there is an unfilled staff position, can it be redefined and filled by hiring a facilitator? Further, can a structure be established that regularly offers assistance, guidance, and, above all, collaborative dialogue to the volunteer teachers?

Identify the Reggio principles that you and the volunteer teams are interested in pursuing. It is worth considering choosing one or two principles initially that can be explored in all of the participating classrooms to provide a shared focus for reflective collaboration across classrooms and across sites. However, just choosing one or two Reggio principles does not add up to "exploring Reggio." *It is important to integrate other principles over time so that you gradually include the whole range of principles* (see Chapter 1, "Exploring Reggio Principles in Chicago Commons Schools").

The experience of the Commons program suggests that image of the child and the learning environment can be good starting points (see Appendix, Year 4). *The image of the child* is the anchor for the Reggio philosophy and provides the reference point for virtually everything else. It is the conceptual building block on which the teacher–child relationship is conceived. Teachers acquire the image of the child through listening to and observing children. Work on the image of the child might begin with teachers observing videotapes to infer children's interests and strengths. Have the teachers follow individual children in the classroom, documenting children's activities in a variety of ways, and, in dialogue with others, inferring what the documentation reveals about the child's learning interests. In this way, the habit of documentation is introduced early. Also, teachers can be encouraged to start dialogues with children that focus on listening to or extending children's learning interests. When these are tape-recorded, brief transcriptions can be made and brought to meetings.

A focus on the *learning environment* has the following advantages: First, it is concrete and relatively immediate; one can see rapid changes. Second, progress on the environment is an enabler; for example, it can encourage children to work in small groups in more focused ways and give the teachers increasing opportunities to work with one group at a time (see Chapter 6). Third, work on the environment connects directly with the image of the child in that it makes visible the identities of the children and facilitates children's agency in their learning (see Chapter 6). Finally, work on the environment is an excellent context for teachers to develop a sense of themselves as researchers. For example, they observe how children are using the environment. They then choose one area of the classroom that's not working well and reflect on why it's not working well. Next, they establish a set of aims for what they want the environment to do, and make a plan for changing it. After making the changes, they reflect on the outcome in relation to their intentions and draw conclusions. Throughout this process, reflection and learning are maximized when teachers document their initial observations, the changes they make, and the results. Children's learning motivations and interests can inspire teacher teams to continually recreate the classroom environment.

Consideration of principles such as documentation, co-construction of understanding, revisiting, exploring materials, and representation will evolve from working on the initial principles of image of the child and the learning environment.

How might you set up a way for staff to dialogue and share their learning across the program? One idea might be something like the monthly meeting described in Chapters 9 and 10. As time moves on, encourage teachers (who are ready) to make presentations to staff and parents. Such presentations can be based on relatively simple sequences of children's learning and can use documentation such as videos, slides, children's dictations, and transcriptions of children's conversations (see Chapter 10).

These presentations also can include teachers' perspectives on their own learning that resulted from reflecting on the learning sequence with the children. Further insights are gained when dialogue follows the presentation.

Karen and her staff found it valuable to have a new focus or initiative for each year, as well as following up on previous initiatives. For example, "Teachers as Researchers" became an initiative one year, and "Parent Partnership" another year. Such foci serve to spark the motivation of the staff as inquirers and as participants in a community of learners, especially when the director of the program shares her ongoing reflections with the staff and engages them in dialogue with her and with one another.

WHY EXPLORE THE REGGIO APPROACH?

In the final analysis, a decision to explore the Reggio ideas about early childhood education is based on values; namely, the value placed on children developing capacities for agency, collaboration, dialogue, taking multiple perspectives, learning how to construct rich understandings of the world, and learning how to communicate their understandings to others.

Why is this important? We believe that these values reflect motives and capacities that are basic to our human nature. The history of the species confirms this point of view. Human culture developed because people engaged with one another and the world to construct new meanings, understandings, and innovations.

Further, there is a quality of life issue. Since the motives and capacities to construct meanings and ideas are basic to our nature, children feel deep satisfaction when they experience their own agency as active, reflective learners. Moreover, this sets the stage for their experiencing a wide range of satisfactions in adulthood.

From a purely practical perspective, the various global pressures that we face in the future require the emergence of human beings who can think and act with multiple perspectives, collaborate with a wide variety of people, and construct and represent complex understandings. In other words, the Earth needs people who can think in terms of contexts, connections, relationships, and wholes, and who have been listened to carefully in their childhood, enabling them to reach out, listen to, and communicate well with others as they move into the wider world.

We want to thank you for reading this book. We are greatly enriched through writing it and we thought of you as we did. Together, we can thank the municipal preschools of Reggio Emilia, which have brought this gift to the world, and thank the Chicago Commons staff who so creatively and energetically embraced it and made this book possible. We are privileged to be part of this dialogue.

Appendix

A Brief History of the Reggio Emilia Exploration at Chicago Commons, 1991–2003

As a context for the events reported in the book, we offer the following history of the Reggio Exploration at Chicago Commons from 1991 through 2003.

Years 1 and 2: In May 1991, Karen made her first visit to Reggio Emilia. During the next 2 school years, she gave slide presentations to teachers and other staff about her visit, explored the ideas with them in small groups, and provided occasional workshops.

Year 3: In Summer 1993, Karen took seven teachers, one from each of the Commons preschool centers, and her education coordinator to a 3-day Reggio workshop in Traverse City, Michigan. At the workshop, educators from Reggio Emilia and American teachers gave presentations.

In Fall 1993, seven volunteer teams were formed to explore Reggio ideas, one at each site. A team consisted of a head classroom teacher, the assistant teacher, the site director, the family worker, and the education coordinator from the central office. The coordinator provided leadership to each of the teams and an ongoing line of communication between Karen and the classrooms. Later that year, Karen introduced monthly meetings to provide a context in which teachers from every site could come together to share experiences, thoughts, and questions about their Reggio-related activities. In 1995, the monthly meetings were extended to include parents.

The explorations of the various teams went in diverse directions. Each team worked on a few Reggio principles, but there was no consistency from one team to another in the principles that they chose to explore. Hence, there was a lack of focus and coherence in the program.

Year 4: In June 1994, Karen made a second visit to Reggio Emilia. There, she met Gunilla Dahlberg, who told her that when their program in Sweden decided to focus on the image of the child, dynamic changes occurred. On her return to Chicago, Karen decided to focus with all of the teachers on two principles: *image of the child* and the *environment.*

Work on image of the child began with engaging the site-based teams in observing classroom videotapes for the purpose of noticing children's capabilities. The teachers' first response to the tapes was to be critical of the teachers and classrooms shown in the tapes, rather than to focus on the children. When they finally did focus on the children, their overriding tendency was to comment on deficits rather than capabilities.

Karen and the coordinators understood that the teachers' response reflected a tendency in American early childhood education to look for deficits to be corrected rather than strengths to be built upon. During the next few months, the weekly team meetings focused on identifying strengths in children. They used videotapes from the participants' classrooms to facilitate teachers observing strengths in children's actions and comments. After several such meetings, the teachers began to observe children more carefully and to notice their capabilities.

Later in the year, Karen and the coordinators started working with teachers on the learning environment (see Chapter 6, "Teachers' Reflections on the Evolution of Their Classrooms"). There were three education coordinators and a studio coordinator.

Year 5: Energies continued to be focused on image of the child and the learning environment.

Year 6: By Fall 1996, the number of participating classrooms had increased to 14. From the beginning of the school year, many of the teams were interested in doing in-depth studies with the children. However, Karen felt that the teachers needed three additional types of learning experiences prior to entering into the in-depth studies: exploring materials to prepare them for scaffolding children's exploration of materials later in the year (see Chapter 4); doing observational studies of children (see Chapter 10); and reflecting on transcripts of teacher–child dialogues during the weekly meetings.

Year 7: In Fall 1997, the number of participating classrooms rose to 20. There were three education coordinators and two studio coordinators. The focus on exploration of materials in the classrooms continued, and the phase of children using the materials to *communicate* was added (see Chapter 4).

In April 1998, the emphasis finally shifted to *in-depth studies*. Each classroom team chose a topic from among four options: the City, Friends, the Family, and the "Big School" (the local school where many of the children would be attending kindergarten after leaving preschool). Out of these initiatives came the Pipes and Windows studies (see Chapters 1 and 2), as well as the Friends and Age Progression studies (see Chapter 4). Through the explorations and breakthroughs involved in planning and implementing the in-depth studies, the program as a whole turned a corner in its development. The shift to in-depth studies emphasized the necessity of teachers bringing documentations systematically to the weekly meetings (see Chapters 1, 2, 5, and 10). The structure of the weekly meetings also became clearer; now they were organized around interpretation of documentations followed by projecting and planning (see Chapters 5 and 10). By the end of Year 7, the program had broadly sketched out the use of Reggio principles, even though greater depth and refinement lay ahead.

Year 8: Ten more classrooms volunteered to join the Reggio Exploration, increasing the total number to 30, including some infant–toddler and after-school classes. The focus of exploration continued to be on image of the child, the learning environment, exploration of materials, listening/observing, documentation, and in-depth studies.

Year 9: In Fall 1999, the 10 classrooms that had not yet joined the Reggio program were asked to join. Karen was concerned that the teachers in these classrooms were feeling isolated and that these classrooms were falling behind in the quality of education that they were offering compared with the classrooms that were pursuing Reggio ideas. Thus, all 40 of the classrooms in the program were now exploring

Reggio Emilia ideas: 26 preschool classrooms, 6 infant–toddler classrooms, and 8 after-school classrooms.

Years 10, 11, and 12: From 2000 to 2003, teachers continued to pursue and integrate the entire range of Reggio principles. By 2000, the original group of coordinators had been replaced by new people. The number of coordinators remained at five. During this period, there was more explicit emphasis on reading/writing literacy and on assessment to meet new federal requirements. There was an increased focus on teachers as researchers

References

Alexander, C., & Cecil, J. (2003). Evolution of learning through observation, interpretation, and documentation. *Innovations in Early Education, 10*(3), 9–17.

Au, K. H. (1997). Ownership, literacy achievement, and students of diverse cultural backgrounds. In J. T. Guthrie & A. Wigfield (Eds.), *Reading engagement: Motivating readers through integrated instruction* (pp. 128–148). Newark, DE: International Reading Association.

Bakhtin, M. M. (1984). *Problems of Dostoevsky's poetics*. Minneapolis: University of Minnesota Press.

Bakhtin, M. M. (1986). *Speech genres and other late essays*. Austin: University of Texas Press.

Bakhtin, M. M. (1990). *Art and answerability*. Austin: University of Texas Press.

Ceppi, G., & Zini, M. (Eds.). (1998). *Children, spaces, relations*. Reggio Emilia, Italy: Reggio Children.

Chicago Commons. (2006). *Adaptations of the Reggio Emilia approach: Deeply rooted in theory and practice*. Chicago: Chicago Commons Association.

Dewey, J. (1958). *Art as experience*. New York: Capricorn Books/Putnam. (Original work published 1934)

Duke, N. (2000). For the rich it's richer: Print experiences and environments offered to children in very low- and very high-socioeconomic status first-grade classrooms. *American Educational Research Journal, 37*(2), 441–478.

Edwards, C., Gandini, L., & Forman, G. (Eds.). (1998). *The hundred languages of children* (2nd ed). Greenwich, CT: Ablex.

Freire, P. (1985). Reading the world and reading the word: An interview with Paolo Freire. *Language Arts, 62*(1), 15–21.

Gandini, L. (1998). Educational and caring spaces. In C. Edwards, L. Gandini, & G. Forman (Eds.), *The hundred languages of children* (2nd ed., pp. 161–178). Greenwich, CT: Ablex.

Gandini, L. (2001). Documentation as a tool for promoting the construction of respectful learning. In L. Gandini and C. Edwards (Eds.), *Bambini: The Italian approach to infant toddler care* (pp. 124–132). New York: Teachers College Press.

Haigh, K. (1997). How the Reggio approach has influenced an inner-city program: Exploring Reggio in Head Start and subsidized child care. In J. Hendrick (Ed.), *First steps toward teaching the Reggio way* (pp. 152–166). Upper Saddle River, NJ: Prentice Hall.

Haigh, K. (2004). Reflections on changes within our learning and living environment at Chicago Commons. In J. Hendrick (Ed.), *Next steps toward teaching the Reggio way* (pp. 197–209). Upper Saddle River, NJ: Pearson.

Haigh, K. (2007). Exploring learning with teachers and children: An administrator's perspective. *Theory and Practice, 46*(1), 57–64.

Halliday, M. L. K. (1994). The place of dialogue in children's construction of meaning. In R. B. Russel, M. R. Ruddell, & H. Singer (Eds.), *Theoretical models and processes of reading* (4th ed., pp. 70–82). Arlington, VA: International Reading Association.

Holquist, M. (1990). *Dialogism: Bakhtin and his world*. New York: Routledge.

Johnson, M. (1987). *The body in the mind: The bodily basis of meaning, imagination, and reason.* Chicago: University of Chicago Press.

Malaguzzi, L. (1998). History, ideas, and basic philosophy. In C. Edwards, L. Gandini, & G. Forman (Eds.), *The hundred languages of children* (2nd ed., pp. 49–97). Greenwich, CT: Ablex.

Meisels, S. J., Dichtelmiller, M. L., Jablon, J. R., & Marsden, D. B. (2001). *Developmental guidelines for four year olds: Work sampling for Head Start.* Ann Arbor, MI: Rebus.

Olds, A. R. (2001). *Child care design guide.* New York: McGraw-Hill.

Reggio Children. (2005). *I cento linguaggi de bambini/The hundred languages of children.* [Documentation of the Hundred Languages of Children traveling exhibit, Italian and English text]. Reggio Emilia, Italy: Reggio Children.

Rinaldi, C. (1998). Projected curriculum constructed through documentation—Progettazione. In C. Edwards, L. Gandini, & G. Forman (Eds.), *The hundred languages of children* (2nd ed., pp. 113–125). Greenwich, CT: Ablex.

Rinaldi, C. (2001). Documentation and assessment: What is the relationship?. In Project Zero/Reggio Children, *Making learning visible: Children as individual and group learners* (pp. 78–89). Reggio Emilia, Italy: Reggio Children.

Rinaldi, C. (2006). *In dialogue with Reggio Emilia: Listening, researching, and learning.* London and New York: Routledge.

Roopnarine, J. L., & Johnson, J. E. (1993). *Approaches to early childhood education* (2nd ed.). New York: MacMillan.

Index

About the Authors

Daniel R. Scheinfeld is an anthropologist and Senior Research Associate at Erikson Institute in Chicago. He holds a Ph.D. in Anthropology from the University of Chicago and an M.A. in Social Anthropology from the London School of Economics. He is now in his 25th year of directing professional development and curriculum outreach programs serving Chicago public elementary schools in the areas of open classrooms (1970–1978), arts integration (1991–2000), and children's collaborative reasoning about texts (2001–2008). In the 1980s, he conducted ethnographic studies of the child rearing practices of Vietnamese refugee families in Chicago, programs serving Cambodian refugee families, and the emotional reactions of psychiatric hospital staff to their adolescent patients. Since 1993, he has collaborated with Sandra Scheinfeld and the staff of the Chicago Commons Child Development Program in studying the Chicago Commons Reggio Exploration.

Karen M. Haigh, assistant professor of early childhood education at Columbia College Chicago, has been in early childhood education for 30 years. She began her career as a preschool teacher at Mary Crane in Chicago. Karen then became Education Coordinator for the Hull House Association, during which time she received an M.A. degree from Erikson Institute. In 1988, she became Director of Child Development at Chicago Commons. In that role, she organized, led, and inspired the Chicago Commons Reggio Exploration during the entire 12-year period described in this book (1991–2003). Since that time, Karen has served as Director of Professional Development for the Early Childhood division of the Chicago Public Schools and as Executive Director for the Governors State University Family Development Center. In both of these positions, she consulted with early childhood classrooms in the Chicago public school system that were interested in exploring the Reggio Emilia Approach, and she will continue this work in her new position at Columbia College. Karen also serves as a consultant to early childhood programs in other parts of the country that are exploring Reggio principles in their own settings. Karen is currently receiving a Ph.D. with a specialization in early childhood education from the Union Institute and University. Her dissertation is on professional development in a Reggio-influenced program.

Sandra J. P. Scheinfeld is a research associate at Erikson Institute and a freelance documenter and consultant for not-for-profit organizations. During the past 20 years, she has documented innovative programs in health care, education, community organizing, micro-enterprise, and environmental studies. In the past decade at Erikson, she played a major role in documenting the Chicago Commons Reggio Exploration. Besides her interest in documentation, she is involved in forestry and gardening pursuits that grew out of her childhood experiences and identity as a New Zealander. She came to Chicago to study urban geography in 1965 and received her Ph.D. from the University of Chicago in 1976.